Recent Progress in
Artificial Neural Networks

Recent Progress in Artificial Neural Networks

Edited by Jeremy Rogerson

CLANRYE
INTERNATIONAL
www.clanryeinternational.com

Clanrye International,
750 Third Avenue, 9th Floor,
New York, NY 10017, USA

ISBN: 978-1-63240-843-3

Cataloging-in-Publication Data

Recent progress in artificial neural networks / edited by Jeremy Rogerson.
  p. cm.
Includes bibliographical references and index.
ISBN 978-1-63240-843-3
1. Neural networks (Computer science). 2. Artificial intelligence. I. Rogerson, Jeremy.
QA76.87 .R43 2019
006.32--dc23

For information on all Clanrye International publications
visit our website at www.clanryeinternational.com

Contents

Preface

Artificial neural networks (ANNs) are computing systems that are motivated by the design and functioning of biological neural networks. Its design is driven by the goal of solving problems in a manner that mimics the working of the human brain. To achieve this, a system of artificial neurons is constructed, which transmits signals through connections. Each neuron and the connections between them have a weight that changes as learning proceeds. This, in turn, influences the strength of a signal at a connection. ANN can be programmed to deliver on the functionalities of data processing, classification, function approximation, robotics and control. Its use, however, requires an understanding of the learning algorithm, choice of model and robustness. Due to its diverse capabilities, ANN has potential applications in medical diagnosis, finance, ocean modeling, vehicle control, face identification, among many others. This book contains some path-breaking studies in the field of artificial neural networks. The ever-growing need of advanced technology is the reason that has fueled the research in the field of artificial neural networks in recent times. Coherent flow of topics, student-friendly language and extensive use of examples make this book an invaluable source of knowledge.

All of the data presented henceforth, was collaborated in the wake of recent advancements in the field. The aim of this book is to present the diversified developments from across the globe in a comprehensible manner. The opinions expressed in each chapter belong solely to the contributing authors. Their interpretations of the topics are the integral part of this book, which I have carefully compiled for a better understanding of the readers.

At the end, I would like to thank all those who dedicated their time and efforts for the successful completion of this book. I also wish to convey my gratitude towards my friends and family who supported me at every step.

Editor

Generalized Regression Neural Networks with Application in Neutron Spectrometry

Ma. del Rosario Martinez-Blanco,

Víctor Hugo Castañeda-Miranda,

Gerardo Ornelas-Vargas,

Héctor Alonso Guerrero-Osuna,

Luis Octavio Solis-Sanchez,

Rodrigo Castañeda-Miranda,

José María Celaya-Padilla, Carlos Eric Galvan-Tejada,

Jorge Isaac Galvan-Tejada,

Héctor René Vega-Carrillo,

Margarita Martínez-Fierro, Idalia Garza-Veloz and

Jose Manuel Ortiz-Rodriguez

Additional information is available at the end of the chapter

Abstract

The aim of this research was to apply a generalized regression neural network (GRNN) to predict neutron spectrum using the rates count coming from a Bonner spheres system as the only piece of information. In the training and testing stages, a data set of 251 different types of neutron spectra, taken from the International Atomic Energy Agency compilation, were used. Fifty-one predicted spectra were analyzed at testing stage. Training and testing of GRNN were carried out in the MATLAB environment by means of a scientific and technological tool designed based on GRNN technology, which is capable of solving the neutron spectrometry problem with high performance and generalization capability. This computational tool automates the pre-processing of information, the training and testing stages, the statistical analysis, and the post-processing of the information. In this work, the performance of feed-forward backpro-pagation neural networks (FFBPNN) and GRNN was compared in the solution of the neutron spectrometry problem. From the results obtained, it can be observed that despite very similar results, GRNN performs better than FFBPNN because the former could be used as an alternative procedure in neutron spectrum unfolding methodologies with high performance and accuracy.

Keywords: artificial intelligence, statistical artificial neural networks, neutron spectrometry, unfolding codes, spectra unfolding

---

1. Introduction

Artificial Intelligence or AI is one of the newest fields of intellectual research that attempts to understand the intelligent entities [1]. Intelligence could be defined by the properties it exhibits: an ability to deal with new situations, to solve problems, to answer questions, to devise plans, and so on [2]. The phrase AI was coined by John McCarthy in the 1940s and to date evades a concise and formal definition [3]. A simple definition might be: AI is the study of systems that act in a way, that to any observer would appear to be intelligent, and involves using methods based on the intelligent behavior of humans and other animals to solve complex problems.

AI has been classified into three periods: the classical, the romantic, and the modern periods [1–4]. The major area of research covered under the classical period, in the 1950s, was intelligent search problems involved in game-playing and theorem proving. In the romantic period, from the mid-1960s until the mid-1970s, people were interested in making machines "understand," by which they usually meant the understanding of natural languages. The modern period started from the latter half of 1970s to the present day and includes research on both, theories and practical aspects of AI. This period is devoted to solving relatively simple or complex problems that are integral to more complex systems of practical interest.

The aim of the study of AI is to use algorithms, heuristics, and methodologies based on the ways in which the human brain solves problems. In the most recent decades, AI areas of particular importance include multi-agent systems; artificial life; computer vision; planning; playing games, chess in particular; and machine learning [5–6].

1.1. Machine learning and connectionism

Learning and intelligence are intimately related to each other. Learning is an inherent characteristic of human beings [3]. By virtue of this, people, while executing similar tasks, acquire the ability to improve their performance with the self-improvement of future behavior based on past experience. In most learning problems, the task is to learn to classify inputs according to a finite, or sometimes infinite, set of classifications [2]. Typically, a learning system is provided with a set of training data, which have been classified by hand. The system then attempts to learn from these training data how to classify the same data, usually a relative easy task, and also how to classify new data that are not seen [7].

The principles of learning can be applied to machines to improve their performance [8]. A system capable of learning is intelligent and is usually expected to be able to learn based on past experience. Such learning is usually referred to as "machine learning" (ML) which is an important part of AI and can be broadly classified into three categories: supervised, unsupervised, and reinforcement learning.

Supervised learning requires a trainer who supplies the input-output training instances. The learning system adapts its parameters using some algorithms to generate the desired output patterns from a given input pattern. In absence of trainers, the desired output of a given input instance is not known; consequently, the learner has to adapt its parameters autonomously. Such type of learning is termed unsupervised learning.

Reinforcement learning bridges the gap between the supervised and unsupervised categories. In reinforcement learning, the learner does not explicitly know the input-output instances, but it receives some form of feedback from its environment. The feedback signals help the learner to decide whether its action on the environment is rewarding or punishable. The learner thus adapts its parameters based on the states (rewarding/punishable) of its actions.

Recently, the connectionist approach for building intelligent machines with structured models like artificial neural networks (ANN) is receiving more attention [9]. Connectionist models are based on how computation occurs in biological neural networks. Connections play an essential role in connectionist models, hence the name *connectionism* [10]. The term connectionism was introduced by Donald Hebb in the 1940s, and it is a set of approaches in the fields of AI that models mental or behavioral phenomena as the emergent processes of interconnected networks of simple units [11]. The central connectionist principle is that mental phenomena can be described by interconnected networks of simple and uniform units.

Figure 1. The unit: the basic information processing structure of a connectionist model.

Units are to a connectionist model what neurons are to a biological neural network: the basic information processing structures. Since the flow of information in a network occurs through its connections, the link through which information flows from one member of the network to the next is known as synapses. Synapses are to neural networks what an Ethernet cable or telephone wire is to a computer network. Without synapses from other neurons, it would be impossible for a neuron to receive input and to send output from and to other neurons, respectively. Given the crucial role that connections play in a network of neurons, synapses in a biological neural network matter as much as the neurons themselves [12].

Most connectionist models are computer simulations executed on digital computers. In a connectionist computer model, units are usually represented by circles as shown in **Figure 1**. Because no unit by itself constitutes a network, connectionist models typically are composed of many units as illustrated in **Figure 2**. However, neural networks are organized in layers of neurons. For this reason, connectionist models are organized in layers of units as shown in **Figure 3**. **Figure 3** is still not a network because no group of objects qualifies as a network unless each member is connected to other members; it is the existence of connections that make a network, as illustrated in **Figure 4** [13].

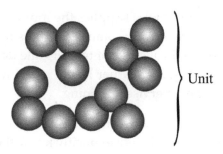

Figure 2. Connectionist model with 11 units.

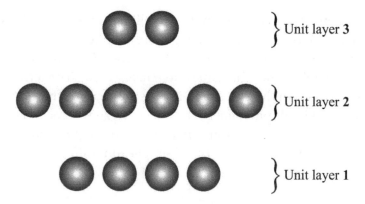

Figure 3. Connectionist model organized in layers.

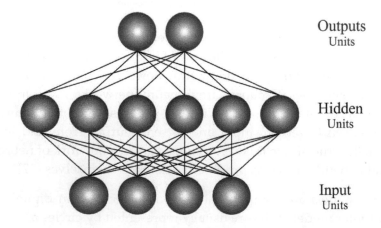

Figure 4. Network connectionist model.

In **Figure 4**, it can be seen that network connections are conduits through which information flows between the members of a network. In the absence of such connections, no group of objects qualifies as a network. There are two kinds of network connections: input and output. An input connection is a conduit through which a member of a network receives information. An output connection is a conduit through which a member of a network sends information. Although it is possible for a network connection to be both an input connection and an output connection, a unit does not qualify as a member of a network if it can neither receive information from other units nor send information to other units.

There are many forms of connectionism, but the most common forms use neural network models [14]. The form of the connections and the units can vary from model to model as shown in **Figures 5–9**, where it can be seen that any number of units may exist within each layer, and each unit of each layer is typically linked via a weighted connection to each node of the next layer. Data are supplied to the network through the input layer.

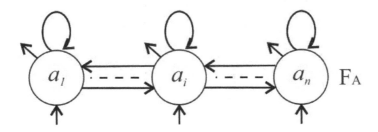

Figure 5. Single-layered recurrent net with lateral feedback structure.

Depending on the nature of the problems, neural network models are organized in different structural arrangements (architectures or topologies) [10]. The neural network architecture defines its structure including the number of hidden layers, number of hidden nodes, and number of nodes at the input and output layers. There are several types of ANN architectures. As illustrated in **Figures 5–9**, most of the widely used neural network models can be divided into two main categories: feed forward neural networks (FFNN) and feedback neural networks (FBNN) [10–14].

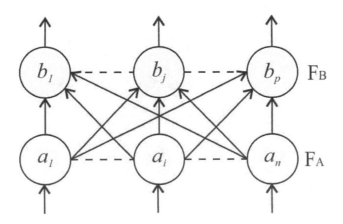

Figure 6. Two-layered feed-forward structure.

As shown in **Figures 6** and **8**, FFNNs allow signals to travel one way only; data enters the inputs and passes through the network, layer by layer, until it arrives at the output. There is no feedback or loops between layers. These networks are extensively used in pattern recognition and classification. FBNN can have signals traveling in both directions by introducing loops in the network as shown in **Figures 5**, **7**, and **9**. FBNNs are dynamic; their state changes continuously until they reach an equilibrium point. They remain at the equilibrium point until the input changes and a new equilibrium needs to be found.

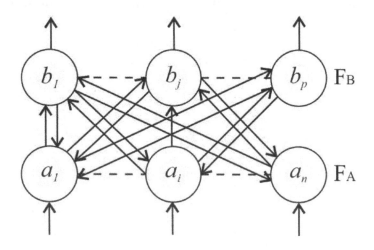

Figure 7. Two-layered feedback structure.

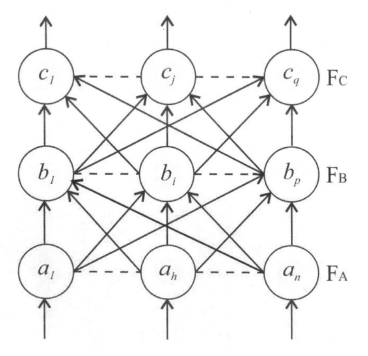

Figure 8. Three-layered feed-forward structure.

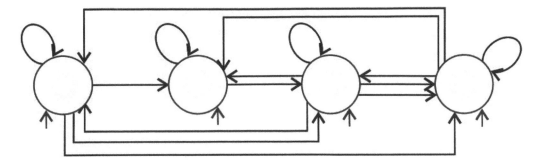

Figure 9. Single-layered recurrent structure.

In most connectionist models, units are organized into three layers: an input layer, one or more "hidden" layers, and an output layer [10–14]. **Figures 4** and **8** show a 3-layered FFNN consisting of 3 layers of units, where each unit is connected to each unit above it, and where information flows "forward" from the network's input units, through its "hidden" units, to its output units. The nodes of the hidden layer process input data they receive as the sum of the weighted outputs of the input layer. Nodes of the output layer process input data they receive as the sum of the weighted output of the units within the hidden layers, and supply the system output.

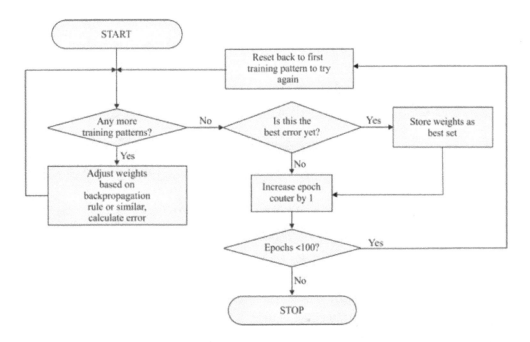

Figure 10. Supervised learning of ANN.

As mentioned earlier, the principles of learning can be applied to machines to improve their performance [15]. In FFNN, network learning is a very important process. The learning situation can be divided into two major categories: supervised and unsupervised. With supervised learning, the ANN must be trained before it becomes useful. Training consists of presenting input and output data to the network. **Figure 10** shows the distinguishing nature of supervised neural network, which incorporates an external trainer in which input and output are known, and its objective is to discover a relationship between the two. In this mode, the actual output of ANN is compared to the desired output.

An important issue concerning supervised learning is the problem of error convergence: the minimization of error between the desired and computed values. The performance of the network is evaluated based on the comparison between the computed (predicted) output and actual (desired) output value [10–15]. There are several types of measurements of prediction accuracy; the most common measurements used are as follows:

1.   Coefficient of determination (R²)

$$R^2 = \frac{\sum_{i=1}^{n}(\hat{Y}_i - \bar{Y})^2}{\sum_{i=1}^{n}(Y_i - \bar{Y})^2} \tag{1}$$

2.   Mean Square Error (MSE)

$$MSE = \frac{1}{n}\sum_{i=0}^{n}(Y_i - \hat{Y}_i)^2 \tag{2}$$

3.   Root Mean Square Error (RMSE)

$$RMSE = \left[\frac{1}{n}\sum_{i=0}^{n}(Y_i - \hat{Y}_i)^2\right]^{\frac{1}{2}} \tag{3}$$

4.   Mean Absolute Percentage Error (MAPE)

$$MAPE\% = \frac{1}{n}\sum_{i=0}^{n}\left|\frac{Y_i - \hat{Y}_i}{Y_i}\right| \times 100 \tag{4}$$

where Y_i is the actual value of output, $\hat{Y}_i$ is the predicted value, and (n) is the number of observations.

Unlike supervised learning, unsupervised neural network uses no external feedback and it is based upon only local information. As can be seen from **Figure 11**, in unsupervised learning only the input is known and the goal is to uncover patterns in the features of the input data. It is also referred to as self-organization, in the sense that it self-organizes data presented to the network and detects their emergent collective properties. Unsupervised learning's goal is to have the computer learn how to do something that we do not tell it how to do. The common applications of unsupervised learning are classification, data mining, and self-organizing maps (SOM), also called Kohonen Neural Network (KNN).

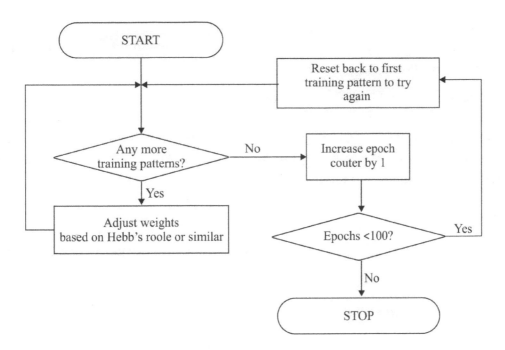

Figure 11. Unsupervised learning of ANN.

In FFNN with supervised training, two very different types of neural networks exist: FFNN trained with Backpropagation (BP) algorithm (FFBPNN) and Statistical Neural Networks (SNN) [10, 11, 14]. FFBPNNs use equations that are connected using weighting factors [11]. The selection of the weighting factors makes these neural nets very powerful. The multilayer perceptron (MLP) is the most common and successful neural network architecture with FFNN topologies, while the most common supervised learning technique used for training artificial neural networks is the multilayer backpropagation (BP) algorithm [10–15].

BP is a systematic method for training multilayer FFNN as shown in **Figure 8**. Since it is a supervised training algorithm, both the input and the target patterns are given (**Figure 10**). For a given input pattern, the output vector is estimated though a forward pass on the network. After the forward pass is over, the error vector at the output layer is estimated by taking the component-wise difference of the target pattern and the generated output vector. A function of errors of the output layered nodes is then propagated back through the network to each layer for adjustment of weights in that layer. The weight adaptation policy in BP algorithm is derived following the principle of steepest descent approach of finding minima of a multi-valued function.

BPFFNNs consist of neurons organized into one input layer and one output layer and several hidden layers of neurons as shown in **Figure 8**. Neurons perform some kind of calculation using inputs to compute an output that represents the system. The outputs are given on to the next neuron. An edge indicates to which neurons the output is given. These arcs carry weights.

Generally, BP learning consists of two passes: a forward pass and a backward pass. In the forward pass, an activity pattern is applied to the sensory nodes of the network. It is at last that a set of outputs is produced as the actual responses of the network. During this path, the synaptic weights are fixed. During backward pass, the synaptic weights are adjusted in accordance with an error correction rule.

BPFFNNs have the desirable characteristic of being very flexible. They can be used for pattern recognition as well as for decision-making problems. Another advantage is that like for every other neural network, the process is highly parallel and therefore the use of parallel processors is possible and cuts down the necessary time for calculations. However, BPNNs have negative characteristics. The training of the network can need a substantial amount of time [16]. The size of the training data for BPFFNN has to be very large. In some instances, it is almost impossible to provide enough training.

On the other hand, SNNs use statistical methods to select the equations within the structure and do not weigh these functions differently [17].

1.2. Statistical neural networks

SNNs are an important and very popular type of neural networks that mainly depend on statistical methods and probability theory [18]. Three of the most important types of these networks are Radial Basis Function Neural Network (RBFNNs), Probabilistic Neural Network (PNNs), and General Regression Neural Network (GRNNs) [19].

1.2.1. Radial basis function neural network

RBFNN was introduced by Broomhead and Lowe in 1988 and is a popular alternative to FFBPNN [20]. The behavior of the network depends on the weights and the activation of a transfer function F, specified for the units [21]. Activation functions are mathematical formulas that determine the output of a processing node [22]. The activation function maps the sum of weighted values passed to them by applying F into the output value, which is then "fired" on to the next layer.

There are several kinds of transfer or activation functions, typically falling into four common categories: Linear function (LF), Threshold function (TF), Sigmoid Function (SF), and Radial Basis Function (RBF) [23]. RBFs are a special class of activation functions which form a set of basis functions, one for each data set. The general form of RBF is:

$$G\left(\|X - \mu\|\right) \tag{5}$$

where G(.) is a positive nonlinear symmetric radial function (kernel); X is the input pattern and μ is the center of the function. Another important property of RBF is that its output is symmetric around the associated center μ. Thus, $f(X_i)$ can be taken to be a linear combination of the outputs of all the basis functions:

$$f(x) = \sum_{i=1}^{n} w_i G(X - \mu) \tag{6}$$

There are several common types of radial basis functions represented in **Table 1** [19–23]:

Function name	Mathematical form
Thin plate spline	$G(x) = (x - \mu)^2 \log(x - \mu)$
Multi-quadratic	$G(x) = \sqrt{(x - \mu)^2 + \sigma^2}$
Inverse multi-quadratic	$G(x) = \dfrac{1}{\sqrt{(x - \mu)^2 + \sigma^2}}$
Gaussian	$G(x) = exp\left(-\dfrac{(x - \mu)^2}{\sigma^2}\right)$

Table 1. Types of radial basis functions.

where these function parameters are the center (μ) and the radius (σ^2). A Gaussian function, also called "bell shaped curve" or normal distribution, is the most common applicable type of RBF. It is suitable not only in generalizing a global mapping but also in refining local features. The Gaussian function tends to be local in its response and is biologically more acceptable than other functions. RBF is unique, because unlike the others, it monotonically decreases with distance from the center, and forms the classic bell shaped curve which maps high values into low ones, and maps mid-range values into high ones. A plot of a Gaussian function is represented in **Figure 12**.

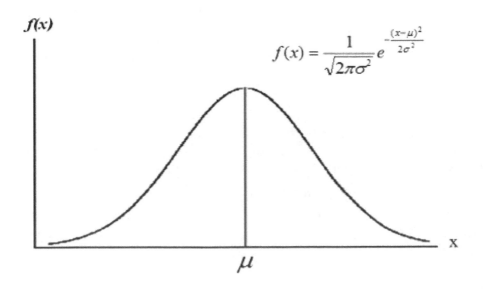

$$f(x) = \frac{1}{\sqrt{2\pi\sigma^2}} e^{-\frac{(x-\mu)^2}{2\sigma^2}}$$

Figure 12. Plot representing a Gaussian function.

The mathematical form of this function for the case of a single variable is given by:

$$f(x) = \frac{1}{\sqrt{2\pi^2}} e^{\frac{(\chi - \mu)^2}{2\sigma^2}} \tag{7}$$

where

$$\mu = E(X) = \int_{-\infty}^{\infty} \chi . f(x) dx \tag{8}$$

$$\sigma^2 = E(X - \mu)^2 = \int_{-\infty}^{\infty} (\chi - \mu)^2 . f(x) dx \tag{9}$$

μ: is the mean (center) of the distribution.

σ^2: is the variance (width or radius) of distribution.

Extending the formula (7) to multiple dimensions, we can get the general Gaussian probability density:

$$f(x) = \frac{1}{(2\pi)^{p/2} |\Sigma|^{p/2}} exp\left(-\frac{1}{2}(\underline{x} - \underline{\mu})^T \Sigma^{-1}(\underline{x} - \underline{\mu}) \right) \tag{10}$$

where p is the number of dimensions, μ is the mean p-dimensional vector and Σ is the covariance p x p matrix.

RBFNNs are useful in solving problems where the input data are corrupted with additive noise and can be used for approximating functions and recognizing patterns [24]. As shown in **Figure 13**, the RBFNN has a feed forward architecture, and it is composed of many interconnected processing units or neurons organized in three successive layers. The first layer is the input layer. There is one neuron in the input layer for each predictor variable. The second layer is the hidden layer. This layer has a variable number of neurons. Each neuron consists of a RBF centered on a point with as many dimensions as there are predictor variables.

The standard euclidean distance is used to measure how far an input vector is located from the center. The value coming out from the neuron in the hidden layer is multiplied by a weight (W_i) associated with the neuron, also a bias value that is multiplied by a weight (W_o), is passed to the summation layer which adds up the weighted values and presents this sum as the network outputs.

The training of RBFNNs is radically different from the training of FFNNs [19–24]. RBFNN training may be done in two stages: First, calculating the RBF parameters, including centers and the scaling parameter. Various parameters, such as the number of neurons in the hidden layer, the coordinates of the center of each hidden layer function, the radius (width) of each function in each hidden unit, and the weights between the hidden and output units, are determined by the training process; second, estimating the weights between the hidden and output layers. Opposed to BPFFNN, in RBFNN training, there is no changing of the weights with the use of the gradient method for function minimization. In RBFNNs, training resolves itself into selecting the centers and calculating the weights of the output neuron.

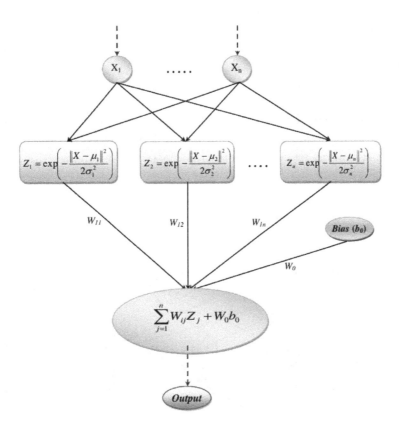

Figure 13. Network architecture of RBFNN.

The center (μ) and width radius (σ) of the radial function and final weights are the parameters of the model. Many algorithms have been designed to determine these parameters by minimizing the error between the target and actual output. Determination of centers is important for the success of the RBFNN and there are several methods to choose suitable centers for network, such as random selection from data set, randomly fixed, and clustering approach.

Determination of the width is very important for the success of the RBFNN. If the width values are large, the model will not be able to closely fit the function; on the other hand, a large width parameter would give better generalization but poorer output. A small width parameter gives good recall of the training patterns but poor generalization, and the model will over fit the data because each training point will have too much influence. There are several methods to determine the width. Two of the common methods for width selection are fixed method and distance averaging.

The number of hidden units is very important and plays a major role in RBFNN performance. It is very difficult to find a suitable number of hidden units. If the number of hidden units is too low, the network cannot reach a desired level of performance because of an insufficient number of hidden neurons. Many researchers assumed that the number of hidden units is fixed and is chose a priori.

There are several types of learning that can be used in RBFNNs, such as General Regression Neural Network (GRNN), Orthogonal Least Squares, K-Means Clustering, and P-Nearest Neighbour.

1.2.2. Probabilistic neural network

Specht first introduced the probabilistic neural network (PNN) in the 1990s. It closely related to "the Bayes Strategy for Pattern Classification" rule and Parzen nonparametric probability density function estimation theory. It performs classification where the target variable is categorical [19–24].

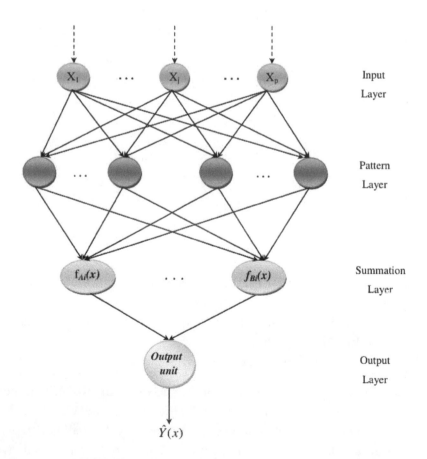

Figure 14. Block diagram of a probabilistic neural network (PNN).

PNNs are often more accurate than FFNNs and it is usually much faster to train PNNs than FFNNs. The greatest advantages of PNNs are the fact that the output is probabilistic which makes interpretation of output easy, and the training speed. Training a PNN is very fast because it requires that each pattern be presented to the network only once during training, unlike BPFFNNs, which require feedback of errors and adjusting weights and many presentations of training patterns. These PNNs, with variation can be used for mapping, classification, and associative memory. The greatest disadvantage is the network size since PNNs require more memory space to store the model.

The general structure of PNN, which is presented in **Figure 14**, consists of four layers. The first layer is the input layer. The input unit nodes do not perform any computation and simply distribute the input to the neurons in the first hidden layer (pattern layer). There is one neuron in the input layer for each predictor variable.

The second layer is the pattern layer. Each pattern unit represents information on one training sample. Each pattern unit calculates the probability of how well the input vector fits into the pattern unit. The neurons of the pattern layer are divided into K groups, one for each category. The i-th pattern neuron in the k-th group computes its output using a Gaussian kernel with the form:

$$f_{Ai}(X) = \frac{1}{(2\pi\sigma^2)^{p/2}} exp\left[-\frac{(X - X_{Ai})^T - (X - X_{Ai})}{2\sigma^2}\right] \qquad (11)$$

where:

i: is the pattern number.

p: denotes the dimension of the pattern vector x.

σ: is the smoothing parameter of the Gaussian Kernel.

X_{Ai}: is the center of the kernel.

The third layer is the summation layer. In the summation layer, there is one pattern neuron for each category of the target variable. The neurons of this layer compute the approximation of the conditional class probability function through a combination of the previously computed densities as the following equation:

$$f_A(X) = \frac{1}{(2\pi\sigma^2)^{p/2}} \frac{1}{M} \sum_{i=1}^{M} exp\left[-\frac{(X - X_{Ai})^T - (X - X_{Ai})}{2\sigma^2}\right] \qquad (12)$$

The fourth layer is the output layer (also called decision layer). At the output layer, we have a hard-limiting threshold: (+1) whenever an input pattern X belongs to category (A), and (-1) if it is from category (B).

The use of PNN is especially advantageous due to its ability to converge to the underlying function of the data with only few training samples available. The additional knowledge needed to get the fit in a satisfying way is relatively small and can be done without additional input by the user. GRNN falls into the category of PNN. This neural network, like other SNNs, needs only a fraction of the training samples a BPFFNN would need, mainly because the data available from measurements of an instance is generally never enough for a BPFFNN. This makes GRNN a very useful tool to perform predictions and comparisons of system performance in practice.

The invention of GRNN was a great turn in the history of neural networks. Researchers from many fields including medicine, engineering, commerce, physics, chemistry, geology, statistics, etc., benefited from this technique for their research.

1.2.3. Generalized regression neural network

GRNN is a type of supervised FFNN and is one of the most popular neural networks. Donald F. Specht first introduced it in 1991. Specht's GRNN is related to his probabilistic neural network (PNN) classifier. Like PNN networks, GRNNs are known for their ability to train quickly on sparse data sets. Rather than categorizing data like PNN, GRNN applications are able to produce continuous valued outputs. An important by-product of the GRNN network is Bayesian posterior probabilities. The training of GRNN networks is very fast because the data only needs to propagate forward once, unlike most other BPNNs, where data may be propagated forward and backward many times until an acceptable error is found [19–24].

GRNNs work well on interpolation problems. However, because they are function approximators, they tend to trade accuracy for speed. The GRNN is used for estimation of continuous variables, as in standard regression techniques. It uses a single common radial basis function kernel bandwidth (σ) that is tuned to achieve optimal learning.

The regression performed by GRNN is in fact the conditional expectation of Y, given X = x. In other words, it outputs the most probable scalar Y given specified input vector x. Let f(x, y) be the joint continuous probability density function of a vector random variable, X, and a scalar random variable, Y. Let x be a particular measured value of the random X. The regression of Y given x (also called conditional mean of Y given x) is given by:

$$E[Y/x] = \int_{-\infty}^{\infty} Y.f(Y/x)dy = \frac{\int_{-\infty}^{\infty} Y.f(x, Y)dy}{\int_{-\infty}^{\infty} (x,Y)dy} \tag{13}$$

If the relationship between independent (X) and dependent (Y) variables is expressed in a functional form with parameters, then the regression will be parametric. Without any real knowledge of the functional form between the x and y, nonparametric estimation method will be used. For a nonparametric estimate of f(x, y), we will use one of the consistent estimators that is a Gaussian function. This estimator is a good choice for estimating the probability density function, f, if it can be assumed that the underlying density is continuous and that the first partial derivatives of the function evaluated at any x are small. The good choice for probability estimator $\hat{f}(x, y)$ is based on sample values x_i and y_i of the random variables X and Y is given by:

$$\hat{f}(x,y) = \frac{1}{(2\pi)^{(p+1)/2} \cdot \sigma^{p+1}} \cdot \frac{1}{n} \sum_{i=1}^{n} \left\{ exp\left[-\frac{(X - X_i)^T (X - X_i)}{2\sigma^2} \right] exp\left[\frac{(Y - Y_i)^2}{2\sigma^2} \right] \right\} \tag{14}$$

p: is the dimension of the vector variable.

n: is the number of training pairs $(x_i \rightarrow y_i)$.

σ: is the single learning or smoothing parameter chosen during network training.

Y_i: is desired scalar output given the observed input x_i.

The topology of GRNN presented in **Figure 15** consists of four layers: The first layer is the input layer that is fully connected to the second layer. The input units are merely distribution units, which provide all of the (scaled) measurement variables X to all of the neurons on the second layer, the pattern units. The second layer is the first hidden layer (also called the pattern layer). This layer consists of N processing elements or nodes, where N is the number of sample within a training data set and each node represents the input vector, Xi, associated with the vector assigned with the jth sample in training data. In each node, each input vector is subtracted from the vector assigned to the node, Xj. This difference is then squared by the node. The result is fed into a nonlinear kernel, which is usually an exponential function. The pattern unit outputs are passed on to the summation units.

Note that the second hidden layer always has exactly one more node than the output layer. When you need a multidimensional (vector) output, the only change to the network is to add one additional node to the second hidden layer, plus an additional node in the output layer for each element of the output vector.

The third layer is the second hidden layer (Summation layer) which has two nodes. The input to the first node is the sum of the first hidden layer outputs, each weighted by the observed output yj corresponding to Xj. The input of the second node is the summation of the first hidden layer activations.

The fourth layer is the output layer. It receives the two outputs from the hidden layer and divides them to yield an estimate for y (or to provide the prediction result).

In the GRNN architecture, unlike other network architectures as in BP, there are no training parameters such as learning rate and momentum, but there is a smoothing factor (σ) that is applied after the network is trained. The choice of smoothing factor (parameter) of the kernel σ is very important. It has the effect of smoothing the training examples. Small values of σ tend to make each training point distinct, whereas large values force a greater degree of interpolation between the training observations. For GRNNs, the smoothing factor must be greater than 0 and can usually range from 0.01 to 1 with good results. We need to experiment in order to determine which smoothing factor is most appropriate for our data.

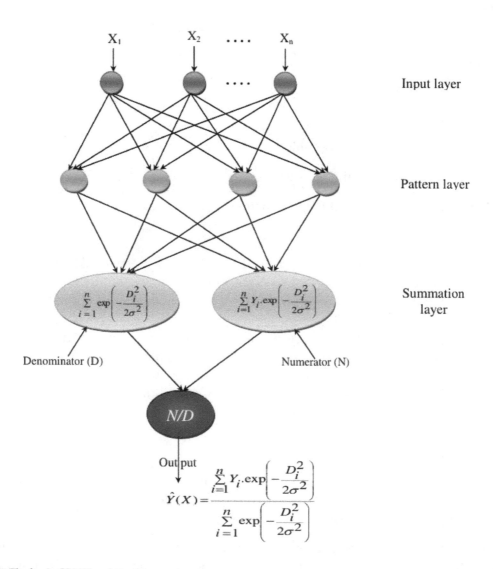

Figure 15. The basic GRNN architecture.

A useful method of selecting an appropriate σ is the Holdout method. For a particular value of σ, the Holdout method consists in removing one sample at a time and constructing a network based on all of the other samples. The network is then used to estimate Y for the removed sample. By repeating this process for each sample and storing each estimate, the mean square error can be measured between the actual sample values Yi and the estimates. The value of σ giving the smallest error should be used in the final network.

Fortunately, in most applications there is a unique σ which produces the minimum MSE between the network output and the desired output for the testing set that can be found quickly by trial and error.

2. Neutron spectrometry by means of generalized regression neural networks

2.1. Neutron spectrometry

In general, neutrons are more difficult to detect than gamma rays because of their weak interaction with matter and their large dynamic range in energy [25]. Neutrons have mass but no electrical charge [26]. Because of this, they cannot directly produce ionization in a detector, and therefore cannot be directly detected. This means that neutron detectors must rely upon a conversion process where an incident neutron interacts with a nucleus to produce a secondary charged particle [27]. These charged particles are then directly detected and from them the presence of neutrons is deduced.

The derivation of the spectral information is not simple because the unknown is not given directly as a result of measurements [28]. The spectral information is derived through the discrete version of the Fredholm integral-differential equation of first type [29]. Normally, researchers solve a discrete version of this equation, which gives an ill-conditioned system of equations which have no explicit solution, may have no unique solution, and are referred to as ill-posed [30].

Since the 1960s, the Bonner Sphere Spectrometer (BSS) has been the most used method for radiological protection purposes [28]. The isotropy of the response, the wide energy range (from thermal to GeV neutrons), and the easy operation make these systems still applicable. BSS consists of a thermal neutron detector located at the center of several high-density polyethylene spheres of different diameters [29]. By measuring the count rates with each sphere individually, an unfolding process can, in principle, provide some information about the energy distribution of the incident neutrons.

The most delicate part of neutron spectrometry based on BSS is the unfolding process [30]. The unfolding spectrum of the neutrons measured consists of establishing the rate of energy distribution of fluency, known as response matrix, and the group of carried-out measures. Because the number of unknowns overcomes the number of equations, this ill-conditioned system has an infinite number of solutions. The process of selecting the solution that has meaning for the problem is part of the unfolding process.

To solve the system of equations for BSS unfolding, several approaches have been used [29]: iterative procedures, Monte Carlo, regularization, and maximum entropy methods. The drawbacks associated with these traditional unfolding procedures have motivated the need for complementary approaches. Novel methods based on AI have been suggested. In neutron spectrometry, the theory of ANN has offered a promising alternative to the classic calculations with traditional methods. Previous researches indicate that BPFFNNs perform well and have been the most popular networks used in neutron spectrometry [30–35].

BPFFNN have the characteristic of being very flexible; the process is highly parallel and can be used to solve diverse problems; however, this neural network topology has some drawbacks: the structural and learning parameters of the network are often determined using the trial-and-error technique [36]. This produces networks with poor performance and generalization capabilities which affect its application in real problems. Training can require a substantial amount of time to gradually approach good values of the weights. The size of the training data has to be very large and often it is almost impossible to provide enough training samples as in the case of the neutron spectrometry problem.

Another drawback is that adding new information requires retraining the network and this is computationally very expensive for BPFFNN, but not for GRNN which belongs to SNNs. GRNNs use a statistical approach in their prediction algorithm given the bases in the Bayes strategy for pattern recognition. To be able to use the Bayes strategy, it is necessary to estimate the probability density function accurately. The only available information to estimate the density functions is the training samples. These strategies can be applied to problems containing any number of categories as in the case of the neutron spectrometry problem.

2.2. Neutron spectrometry by means of generalized regression neural networks

A GRNN has certain differences compared to BPFFNN approach [24]. The learning of BPFFNN can be described as trial and error. This is no longer the case of the GRNNs because they use a statistical approach in their prediction algorithm which is capable of working with only few training samples. The experience is learned not by trial but by experience others made for the neural network. GRNNs are very flexible and new information can be added immediately with almost no retraining. The biggest advantage is the fact that the probabilistic approach of GRNN works with one-step-only learning.

A further big difference that exists between BPFFNN and GRNN is the difference in the process inside the neurons. A GRNN uses functions that are based on knowledge resulting from the Bayes strategy for pattern classification. The structure of the calculations for the probabilistic density function in GRNN has striking similarities to a BPFFNN. The strength of a GRNN lies in the function that is used inside the neuron.

It would be desirable to approach the parameters in one-step-only approach. The Bayes strategy for pattern classification extracts characteristics from the training samples to come to knowledge about underlying function.

In this work, both BPFFNN and GRNN architectures were trained in order to solve the neutron spectrometry problem using customized technological tools designed with this purpose. A comparison of the performance obtained using both architectures was performed. Results obtained show that the two architectures solve the neutron spectrometry problem well, with high performance and generalization capabilities; however, the results obtained with GRNN are better than those obtained with BPFFNN, mainly because GRNN does not produce negative values and oscillations around the target value.

As mentioned, a GRNN is a BPFFNN based on non-linear regression. It is suited to function approximation tasks such as system modeling and prediction. While the neurons in the first three layers are fully connected, each output neuron is connected only to some processing units in the summation layer. The function of the pattern layers of the GRNN is a Radial Basis Function (RBF), typically the Gaussian kernel function.

In this work, a neutron spectrum unfolding computer tool based on neural nets technology was designed to train a GRNN capable of solving the neutron spectrum unfolding problem with high performance and generalization capabilities. The code automates the pre-processing, training, testing, validation, and post-processing stages of the information regarded with GRNN. The code is capable of training, testing, and validating GRNN. After training and testing the neural net, the code analyzes, graphs, and stores the results obtained.

2.3. Methods

The use of GRNN to unfold the neutron spectra from the count rates measured with the BSS is a promising alternative procedure; however, one of the main drawbacks is the lack of scientific and technological tools based on this technology. In consequence, a scientific computational tool was designed to train, to test, to analyze, and to validate GRNN in this research domain.

Statistical methods tend to put more emphasis on the structure of the data. For neural network methods, the structure of the data is secondary. Therefore, the amount of data needed for statistical methods is a lot smaller than the amount of data needed for ANN approaches. GRNNs are frequently used to classify patterns based on learning from examples. PNNs base the algorithm on the Bayes strategy for pattern recognition.

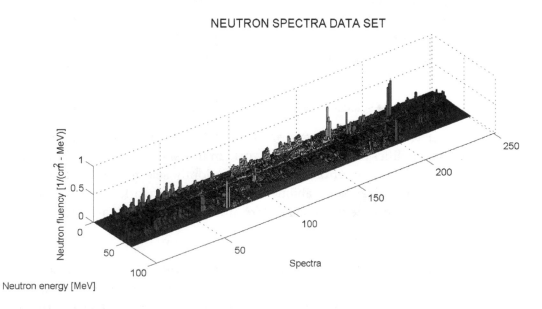

Figure 16. Neutron spectra data set expressed in energy units, used to train the GRNN.

In order to train both BPFFNNs and GRNNs, the only available information is a neutron spectra compilation of the International Atomic Energy Agency (IAEA) which contains a collection of 251 different neutron spectra [37]. This compendium was made with the aim to provide specific technical information that could be used by radiation protection specialists for proper selection of dosimeters and survey instruments, and for interpretation of data obtained with these detectors.

The developed code based on GRNNs technology utilizes these 251 neutron spectra and both, the response matrixes from IAEA's compilation and those that could be introduced by the user. The designed technological tool automates the following activities:

- Read the neutron spectra data set coming from IAEA's compendium, which are expressed in 60 energy bins.

- Read a response matrix used to train the neural network.

- Because the neutron spectra coming from IAEA's compendium are expressed in lethargy units, the code converts these spectra in energy units.

- The neutrons expressed in energy units are multiplied by the selected response matrix in order to calculate the count rates.

- To train the GRNN, the code uses the 251 calculated count rates as entrance data, and their corresponding neutron spectra are expressed in energy units as the output data as shown in **Figure 16**.

- The code randomly generates the training data set, 80% of the whole data, and the testing data set, remaining 20%, as shown in **Figure 17**.

- Using the earlier calculated information, the following stage is to determine the spread constant value. To calculate this value, the computer tool trains several neural networks varying this value from 0 in increments of 0.01 through 2 and compares the mean square error (MSE), which is used to determine the performance of the network. The minimum value obtained is selected as the spread constant value (**Figure 18**).

- After the developed code selects the spread constant value, a final GRNN is trained.

- After training, a testing stage is performed in order to analyze the performance and generalization capabilities of the trained network. In this stage only the input is proportionated to the network. Fifty neutron spectra are randomly selected by the code to test the performance and generalization capabilities of the trained network. In order to analyze the performance of the trained network, chi square and correlation tests are performed.

- Finally, the code plots and stores the generated information.

In this work, a comparison of the performance obtained in the solution of the neutron spectrometry problem using two different neural network architectures, BPFFNN and GRNN, is presented. Both BPFFNN and GRNN were trained and tested using the same information: 251 neutron spectra, extracted from IAEA's compilation. Eighty percent of the whole data set, randomly selected, was used at training stage and remaining 20% at testing stage. Fifty neutron spectra were used as testing data set.

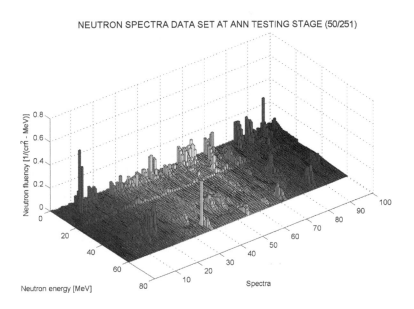

Figure 17. Neutron spectra data set used at testing stage, compared with target spectra.

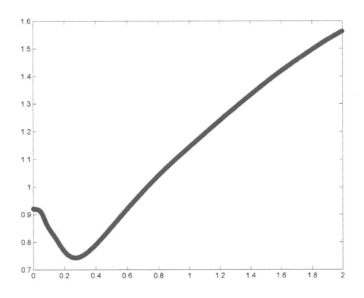

Figure 18. Optimum spread constant value, sigma, and determination.

The architectural and learning parameters of BPFFNN were optimized using a statistical methodology known as Robust Design of Artificial Neural Networks Methodology (RDANNM) [36]. In GRNN, the only parameter determined was the spread constant value, known as sigma. For both architectures, BPFFNN and GRNN, customized scientific computational tools were used for the training, testing, analysis, and storage of the information generated in the whole process of both network architectures. It can be observed from the results obtained that although the two network architectures present very similar performance and generalization capabilities, GRNN performs better than BPFFNN in the solution of the neutron spectrometry problem. BPFFNNs produce negative values and high oscillations around the target values, which makes this type of network unusable in the solution of the problem mentioned.

2.4. Results

In this work, by using two different technological tools, two different artificial neural networks architectures, BPFFNN and GRRN, were trained and tested using the same information. The performance of the networks was compared. From the results obtained, it can be observed that GRNN performs better than BPFFNN in the solution of the neutron spectrometry problem.

Network parameters	BPNN (trial and error)	BPNN (RDANNM)	GRNN
Networks tested before training	Undetermined	50 in 150 minutes	2000 in 154 seconds
Hidden layers	Undetermined	1	Fixed architecture
Neurons in hidden layer	Undetermined	10	According input
Training algorithm	Undetermined	Trainscg	Statistical methods
Learning rate	Undetermined	0.1	–
Momentum	Undetermined	0.01	–
Spread constant	–	–	0.2711
Performance (MSE)	Undetermined	2.12E-4	2.48E-4
Training time (seconds)	Several hours	170.40	0.058
Epochs	Often millions	50E3	1
Best chi-square test BPNN Statistical margin 34.7	–	2.3525	0.049
Best correlation test BPNN Statistical margin 1	–	0.9928	0.99571
Worst chi-square test BPNN	–	0.44704	0.3223
Worst correlation test BPNN	–	0.2926	0.46023

Table 2. Comparison between BPFFNN and GRNN values in neutron spectrometry.

By using the RDANNM, around 50 different network architectures were trained in 150 minutes average, before the selection of the near-optimum architecture. By testing different network architectures according to RDANNM, each network was trained in 50E3 epochs and 180 seconds average, stopping the training when the network reached the established mean square error (MSE) equal to 1E-4, the value used to measure the network performance. After selecting the near-optimum architectural and learning parameters of the BPFFNN, the network was trained and tested using the values shown in **Table 2**: one hidden layer with 10 neurons, a trainscg training algorithm, and a learning rate and momentum equal to 0.1 and 0.01, respectively.

As can be seen in **Table 2**, contrary to BPFFNN the spread constant or sigma was the only value determined in GRNN. Using the same training and testing data sets used for BPFFNN, around 2000 neural networks were trained in 154 seconds average in order to determine the spread constant equal to 0.2711. Each GRNN was trained in 0.058 seconds average in only one-step-only learning. Further, a final GRNN was trained and tested in 0.058 seconds average in only one epoch.

Table 2 shows the values obtained after training the two network architectures compared in this work. As can be seen, when the trial-and-error technique is used, it is very difficult to determine if the performance of the network is good or bad, mainly because a scientific and systematic methodology is not used for determining the near-optimum learning and architectural values as when RDANNM is used.

As can be appreciated in **Table 2**, after training both network architectures, BPFFNN was optimized using RDANNM and GRNN, the performance, MSE, reached by the two networks is very close to each other. In BPFFNNs, the MSE is a value optimized by the network designer using RDANNM; in GRNN network the value was automatically obtained by the network based on the training information used by the automated code. The anterior demonstrates the powerful RDANNM in the optimization of the near-optimum values of BPFFNN architectures.

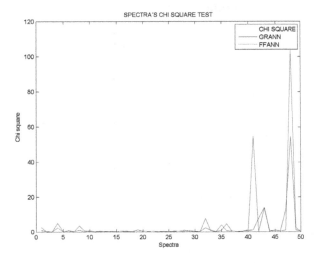

Figure 19. Chi-square test comparison for BPFFNN and GRNN.

Figures 19 and **20** show that at testing stage, the chi square and correlation tests are very close in both BPFFNN and GRNN network architectures. The same 50 neutron spectra were used for testing the two network architectures. At testing stage, only the count rates were proportionated to the trained networks. The output produced by the networks was compared with the expected neutron spectrum taken from IAEA's compilation by means of chi square and correlation tests. In the trained networks, two spectra are above the statistical margin of the chi-square test. In correlation tests, two values are below 0.5. This shows the high performance of the networks.

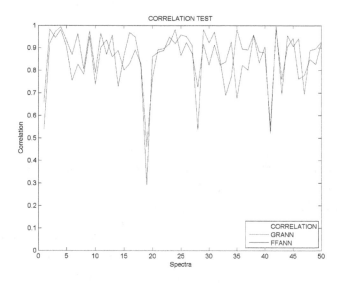

Figure 20. Correlation test comparison for BPFFNN and GRNN.

As can be seen from **Figures 19** and **20**, the 50 chi-square and correlation tests of trained networks are very similar. In both cases, the average value is around 0 and 0.8 respectively, which is near the optimum values equal to 0 and 1. This means that BPFFNN and GRNN have high performance and generalization capabilities and demonstrates the effectiveness of the RDANNM in the design of near-optimum architectures of BPFFNN.

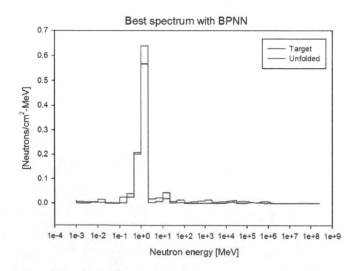

Figure 21. Best spectrum obtained with BPFFNN.

As mentioned earlier, 50 neutron spectra were randomly selected at the testing stage. The same training and testing data sets were used to train and to test the performance and generalization capability of the networks. The best and the worst cases for both BPFFNN and GRNN are showed in **Figures 21–28**. **Figures 21–22** and **23–24** show the best cases observed at testing stage for BPFFNN and GRNN, respectively. From these figures, it can be observed that the chi-square and correlations tests for both BPFFNN and GRNN are near 0 and 1, respectively, which means that the compared neutron spectra are very similar.

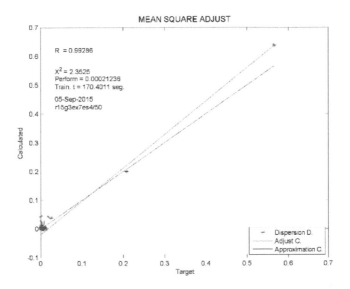

Figure 22. Best chi-square and correlation tests for spectrum obtained with BPNN.

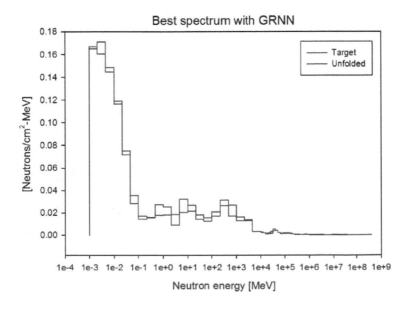

Figure 23. Best spectrum obtained with GRFFNN.

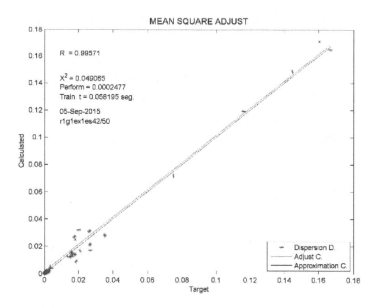

Figure 24. Best chi-square and correlation tests for spectrum obtained with GRNN.

As can be appreciated in **Figures 21–28**, despite the good results obtained with BPFFNN, one drawback is that the calculated neutron spectra produce negative values which have no meaning in real problems. These negative values are eliminated from the output produced by the network; however, when the BPFFNN is applied in real workplaces, because the training received, the network tends to produce negative values and oscillations around the target value. GRNN networks do not produce these negative values and oscillations and therefore the performance is better than BPFFNN in the solution of the neutron spectrometry problem.

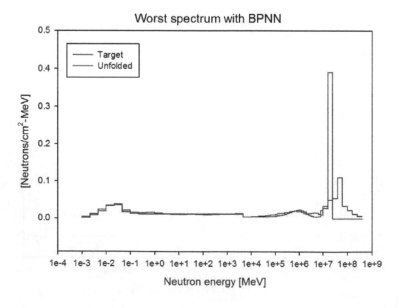

Figure 25. Worst spectrum obtained with BPFFNN.

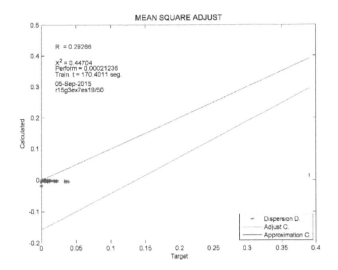

Figure 26. Worst chi-square and correlation tests for spectrum obtained with BPNN.

Figures 25–28 show the worst case observed at the testing stage for BPFFNN and GRNN networks, respectively. As can be seen from these figures, both BPFFNN and GRNN selected the same neutron spectra as the worst. This could be because of the 50 energy bins that the neural networks calculated; 49 values are very similar and only one value is far from the expected target value, which causes that the chi-square and correlation tests to produce low values. From **Figures 25–28**, it can be observed that in the GRNN architecture, the output is closer to the target values of the neutron spectra if compared with BPFFNN. This shows that in the worst case, GRNNs have better performance than BPFFNN.

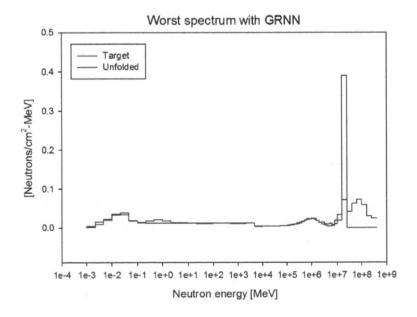

Figure 27. Worst spectrum obtained with BPFFNN.

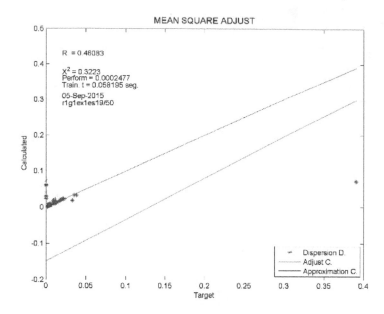

Figure 28. Worst chi-square and correlation tests for spectrum obtained with GRNN.

The results observed in this work indicate that GRNN is able to predict the unknown neutron spectrum presented to the network with good accuracy. As can be seen from **Figures 21–24**, due to proper selection of the spread constant value, the GRNN calculated values, each one of the 60 energy bins of the spectrum, are around the target value (the spectrum from IAEA's compendium). As opposed to BPFFNN, non-negative values and oscillations around the target value are generated when GRNNs are used.

Since there is only one parameter in GRNN, this type of ANN is also called a nonparametric model. It stores the training data as the parameter, rather than calculating and modifying the weights and bias in each hidden layer as the input data imported into the model. When the query comes, the model will calculate the value by summing the values of the other points weighted by the RBF function. Therefore, unlike parametric models such as BP, there are no weights and bias information produced to characterize the trained model.

3. Discussion and conclusions

Different approaches exist to model a system with available data. Each one of them has its own qualities and therefore advantages. GRNN falls into the category of PNN. This neural network, like other PNNs, needs only a fraction of the training samples a BPNN would need. The data available from measurements of an instance is generally never enough for a BPNN. Therefore, the use of GRNN is especially advantageous due to its ability to converge to the underlying function of the data with only few training samples available. The additional knowledge needed to get the fit in a satisfying way is relatively small and can be done without additional input by the user.

Statistical methods tend to put more emphasis on the structure of the data. For neural network methods, the structure of the data is secondary. Therefore, the amount of data needed for statistical methods is a lot smaller than the amount of data needed for ANN approaches.

Most methods are asymptotically good but most of them have severe drawbacks as well. BPNNs need a very large number of training samples and need a lot of time to gradually approach good values of the weights. Addition of new information requires retraining and this is computationally very expensive for BPNN but not for PNN. PNNs have the big advantage that the prediction algorithm works with only few training samples. Other big advantage is that they are very flexible and new information can be added immediately with almost no retraining.

PNNs use a statistical approach in their prediction algorithm. The bases for the statistical approach are given in the Bayes strategy for pattern recognition. These strategies can be applied to problems containing any number of categories as in the case of the neutron spectrometry problem. To be able to use the Bayes strategy, it is necessary to estimate the probability density function accurately. The only available information to estimate the density functions is the training samples.

The structure of the calculations for the probabilistic density function has striking similarities to a backpropagation feed-forward neural network. PNNs are frequently used to classify patterns based on learning from examples. PNNs base the algorithm on the Bayes strategy for pattern classification. Different rules determine patterns statistics from the training samples. BPNN uses methods that are not based on statistical methods and need a long time and many iterations and feedback until it gradually approaches the underlying function. It would be desirable to approach the parameters in one-step-only approach. The Bayes strategy for pattern classification extracts characteristics from the training samples to come to knowledge about underlying function.

In this work, two different artificial neural networks architectures, BPNN and GRRN, were trained and tested using the same information. The performance of the networks was compared. From the results obtained, it can be observed that GRNN performs better than BPNN in the solution of the neutron spectrometry problem.

PNNs have a very simple structure and are therefore very stable procedures. PNNs perform very well for only few available training samples and the quality increases as the number of training samples increases. This makes GRNN a very useful tool to perform predictions and comparisons of system performance in practice. GRNN is a promising technological tool that can be applied to solve with high efficiency the problems related to neutron spectrometry.

Acknowledgements

This work was partially supported by Fondo Sectorial de Investigación para la Eduación under contract 241771, Fondos Mixtos SEP-CONACYT under contract ZAC-C03-2015-26357-4, and PROSOFT under contract 201513723. The first and second authors want to thank the Doctorate scholarships, with scholarship holder numbers 23386 and 23385, respectively, received by Fondo Sectorial de Investigación para la Eduación under contract 241771. The third and fourth authors want to thank the Doctorate scholarships received by Fondos Mixtos SEP-CONACYT under contract ZAC-C03-2015-26357-4. The seventh author want to thank conacyt for the post-doctoral scholarship number 24296. The authors want to thank the active and determined participation and collaboration on several activities on this research project of the undergraduate students: Ana Isabel Ortiz Hernández, Miguel Ángel Acosta García, Fabian García Vázquez, Edgar Viveros Llamas, and Rogelio Osbaldo Reyes Vargas.

Author details

Ma. del Rosario Martinez-Blanco[1,3], Víctor Hugo Castañeda-Miranda[1,3], Gerardo Ornelas-Vargas[1,3], Héctor Alonso Guerrero-Osuna[1,3], Luis Octavio Solis-Sanchez[1,3], Rodrigo Castañeda-Miranda[1,3], José María Celaya-Padilla[1,3], Carlos Eric Galvan-Tejada[3], Jorge Isaac Galvan-Tejada[3], Héctor René Vega-Carrillo[4], Margarita Martínez-Fierro[1,5], Idalia Garza-Veloz[1,5] and Jose Manuel Ortiz-Rodriguez[1,3,2]*

*Address all correspondence to: morvymm@yahoo.com.mx

1 Centro de Investigación e Innovación Tecnológica Industrial (CIITI), Universidad Autónoma de Zacatecas, Zacatecas, México

2 Laboratorio de Innovación y Desarrollo Tecnológico en Inteligencia Artificial (LIDTIA), Universidad Autónoma de Zacatecas, Zacatecas, México

3 Unidad Académica de Ingeniería Eléctrica (UAIE), Universidad Autónoma de Zacatecas, Zacatecas, México

4 Unidad Académica de Estudios Nucleares (UAEN), Universidad Autónoma de Zacatecas, Zacatecas, México

5 Laboratorio de Medicina Molecular, Unidad académica de Medicina Humana y Ciencias de la Salud (UAMHCS), Universidad Autónoma de Zacatecas, Zacatecas, México

References

[1] Fritzsche P. Tools in artificial intelligence. Viena, Austria: InTech; 2008.

[2] Negnevitsky M. Artificial intelligence, a guide to intelligent systems. Reading, MA, USA: Addison Wesley; 2005.

[3] Coppin B. Artificial intelligence illuminated. Burlington, MA, USA: Jones and Barttlet Publishers; 2004.

[4] Russell S.J., Norvig P. Artificial intelligence a modern approach. Mexico: Prentice Hall; 2004.

[5] Luger G.F. Artificial intelligence structures and strategies for complex problem solving. Reading, MA, USA: Addison-Wesley; 2005.

[6] Baldi P., Brunak S. Bioinformatics, the machine learning approach. Cambridge, MA, USA: Mit Press; 2001.

[7] Yu W. Recent advances in intelligent control systems. London: Springer-Verlag; 2009.

[8] Munakata T. Fundamentals of the new artificial intelligence, neural, evolutionary, fuzzy and more. London: Springer; 2008.

[9] Chennakesava R.A. Fuzzy logic and neural networks, basic concepts and applications. New Delhi,India: New Age International Publishers; 2008.

[10] Arbib M.A. Brain theory and neural networks. Cambridge, MA, USA: The Mit Press; 2003.

[11] Haykin S. Neural networks: a comprehensive foundation. Mexico: Prentice Hall; 1999.

[12] Zupan J. Introduction to artificial neural network methods: what they are and how to use them. Acta Chimica Slovenica. 1994;41(3):327–352.

[13] Jain A.K., Mao J., Mohiuddin K.M. Artificial neural networks: a tutorial. IEEE: Computer. 1996;29(3):31–44.

[14] Lippmann R. An introduction to computing with neural nets. IEEE ASSP Magazine. 1987;4(2):4–22.

[15] Floreano F., Mattiussi C. Bio-inspired artificial intelligence, theories, methods and technologies. Cambridge, MA, USA: The MIT Press; 2008.

[16] Gupta M., Jin L., Homma N. Static and dynamic neural networks: from fundamentals to advanced theory. New Jersey, USA: John Wiley Sons; 2003.

[17] Huang D.S. Radial basis probabilistic neural networks: model and applications. International Journal of Pattern Recognition and Artificial Intelligence. 1999;13(7):1083–1101.

[18] Mao K., Tan K., Ser W. Probabilistic neural network structure determination for pattern classification. IEEE Transactions on Neural Networks. 2000;11(4):1009–1016.

[19] Spetch D.F. Probabilistic neural networks for classification, mapping or associative memory. IEEE International Conference on Neural Networks. 1998;1:525–532.

[20] Spetch D.F. Probabilistic neural networks. Neural Networks. 1990;3(1):109–118.

[21] Spetch D.F. Enhancements to probabilistic neural networks. International Joint Conference on Neural Networks. 1992;1:761–768.

[22] Taylor J.G. Mathematical approaches to neural networks. Holland: North-Holland Mathematical library; 1993.

[23] Spetch D.F., Romsdhal H. Experience with adaptive probabilistic neural networks and adaptive general regression neural networks. IEEE International Conference on Neural Networks. 1994;2:1203–1208.

[24] Spetch D.F., Shapiro P. Generalization accuracy of probabilistic neural networks compared with backpropagation networks. IJCNN-91-Seattle International Joint Conference on Neural Networks. 1991;1:887–892.

[25] Attix F.H. Introduction to radiological physics and radiation dosimetry. New Jersey, USA: Wiley-VCH; 2004.

[26] Lilley J. Nuclear physics, principles and applications. New Jersey, USA: John Wiley & Sons, Ltd.; 2001.

[27] Bromley D.A. Detectors in nuclear science. Nuclear Instruments and Methods. 1979;162:431–476.

[28] Bramblett R.L., Ewing R.I., Bonner T.W. A new type of neutron spectrometer. Nuclear Instruments and Methods. 1960;9:1–12.

[29] Thomas D.J. Neutron spectrometry for radiation protection. Radiation Protection Dosimetry. 2004;110(1–4):141–149.

[30] Matzke M. Unfolding procedures. Radiation Protection Dosimetry. 2003;107(1–3):155–174.

[31] Braga C.C., Dias M.S. Application of neural networks for unfolding neutron spectra measured by means of Bonner spheres. Nuclear Instruments and Methods in Physics Research Section A. 2002;476(1–2):252–255.

[32] Kardan M.R., Setayeshi S., Koohi-Fayegh R., Ghiassi-Nejad M. Neutron spectra unfolding in Bonner spheres spectrometry using neural networks. Radiation Protection Dosimetry. 2003;104(1):27–30.

[33] Kardan M.R., Koohi-Fayegh R., Setayeshi S., Ghiassi-Nejad M. Fast neutron spectra determination by threshold activation detectors using neural networks. Radiation Measurements. 2004;38:185–191.

[34] Vega-Carrillo H.R., et al. Neutron spectrometry using artificial neural networks. Radiation Measurements. 2006;41:425–431.

[35] Vega-Carrillo H.R., Martinez Blanco M.R., Hernandez Davila V.M., Ortiz Rodriguez J.M. Ann in spectroscopy and neutron dosimetry. Journal of Radioanalytical and Nuclear Chemistry. 2009;281(3):615–618.

[36] Ortiz-Rodriguez J.M., Martinez-Blanco H.R., Vega-Carrillo H.R. Robust design of artificial neural networks applying the Taguchi methodology and DoE. Proceedings of the Electronics, Robotics and Automotive Mechanics Conference (CERMA'06), IEEE Computer Society. 2006;1:1–6.

[37] IAEA. Compendium of neutron spectra and detector responses for radiation protection purposes. Technical Report 403; Vienna, Austria: International Atomic Energy Agency (IAEA); 2001.

2

Artificial Neural Networks in Production Scheduling and Yield Prediction of Semiconductor Wafer Fabrication System

Jie Zhang, Junliang Wang and Wei Qin

Additional information is available at the end of the chapter

Abstract

With the development of artificial intelligence, the artificial neural networks (ANN) are widely used in the control, decision-making and prediction of complex discrete event manufacturing systems. Wafer fabrication is one of the most complicated and high competence manufacturing phases. The production scheduling and yield prediction are two critical issues in the operation of semiconductor wafer fabrication system (SWFS). This chapter proposed two fuzzy neural networks for the production rescheduling strategy decision and the die yield prediction. Firstly, a fuzzy neural network (FNN)-based rescheduling decision model is implemented, which can rapidly choose an optimized rescheduling strategy to schedule the semiconductor wafer fabrication lines according to the current system disturbances. The experimental results demonstrate the effectiveness of proposed FNN-based rescheduling decision mechanism approach over the alternatives (back-propagation neural network and Multivariate regression). Secondly, a novel fuzzy neural network-based yield prediction model is proposed to improve prediction accuracy of die yield in which the impact factors of yield and critical electrical test parameters are considered simultaneously and are taken as independent variables. The comparison experiment verifies the proposed yield prediction method improves on three traditional yield prediction methods with respect to prediction accuracy.

Keywords: semiconductor wafer fabrication system, rescheduling, fuzzy neural networks, yield prediction, decision mechanism

1. The production scheduling and yield prediction of semiconductor wafer fabrication system (SWFS)

The semiconductor wafer fabrication system (SWFS) is one of the most sophisticated manufacturing systems. This kind of manufacture system is characterised by a different type of wafer process (batch and single process), hundreds of process steps, the large and expensive device, production unforeseen circumstances and re-entrant flow [1]. Semiconductor manufacturing orders are usually global, dynamic and customer driven since the 1990s. As a result, semiconductor manufacturers strive to achieve high-quality products using advance manufacturing technologies (such as process planning and scheduling and digitized indicators' prediction technologies) [2]. In recent years, production scheduling and yield prediction are always two issues above all in the complex SWFS.

An organization's competitive advantage is increasingly dependent on its response to market changes and opportunities, and in response to unforeseen circumstances (i.e. Machine breakdown, rush orders), so it is important to reduce inventory and cycle time, and improve resource utilization. Therefore, production scheduling is required to optimize the operation of SWFS and has been reviewed by Uzsoy and his colleagues [3]. SWFS operates in uncertain dynamic environments, facing with a lot of disturbances, such as machine failure, a lot of rework and rush orders [4]. Production rescheduling has been viewed as an efficient approach in responding to these uncertainties raised by the external environment and internal conditions of production [5]. In job shop and flow shop, heuristic algorithms and discrete event simulation methods are mainly applied in production scheduling problems [6–8]. However, the SWFS is large-scaled, complicated system with re-entrant flows, which is different from typical job and flow shop. Many rescheduling strategies improving traditional job shop rescheduling methods have been proposed and applied in SWFS in the recent decade [9, 10]. These methods using a single rescheduling strategy are not enough for the real-time dynamic manufacturing environment, which is more complex with disruptive events every day. For this reason, a layered rescheduling framework is needed to select rescheduling methodologies in SWFS according to the present system status.

Yield prediction plays an indispensable role in the semiconductor manufacturing factory for its powerful function of reducing cost, increasing production and maintaining a good relationship with customers. Before a malfunction is detected, the accurate prediction model of yield will serve as a warning role and help people take proactive measures to reduce the number of defect's wafers and increase the total yield of SWFS. An accurate prediction of yield plays a useful role in releasing the plan of production and optimizing the process of production, which will make the cycle time shorter and reduce fabrication cost of average units. To offer a reasonable and acceptable price and satisfy the customers, the prediction of manufacturing costs for products is necessary if they are still under development and the accurate prediction of yield can provide some advice for Ref. [11]. To maintain the good relationship with the customers, the order's due data should be guaranteed and the accurate prediction of yield is also useful in this aspect. Some organic problems located on the wafer such as microscopic particles, cluster defects, photo-resist, critical processing parameters would be the factors which affect the yield of the semiconductor wafer. With the statistic analysis models [12] and traditional artificial neural network (ANN) models [13], the prediction of semiconductor fabrication system's yield is difficult. A fuzzy neural network (FNN)-based yield model for yield prediction of semiconductor manufacturing systems is proposes in this chapter. In this system, the impacted factors, which are cluster defects, the defect's key attributed parameters, key electrical test parameters, should be considered in the same time. By this way, the precision of the wafer yield's prediction is improved.

2. The application of ANN in production scheduling and yield prediction of the SWFS

For selecting a scheduling strategy, the FNN approach is widely used. FNN is also an effective methodology for prediction of discrete event manufacturing systems, control and decision-making [14, 15]. For demonstrating the relationship between the monitoring features of a flexible manufacturing system and the conditions of tools, Li et al. [16] presented a fuzzy neural network approach. For controlling manufacturing process, Zhou et al. [17] used a fuzzy neural network approach. Chang et al. [18] created a FNN model of flow time estimation with data, which are generated from a foundry service company. The product design time was estimated with the FNN approach by Xu and Yan [19]. Chang et al. [20] used FNN approach to estimate the influence of the process on the results of the wafer fabrication in SWFS. However, the FNN approach has not been used to solve the problem of SWFS rescheduling problem. This chapter proposes the FNN-based rescheduling decision mechanism for SWFS. This methodology can solve the uncertainty problem and express the expert knowledge in weighted values. In the neural network, the evaluation of local weight values is the knowledge modelling of control rules. Rescheduling strategies, SWFS state parameters, disturbance parameters can be identified and analysed in this model. In this model, we can build the nonlinear relationship between these three components. With this approach, the layered rescheduling approach will be selected that make the yields rapid responsiveness and high productivity of the SWFS in an environment full of randomness.

To predict the wafer yield, Tong et al. [21] proposed a neural network-based approach through considering the clustering phenomenon of the defects in integrated circuit manufacturing. It was proved that the proposed approach was effective. For predicting wafer yield for integrated circuit with clustered defects, Tong and Chao [22] used a general regression neural network (GRNN) approach. Defect clustering patterns are simulated from three aspects: the size of chip, percentage of defects and the cluster pattern. A case study demonstrated the effectiveness of the approach of the model. For the lack of reliability and accuracy in the prediction of yield, an approach of a fuzzy set for yield learning was proposed by Chen and Wang [23]. A few of examples enhanced the reliability and precision of the forecasting of the yield. Chen and Lin [24] proposed a fuzzy-neural system with expert opinions, which can increase the precision of semiconductor yield prediction. The artificial intelligent-based yield forecasting models demonstrated above have some limitations that it only takes consideration of the physical parameters of wafer and the important attributed parameters of defects in wafer without considering the influence of variation of the key electrical test parameters. With the combining of neural network (NN) and memory-based reasoning (MBR), an integrated framework for a yield management system with techniques of hybrid machine learning was given by Chung and Sang [25]. In the forecasting model of the yield, some key electrical test parameters have been taken into consideration. With the use of wafer level electrical test data, a parametric neural forecasting model was constructed by Kim et al. [26] and Kim [27]. However, these yield forecasting models have not taken the attributed parameters of defects in wafer into consideration. This chapter proposes a yield forecasting model with the consideration of the wafer electrical test parameters and important attributed parameters of defects in wafer.

3. Artificial neural network for rescheduling decision mechanism in the SWFS

3.1. Layered rescheduling framework of SWFS

A layered rescheduling framework is proposed in order to reschedule the SWFS for the unstable environment which is shown in **Figure 1**. In the process of rescheduling framework, a three layers of rescheduling strategies are used. a three layers are machine group layer, machine layer and the system layer. The strategies of the rescheduling implement the dynamic scheduling, the global scheduling of SWFS and the machine scheduling. To choose the particular rescheduling strategy, the optimal rescheduling decision mechanism based on FNN approach. The layered rescheduling framework is described in detail in the following paragraph.

Global scheduling of SWFS. If there are some changes in the large-scale SWFS's condition or there are some disturbances, the rescheduling is needed and the global rescheduling of SWFS is managed for the adjustment of the global scheduling [28]. With the machine group layer's adjusted scheduling objectives, a local dynamic scheduling algorithm is applied for scheduling in the machine group layer [29]. In the end, with the machine group layer's adjusted scheduling objectives, machine scheduling is processed in real-time and the optimal machine real-time scheduling solutions are achieved.

Dynamic scheduling of SWFS. If there are some changes in the medium-scale SWFS's condition or there are some disturbances, the rescheduling in the machine group layer is needed and the local dynamic scheduling of SWFS is managed. In order to adjust the local scheduling of a machine group, a local dynamic scheduling algorithm is applied. With the adjusted scheduling objectives of the machine layer taken into consideration, machine scheduling of SWFS is processed.

Machine scheduling of SWFS. If there are some changes in the large-scale SWFS's condition or there are some disturbances, the rescheduling is just accomplished and in the same time, the machine scheduling is processed. Though they are same in the operation sequences of the lots, they are different in the operation start times of delayed lots.

FNN-based optimal rescheduling decision mechanism. With the consideration of the statuses and disturbances to SWFS, the rescheduling layer is chosen by optimal rescheduling decision mechanism. According to the fuzzy neural network, an algorithm for the system is stated in this paper.

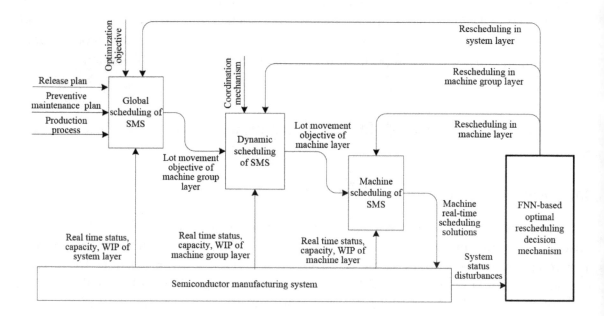

Figure 1. Layered rescheduling framework of SWFS.

3.2. FNN-based decision mechanism for rescheduling

Fuzzy neural network (FNN) is an ingenious combination of fuzzy logic and neural network, which inherits the advantages from both fuzzy system and neural network. The FNN has the characteristics of processing fuzzy information with fuzzy algorithms and learning with a high-speed parallel structure. The FNN approach is therefore adaptable and robust, and is well suited for the SMS rescheduling problem.

The FNN-based rescheduling decision model consists of an input layer, several hidden layers and an output layer. Input parameters connected with disturbances and state parameters are accepted in the input layer. The hidden layers calculate and transform the input parameters using fuzzy logic theory. The output layer produces the decision-making response of the rescheduling model. More details of this method are described.

3.2.1. Input factors in the proposed FNN model

The SMS's state and disturbance parameters are treated as input of the FNN, which can be detailed as: system disturbances parameter, average queue length, stability of SMS, average relative load and average slack time.

3.2.1.1. System disturbances parameter

Since the operating environments of SMS are uncertain and dynamic, disturbances mainly include: machine failures, lot reworks and rush orders. Once a disturbance has happened, an optimal rescheduling strategy must be selected and carried out to guarantee the stability and efficiency of SMS. Disturbances are converted into machine work times to quantify their effect. The mapping of disturbances to machine work times is defined as follows.

(1) Machine failures. The processing time in SMS increases if machine failures happen. Suppose that t^f refers to the increased process time caused by all machine failures, then,

$$t^f = \sum_{M_j^f \in F^f} \sum_{m_{ji} \in M_j^f} t^f_{ji} \qquad (1)$$

where M_j^f is the failed machine group j, m_{ji} refers to the failed machine i of machine group j, t^f_{ji} represents the repair time of machine i of machine group j, and F^f is the set of failed machine group.

(2) Lot reworks. Lot reworks raise the output requirement of SMS. Suppose that t^r is the additional process time incurred by all lot reworks, then,

$$t^r = \sum_{M_j^r \in F^r} \sum_{p_{jk} \in R_j^r} t^r_{jk} \qquad (2)$$

where M_j^r refers to the machine group j operating the rework lots, R_j^r refers to the set of the rework lots operated by the machine group j, p_{jk} refers to the rework lot k operated by the machine group j, t^r_{jk} refers to the process time of the rework lot k operated by the machine group j, F^r refers to the set of the machine group that operate rework lots.

(3) Rush orders. Rush orders also demand more of the production requirement of SMS. Suppose that t^o is the process time required by all rush orders, then,

$$t^o = \sum_{M_j^o \in F^o} \sum_{q_{jk} \in R_j^o} t^o_{jk} \qquad (3)$$

where M_j^o represents the machine group j, that operates the rush orders in current plan time phase, R_j^o represents the set of the lots operated by machine group j in the rush orders; q_{jk} represents the lot k in the rush orders operated by machine group j, t^o_{jk} is the process time of the lot k operated by the machine group j in the rush orders, F^o represents the set of the machine group which are related with rush orders.

(4) System disturbances parameter. Suppose that td is the system disturbances parameter, denoting the total effect of disturbances on SMS scheduling. The formula to calculate td is shown as the (4).

$$td = t^f + t^r + t^o \tag{4}$$

3.2.1.2. Average queue length

Average queue length of machine groups reflecting the utility of the machine group is affected by disturbances. L is the average queue length of machine groups affected by disturbances; and the formula is shown in (5).

$$L = \frac{\sum\limits_{M_j \in (F^r \cup F^f \cup F^o)} L_j}{N} \tag{5}$$

where M_j denotes the machine group j, L_j means queue length of machine group M_j, N refers to the number of machine group that affected by disturbances.

3.2.1.3. Stability of SMS

The stability of SMS is defined as the deviation in predicted average start time of a rescheduled strategy from the real start time. β denotes the stability of SMS, which is shown in (6).

$$\beta = \frac{\sum\limits_{\substack{(i,s)\in S \\ tc_{is} \le tc}} \left| tc'_{is} - tc_{is} \right|}{\sum\limits_{\substack{(i,s)\in S \\ tc_{is} \le tc}} q_{is}} \tag{6}$$

where tc'_{is} is practical start time of process stage s of product i, tc_{is} is computational start time of process stage s of product i which optimized with a global scheduling algorithm or re-scheduling strategy, q_{is} is the number of process stage s of product i, tc is the current time when disturbance happens, S is set of tasks of all machine group in SMS.

3.2.1.4. Average relative loads

Average relative loads denote the loads of machine groups measured from the current time to the end of the scheduling horizon which can be affected by disturbances. Let η represent the average relative loads, the formula for calculation is shown in (7).

$$\eta = \frac{\displaystyle\sum_{\substack{(i,s)\in S_d \\ t_e \geq t_{is} \geq t_c}} tp_{is}}{\displaystyle\sum_{M_j \in (F^r \cup F^f \cup F^o_3)} n_j(te - tc)} \tag{7}$$

where tp_{is} denotes process time of process stage s of product i, te denotes the time point when scheduling is ended, n_j denotes the number of machine of machine group M_j, S_d represents set of tasks of machine group which affected by disturbances.

3.2.1.5. Average slack time

Average slack time represents the space that the machine groups can be adjusted when disturbances happen. Suppose ts is the average slack time, shown in (8).

$$ts = \frac{\displaystyle\sum_{\substack{(i,s)\in S_d \\ t_e \geq t_{is} \geq tc}} \left(t_{i(s+1)} - t_{is} - tp_{is} \right)}{\displaystyle\sum_{\substack{(i,s)\in S_d \\ t_e \geq t_{is} \geq tc}} q_{is}} \tag{8}$$

3.2.2. Output variables

The output variables in the FNN output layer are related to the layered rescheduling strategies, which consists of the rescheduling in system layer, machine group layer, and machine layer. If a particular layered rescheduling strategy is selected, then the corresponding output variable is close to 1, otherwise it equals to 0. In FNN-based rescheduling decision model, suppose that y_1, y_2, y_3 are defined as output variables, then y_1, y_2, y_3 correspond to the rescheduling in system layer, rescheduling in machine group layer, and rescheduling in machine layer, respectively.

3.2.3. The structure of FNN

There are five layers in the rescheduling decision model based on FNN, as illustrated in **Figure 2**.

a. The input vector is $X = [x1, x2, x3, x4, x5]T = [L, \beta, \eta, ts, td]T$. The function of node input-output is:

$$f_{i(1)} = x_{i(0)} = x_i; x_{i(1)} = g_{i(1)} = f_{i(1)}; i = 1, 2, \cdots 5 \tag{9}$$

b. In the second layer which is the fuzzifer layer, the function of the Gauss membership is adopted.

$$u_{ij} = e^{-\frac{(x_i - c_{ij})^2}{\sigma_{ij}^2}}, i = 1, 2, \cdots, 5,$$
$$j = 1, 2, \cdots, k_i \tag{10}$$

In this formula, cij is the centre and σ_{ij} is width. The node input–output function is:

$$f_{ij(2)} = -\frac{(x_i - c_{ij})^2}{\sigma_{ij}^2};$$

$$x_{ij(2)} = u_{ij} = g_{ij(2)} = e^{f_{ij(2)}} = e^{-\frac{(x_i - c_{ij})^2}{\sigma_{ij}^2}};$$
$$i = 1, 2, \cdots 5, j = 1, 2, \cdots, k_i \tag{11}$$

c.   In the third layer as the rule layer, each node in the layer is a fuzzy rule which not only matches the front part of the fuzzy rule but also calculates the adaptive of the rule,

$$a_j = \prod_{l=1}^{5} u_{li_l}(x_{li_l}),$$
$$j = 1, 2, \cdots, n \tag{12}$$

In this layer, the input--output function is:

$$f_{j(3)} = \prod_{l=1}^{5} x_{li_l(2)} = \prod_{l=1}^{5} u_{li_l}(x_{li_l}); x_{j(3)} = g_{j(3)} = f_{j(3)};$$
$$j = 1, 2, \cdots, nx_{j(3)} = g_{j(3)} = f_{j(3)}; j = 1, 2, \cdots, n \tag{13}$$

d.   In the fourth layer which is the normalized layer. In this layer, the node numbers are the same in the third layer. It normalized the adaptive values of these rules. And the input-output function is:

$$f_{j(4)} = \frac{x_{j(3)}}{\sum\limits_{i=1}^{n} x_{i(3)}} = \frac{a_j}{\sum\limits_{i=1}^{n} a_i};$$
$$x_{j(4)} = g_{j(4)} = f_{j(4)}; j = 1, 2, \cdots, n \tag{14}$$

e.   The last layer is the output layer. It defuzzify the output variables. And each node describes a rescheduling strategy. While a rescheduling strategy is chose, the corresponding output is 1 or 0. The input-output function is:

$$f_{i(5)} = \sum_{j=1}^{n} w_{ij} x_{j(4)} \quad = \sum_{j=1}^{n} w_{ij} b_j; x_{j(5)} = g_{j(5)} = f_{j(5)} \quad ; i = 1,2,3$$

$$x_{j(5)} = g_{j(5)} = f_{j(5)} \quad ; i = 1,2,3 \tag{15}$$

$$x_{j(5)} = g_{j(5)} = f_{j(5)} \quad ; i = 1,2,3$$

where w_{ij} is the connection weight parameter.

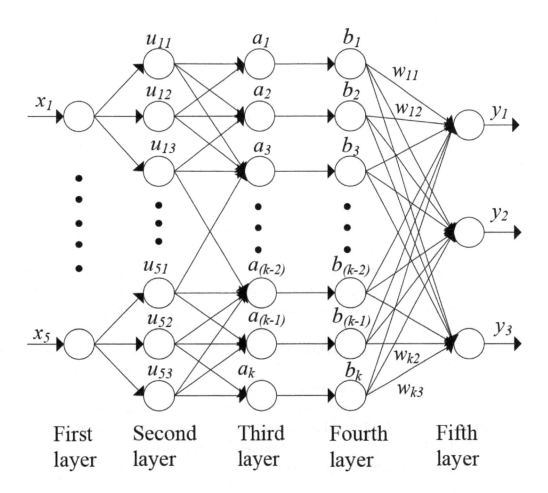

Figure 2. FNN structure.

3.2.4. The strategy of the fuzzy inference

The Mamdani-based fuzzy inference is applied in this FNN-based rescheduling decision model with a assumption that the fuzzy rule Ri describes the relationship between input and output. Then,

Ri:

IF x1 is A1i and x2 is A2i and … and xm is Ami,

THEN y1 is B1i and y2 is B2i and … and ym is Bki,

where

i = 1, 2, …, n.

n: number of rules.

m: number of input variables.

k: number of output variables.

A_{ji}: value of fuzzy linguistic variable xj.

B_{ji}: value of fuzzy linguistic variable yj.

3.3. Result and discussion

3.3.1. Experiment on the proposed FNN approach

In this section, the experiments are conducted to evaluate the effectiveness of the proposed FNN rescheduling decision mechanism. A discrete event simulation model is run to gather the experiment data, which is based on a 6-in. SWFS in Shanghai. This SWFS is composed by eleven machine groups, which add up to thirty-four machines in total. And three types of wafers are put into the SWFS. The processes of all three types of wafer lots are divided into dozes of stages, which is composed by a key step and several successive normal steps. One hundred and fifty records of rescheduling decision are collected from the simulation model, and shown in **Table 1**. Ninety records are used in model training, and 60 are taken to evaluate the model. The presented FNN approach is compared with the back propagation network (BPN) approach and the multivariate regression methodology, since the BPN and multivariate regression approaches are widely used in the rescheduling strategy decision and proven to be competitive [30, 31]. Furthermore, the detail numerical comparison of the FNN approach, BPNN approach and multivariate regression are demonstrated as follows.

Now, it's going to compare the experimental results which are made by these three methods. **Figure 3** shows the optimal rescheduling decision value and the model outputs. It shows that the FNN rescheduling method has the best convergence. We also contrast the RMSE and the decision coefficients R^2 of these three methodologies in **Table 2**. The FNN has the best performance for the RMSE which is 0.042 and has the largest of the R^2 values which is 0.9941. Hence, the rescheduling decision based on FNN has the best performance in these three methods.

Samples no	Average queue length of disturbed machine stations x_1 (lot)	Stability of scheduling x_2 (h)	Average load of disturbed machine stations x_3 (100%)	Average slack time of disturbed machine stations x_4 (h)	Disturbance x_5 (h)	Optimal rescheduling decision objective		
						Rescheduling in machine layer y_1	Rescheduling in machine group layer y_2	Rescheduling in system layer y_3
1	1	1.10	0.59	6.42	2.14	1	0	0
2	2	0.78	0.52	6.51	2.01	1	0	0
3	0	0.81	0.46	5.16	1.76	1	0	0
4	0	0.48	0.1	5.81	1.21	1	0	0
5	2	0.49	0.14	4.62	1.42	1	0	0
6	1	0.52	0.12	5.54	1.79	1	0	0
7	2	0.74	0.17	5.16	1.13	1	0	0
8	0	0.76	0.07	4.49	1.64	1	0	0
9	6	0.38	0.29	4.86	1.4	1	0	0
10	5	0.37	0.26	5.17	2.21	1	0	0
..	..	..	..	..	..	..	..	..
141	6	4.23	0.75	3.81	9.81	0	0	1
142	4	4.15	0.76	5.64	9.18	0	0	1
143	5	4.01	0.76	4.97	9.77	0	0	1
144	2	0.81	0.38	1.87	9.87	0	0	1
145	4	0.87	0.37	2.41	10.11	0	0	1
146	2	0.68	0.42	2.18	9.42	0	0	1
147	2	0.72	0.35	2.18	9.76	0	0	1
148	2	0.91	0.23	2.7	9.13	0	0	1
149	1	0.87	0.21	2.97	9.73	0	0	1
150	2	0.87	0.31	2.77	10.18	0	0	1

Table 1. One hundred and fifty records for numerical experiments.

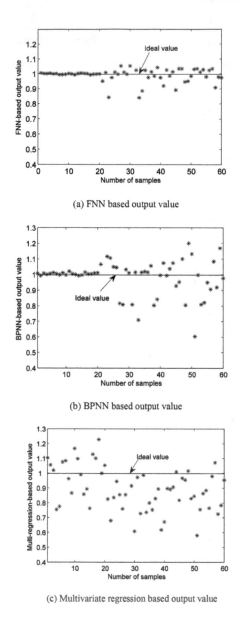

(a) FNN based output value

(b) BPNN based output value

(c) Multivariate regression based output value

Figure 3. The relationship between the rescheduling strategy output and ideal target output for the FNN, BPNN and multivariate regression methods. (a) FNN-based output value, (b) BPNN-based output value and (c) multivariate regression-based output value.

Rescheduling strategy model	RMSE	R^2		
		$R^2_{Y_1}$	$R^2_{Y_2}$	$R^2_{Y_3}$
FNN	0.0042	0.9880	0.9762	0.9941
BPNN	0.0132	0.9745	0.9178	0.9274
Multivariate regression	0.0897	0.85887	0.75566	0.70813

Table 2. Comparison of RMSE and decision coefficients among the FNN, BPNN and multivariate regression methods.

3.3.2. Experiment on the proposed rescheduling decision mechanism

The FNN rescheduling decision mechanism is used in our layered rescheduling method (Method 1). There are two other different rescheduling methods. One is the monolayer-based rescheduling approach (Method 2). Another one is the first come first served (FCFS) approach (Method 23). In our method, the FNN rescheduling decision mechanism figures out the optimal rescheduling approaches which include the global scheduling of SWFS, the dynamic scheduling and the machine scheduling. By contrast, the Method 2 only considers the rescheduling of the machine group layer. But in practice, the Method 3 is widely used in the Fab. In order to prove the efficiency of our approach, we also compared these three rescheduling methods in terms of the machine utilization and the daily movement, which are the important system targets for SWFS.

In the case study, the data are collected from a 6-in. SWFS in Shanghai. It products three kinds of lots which are renamed as A, B and C. The whole process is shown in **Table 4**. This SWFS has eleven key machine groups (shown in **Table 3**). which has 34 machines with MTTF and MTTR parameters. They are explained in Section 5. The SWFS simulation model is built by eM-plant 7.0 software. In the simulation, it took 12 days, including a 5-day warm-up. Ten times repeated trials of the same stimulation, in which the initiated loads of machines were different, were performed (3 rescheduling methods 10 replications). The results are shown in **Figures 4** and **5**, which illustrate:

1. Method 1 performs well in the rescheduling decision in the SWFS.

2. Method 1 outperforms method 2 and 3, which indicates the layered rescheduling method is more suitable than the conventional FCFS rescheduling approach and monolayer-based rescheduling approach in the complex SWFS.

Machine group number	Processing type	Number of machine	Batch size	MTBF	MTTR
1	Ion implant	3	1	70	1
2	Ion implant	4	1	70	1
3	Diffusion	3	5	100	2
4	Diffusion	4	5	110	2
5	Etching	2	1	90	1
6	Etching	4	1	80	1
7	Etching	3	1	60	1
8	Etching	2	1	70	1
9	Lithography	4	1	90	1
10	Lithography	3	1	80	1
11	Lithography	2	1	100	1

Table 3. Configuration of SWFS.

Stage number	Number of time period by product A	Machine group number of product A	Process time of product A by key machine t/hour	Number of time period by product B	Machine group number of product B	Process time of product B by key machine t/hour	Number of time period by product C	Machine group number of product C	Process time of product C by key machine t/hour
1	1	8	1	1	10	1	1	10	1
2	1	7	1	1	8	1	1	8	1
3	1	10	1	4	5	1	2	5	1
4	1	9	1	1	10	1	1	8	1
5	5	0	1	1	1	1	1	0	1
6	3	0	1	1	6	1	4	3	6
7	4	2	4	1	10	1	1	8	1
8	1	8	1	1	9	1	2	5	1
9	1	5	1	6	0	1	2	2	3
10	1	3	3	1	0	1	1	8	1
11	1	0	1	1	4	1	2	5	3
12	2	10	1	1	8	1	1	0	1
13	1	0	1	2	1	1	2	3	6
14	4	4	2	3	2	3	1	8	1
15	1	6	1	1	10	1	2	9	1
16	2	1	1	1	8	1	2	4	1
17	3	4	2	2	5	2	3	0	1
18	1	9	1	1	3	1	1	8	1
19	1	5	1	2	5	1	3	6	1
20	1	8	1	1	9	1	2	1	1
21	3	3	3	1	1	1	1	8	1
22	1	5	1	2	5	1	3	7	1
23	4	2	4	1	9	1	2	2	3
24	1	9	1	3	0	1	2	5	1
25	3	4	2	3	2	3	1	0	1
26	2	0	1	2	10	1	1	9	1
27	1	8	1	2	7	1	2	4	1
28	1	7	1	–	–	–	1	1	1
29	2	3	3	–	–	–	–	–	–
30	1	2	1	–	–	–	–	–	–

Table 4. Lot products whole process.

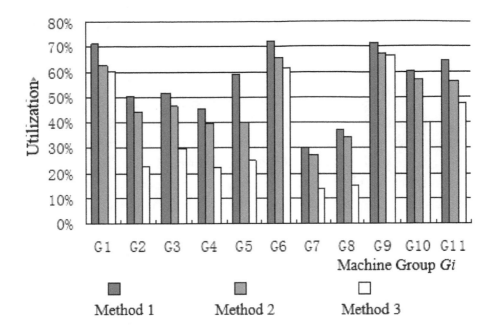

Figure 4. The utilization of machine group.

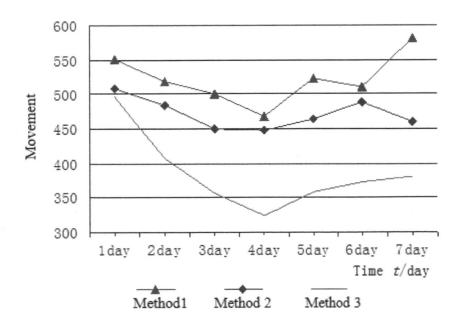

Figure 5. The utilization of machine group.

4. Artificial neural network approach for die yield prediction in the SWFS

4.1. FNN-based yield prediction model

The yield prediction model based on FNN is composed of three parts, which are an input layer, an output layer and several hidden layers. The three parts do the different jobs respectively. The input layer serves to accept input parameters connected with yield. The output layer does the job to get the yield response of the prediction model. The hidden layers are applied to compute and convert the input parameters which are on the basis of fuzzy logical theory. The following sections show a more detailed yield prediction model based on FNN.

4.1.1. Variables in FNN input layer

The input variables in the FNN prediction model include the following parameters: the critical electrical test parameters, wafer physical parameters and key parameters of defects in wafer. Critical process parameters refer to those electrical test parameters which are generally tested at the end of the wafer processing, and they have notable influences on the yield. Wafer physical parameters mainly refer to the size of the chip. Key parameters of defects in wafer Contain a number of defects, clustering parameter, mean number of defects in each chip and mean a number of defects in each unit area. Among these input variables, the critical electrical test parameters and clustering parameters are complex, and we will discuss them in the following sections.

4.1.1.1. Critical electrical test parameters

In the process of fabricating complex semiconductor wafer, there are more than one hundred electrical test parameters related to the probed wafer. This paper mainly does the research on establishing the exact relationship of a small number of critical electrical test parameters with yield. These critical electrical test parameters have significant influence on yield, and they have high correlating coefficients or exhibit a 'cliff' in the correlation graphs which means they can quickly improve the yield. Wong [32] proposed the hybrid statistical correlation analysis method, and the critical electrical test parameters are identified based on this method. Here, we remove some details of these electrical test parameters for confidentiality.

4.1.1.2. Clustering parameter

Clustering parameter displays cluster or clumps degrees of wafer defects in the defect map [33]. Suppose that the clustering parameter is expressed by c, shown in Eq. (1).

$$c = \min\left\{ \frac{s_v^2}{\bar{v}^2}, \frac{s_w^2}{\bar{w}^2} \right\}$$

(22)

where the sample mean and variance of V_i is represented by $\bar{V}^2$ and s_v^2; and the sample mean and variance of W_i are represented by s_w^2. V_i and W_i are a series of defect intervals on the x and y axis defined as:

$$V_i = x_{(i)} - x_{(i-1)}, \ i = 1, 2, ..., n \tag{23}$$

$$W_i = y_{(i)} - y_{(i-1)}, \ i = 1, 2, ..., n \tag{24}$$

where $x_{(i)}$ refers to the ith smallest defect coordinates on x axis, and similarly, $y_{(i)}$ refers to the ith smallest defect coordinates on y axis, $x(0) = y(0) = 0$, and n refers to the quantity of defects on one wafer. If the defects are randomly scattered, the value of CI is close to 1, and when clustering of defects appears, the value of CI is likely to be greater than 1.

4.1.2. FNN structure

There are five layers in the rescheduling decision model based on FNN, as illustrated in **Figure 6**.

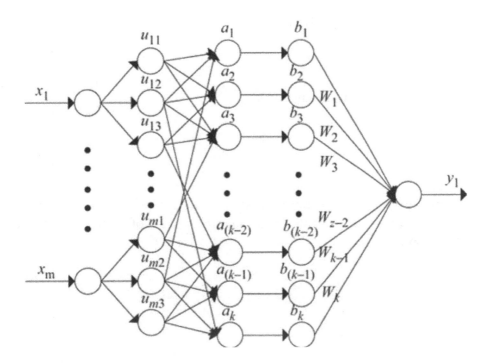

Figure 6. FNN model structure.

a.   The input vector is $X = [x_1, x_2, x_3, ..., x_m]$. The function of node input-output is:

$$f_i^{(1)} = x_i; \ x_i^{(1)} = g_i^{(1)} = f_i^{(1)}; i = 1,2,\cdots m \tag{4-4}$$

b.   In the second layer which is the fuzzifer layer, the function of the Gauss membership is adopted.

$$u_{ij}(x_i) = e^{-\frac{(x_i - c_{ij})^2}{\sigma_{ij}^2}} \tag{25}$$

In this formula, cij is the centre and σ_{ij} is width. The node input-output function is:

$$f_{ij}^{(2)} = -\frac{(x_i^{(1)} - c_{ij})^2}{\sigma_{ij}^2}; x_{ij}^{(2)} = u_{ij}(x_i^{(1)}) = g_{ij}^{(2)} = e^{f_{ij}^{(2)}} = e^{-\frac{(x_i - c_{ij})^2}{\sigma_{ij}^2}} \tag{26}$$

where $i = 1,2,\cdots m$ and $j = \mathbf{1, 2, \cdots, l_i}$.

c.

In the third layer as the rule layer, each node in the layer is a fuzzy rule which not only matches the front part of the fuzzy rule but also calculates the adaptive of the rule,

$$a_j = \prod_{i=1}^{m} u_{il_i}(x_i^{(1)}), j = 1,2,\cdots, n \tag{27}$$

In this layer, the input-output function is:

$$f_j^{(3)} = \prod_{i=1}^{m} x_{il_i}^{(2)} = \prod_{i=1}^{m} u_{il_i}(x_i^{(1)}); \ x_j^{(3)} = a_j = g_j^{(3)} = f_j^{(3)}; j = 1,2,\cdots, n \tag{28}$$

d.

In the fourth layer which is the normalized layer. In this layer, the node numbers are the same in the third layer. It normalized the adaptive values of these rules. And the input-output function is:

$$b_j = \frac{a_j}{\sum_{i=1}^{n} a_i}, j = 1,2,\cdots, n \tag{29}$$

Node input-output function in this layer is as follows.

$$f_j^{(4)} = \frac{x_j^{(3)}}{\sum_{i=1}^{n} x_i^{(3)}} = \frac{a_j}{\sum_{i=1}^{n} a_i}; \ x_j^{(4)} = b_j = g_j^{(4)} = f_j^{(4)}; j = 1, 2, \cdots, n \tag{30}$$

e.   The last layer is the output layer. It defuzzify the output variables. And each node describes a rescheduling strategy. While a rescheduling strategy is chose, the corresponding output is 1 or 0. The input-output function is:

$$f^{(5)} = \sum_{j=1}^{n} w_j x_j^{(4)} = \sum_{j=1}^{n} w_j b_j; \ O_{out} = x^{(5)} = g^{(5)} = f^{(5)} \tag{31}$$

where W_j is connection weight parameter of output layer, and O_{out} is the output of FNN model.

4.2. Case study

In this section, the experiments are conducted to evaluate the effectiveness of the proposed FNN method. This section presents a numerical experiment study to demonstrate the effectiveness of the approach proposed. Seven hundred and twenty wafer samples are obtained from a 6 in. SWFS in Shanghai, and each sample includes 360 records of wafer yield. Five hundred and fifty-two records are used in model training, and 168 are taken to evaluate the model. The attributes contained in each record are, in order, number of defects, clustering parameter, die yield, mean number of defects per unit area, chip size parameter, mean number of defects per chip, and 28 electrical test parameters, which is shown in **Table 5**. Each feature is acquired by test during the critical manufacturing process. The presented FNN approach is compared with the Poisson model, negative binomial model and BPNN approaches, since the three approaches are widely used in research on yield predicting and have been proved to be competitive [34–36]. Furthermore, the detail numerical comparison of the FNN approach, Poisson model, negative binomial model and BPNN approaches are demonstrated as follows.

Record	Number of defects	Mean number of defects/ chip	...	Chip size parameter (cm²)	Clustering parameter	Process parameter 1	Process parameter 2	...	Process parameter 28	Yield (%)
1	21	0.14094	...	1	0.51836	322.7498	0.060865	...	1.169573	0.86577
2	45	0.30201	...	1	0.70814	324.4634	0.061573	...	1.172481	0.73826
3	16	0.10738	...	1	0.65597	322.1903	0.060648	...	1.176223	0.89262
4	21	0.14094	...	1	1.0277	313.9659	0.065036	...	1.162216	0.87248

Record	Number of defects	Mean number of defects/ chip	...	Chip size parameter (cm²)	Clustering parameter	Process parameter 1	Process parameter 2	...	Process parameter 28	Yield (%)
5	46	0.30872	...	1	0.59023	313.0953	0.068286	...	1.183461	0.73826
6	35	0.2349	...	1	0.73168	323.9832	0.061867	...	1.164384	0.81879
7	7	0.04698	...	1	0.73807	315.9001	0.059539	...	1.177436	0.95302
8	49	0.32886	...	1	0.75913	310.9356	0.060887	...	1.180799	0.72483
9	9	0.060403	...	1	0.57871	310.6571	0.06439	...	1.168414	0.9396
10	33	0.22148	...	1	0.83289	310.0921	0.068695	...	1.179983	0.80537
11	37	0.24832	...	1	0.69348	322.2567	0.068536	...	1.160716	0.77181
12	48	0.32215	...	1	0.9089	323.7277	0.069959	...	1.162259	0.73154
13	12	0.080537	...	1	0.6154	321.1246	0.067403	...	1.176334	0.91946
14	33	0.22148	...	1	0.85056	313.0574	0.068778	...	1.170839	0.78523
15	47	0.31544	...	1	1.0109	313.5133	0.063245	...	1.172714	0.72483
...	...	...	...	...	...	...	...	...	...	...
705	31	0.31959	...	1.44	1.0678	310.2484	0.065854	...	1.168734	0.82474
706	35	0.36082	...	1.44	0.67849	321.1613	0.06883	...	1.166041	0.83505
707	61	0.62887	...	1.44	1.00661	314.3752	0.066945	...	1.184936	0.75258
708	71	0.73196	...	1.44	0.95411	321.3472	0.061456	...	1.164627	0.7732
709	82	0.84536	...	1.44	1.5379	311.5562	0.060457	...	1.160369	0.73196
710	32	0.3299	...	1.44	1.2404	313.4114	0.067197	...	1.160229	0.80412
711	79	0.81443	...	1.44	1.5407	317.3192	0.067454	...	1.175912	0.7732
712	72	0.74227	...	1.44	2.4467	323.099	0.062285	...	1.171942	0.76289
713	58	0.59794	...	1.44	2.32601	318.6861	0.068344	...	1.174814	0.76289
714	57	0.58763	...	1.44	1.0014	316.3194	0.065981	...	1.173957	0.79381
715	73	0.75258	...	1.44	1.3139	322.1991	0.065962	...	1.180853	0.73196
716	46	0.47423	...	1.44	1.6882	320.4291	0.069517	...	1.166221	0.79381
717	80	0.82474	...	1.44	1.57021	316.6195	0.062461	...	1.16293	0.74227
718	38	0.39175	...	1.44	2.0034	317.0604	0.06606	...	1.171795	0.79381
719	18	0.18557	...	1.44	0.81646	323.2213	0.064985	...	1.167234	0.8866
720	72	0.74227	...	1.44	0.95479	319.6768	0.068621	...	1.175982	0.73196

Table 5. Partial wafer measurements parameters and yield.

4.2.1. Experiment on fuzzy neural network

The algorithm was programmed in Matlab 6.5, and ten factors were treated as input of the model, which are mean number of defects per chip, chip size, clustering parameter, mean number of defects per unit area, the number of defects per wafer and another five critical electrical test parameters.

Twenty-six rules for classification were identified the fuzzifier layer in the model. The 552 samples were utilized in the training of the FNN model with fivefold cross-validation. The learning process was explored in **Figure 7**. Afterward, the trained model was assessed by another 168 samples, which is demonstrated in **Table 6**. Furthermore, the linear regression analysis of the output of the FNN model is detailed in **Figure 8**.

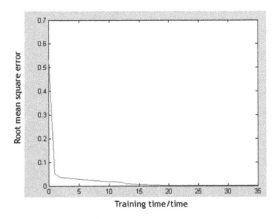

Figure 7. Fuzzy neural network learning curve.

Samples	The actual yield	The predicted yield	Relative error
1	0.72483	0.72514	0.000432
2	0.69128	0.69118	0.000146
3	0.8255	0.8337	0.009929
4	0.75168	0.74329	0.011168
5	0.75839	0.758	0.000513
6	0.73154	0.73031	0.001677
7	0.89933	0.89876	0.000632
8	0.75168	0.75211	0.000576
9	0.74497	0.74409	0.001179
10	0.75168	0.75002	0.002209
11	0.7651	0.7637	0.001824

Samples	The actual yield	The predicted yield	Relative error
12	0.85235	0.85658	0.004967
13	0.89933	0.90485	0.006143
14	0.9396	0.93918	0.000452
15	0.81208	0.81559	0.00432
...	...	...	...
160	0.75258	0.73323	0.025707
161	0.86598	0.84315	0.026365
162	0.74227	0.74376	0.002008
163	0.8866	0.88606	0.000609
164	0.73196	0.72817	0.005175
165	0.7732	0.76827	0.006381
166	0.75258	0.7456	0.009278
167	0.82474	0.83413	0.011391
168	0.83505	0.82249	0.01504

Table 6. The predicted yield based on FNN.

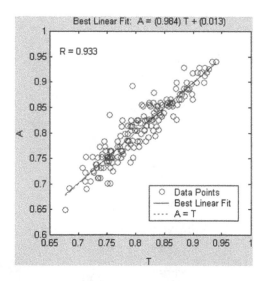

Figure 8. The linear regression analysis of the output of the FNN model.

4.2.2. Experiment of Poisson model

The Poisson model was built to predict wafer yield as follows.

$$Y = e^{-D_0 A}$$

(38)

In the model, Y means the wafer yield, D_0 denotes the defect density, and A is the chip size. The yield was forecasted by Poisson model, and the results of 168 samples can be found in **Table 7**. The lineal correlation analysis between the actual wafer yield and the prediction value is shown in **Figure 9**.

Samples	The actual yield	The predicted yield	Relative error
1	0.72483	0.57675	0.20429
2	0.69128	0.48117	0.30395
3	0.8255	0.79597	0.035769
4	0.75168	0.6552	0.12836
5	0.75839	0.66853	0.11849
6	0.73154	0.58064	0.20627
7	0.89933	0.89218	0.007953
8	0.75168	0.65081	0.13419
9	0.74497	0.61679	0.17206
10	0.75168	0.61267	0.18493
11	0.7651	0.59644	0.22044
12	0.85235	0.83988	0.014634
13	0.89933	0.87439	0.027733
14	0.9396	0.92883	0.011459
15	0.81208	0.74932	0.077284
...	...	...	...
160	0.75258	0.55222	0.26623
161	0.86598	0.75422	0.12905
162	0.74227	0.49038	0.33936
163	0.8866	0.84934	0.042026
164	0.73196	0.40431	0.44763
165	0.7732	0.48316	0.37512
166	0.75258	0.43547	0.42137
167	0.82474	0.75422	0.085502
168	0.83505	0.74311	0.1101

Table 7. The predicted yield based on the Poisson model.

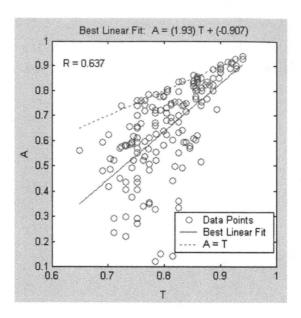

Figure 9. The linear regression analysis of the output of the Poisson model.

4.2.3. Experiment of negative binomial model

The negative binomial model is built to predict wafer yield as follows.

$$Y = \frac{1}{\left(1+D_0 A/a\right)^a} \tag{38}$$

In this model, Y means the defect-limited wafer yield, D_0 denotes the defect density, and A is the cluster coefficient. The yield was forecasted by negative binomial model and the results of 168 samples can be found in **Table 8**. The lineal correlation analysis between the actual wafer yield and the prediction value is shown in **Figure 10**.

Samples	The actual yield	The predicted yield	Relative error
1	0.72483	0.6395	0.11772
2	0.69128	0.57001	0.17543
3	0.8255	0.81257	0.015659
4	0.75168	0.69885	0.070289
5	0.75839	0.70919	0.064881
6	0.73154	0.64239	0.12187
7	0.89933	0.89708	0.002499
8	0.75168	0.69546	0.074787

Samples	The actual yield	The predicted yield	Relative error
9	0.74497	0.66949	0.10132
10	0.75168	0.66637	0.11349
11	0.7651	0.65417	0.14499
12	0.85235	0.85037	0.002326
13	0.89933	0.88098	0.020408
14	0.9396	0.93102	0.009135
15	0.81208	0.7737	0.047256
...	...	...	...
160	0.75258	0.61346	0.18486
161	0.86598	0.7748	0.10529
162	0.74227	0.5669	0.23626
163	0.8866	0.85746	0.032863
164	0.73196	0.50341	0.31225
165	0.7732	0.56152	0.27377
166	0.75258	0.52626	0.30072
167	0.82474	0.7748	0.06055
168	0.83505	0.76546	0.083336

Table 8. The predicted yield based on the negative binomial model.

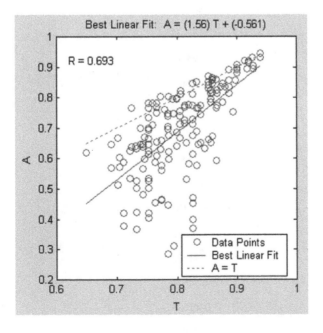

Figure 10. The linear regression analysis of the output of the negative binomial model.

4.2.4. Experiment of back-propagation neural network

A three layer BPNN is applied to predict wafer yield with ten input factors as same as the proposed FNN. The number of hidden neurons is determined by the empirical formula and selected to be 35. The yield was forecasted by BPNN and the results of 168 samples can be found in **Table 9**. The lineal correlation analysis between the actual wafer yield and the prediction value is shown in **Figure 11**.

Samples	The actual yield	The predicted yield	Relative error
1	0.72483	0.73495	0.013962
2	0.69128	0.7263	0.050661
3	0.8255	0.82385	0.001994
4	0.75168	0.76318	0.015293
5	0.75839	0.75985	0.001919
6	0.73154	0.75042	0.025807
7	0.89933	0.89876	0.000632
8	0.75168	0.76104	0.012456
9	0.74497	0.75932	0.019268
10	0.75168	0.73971	0.015921
11	0.7651	0.76666	0.002033
12	0.85235	0.83068	0.025423
13	0.89933	0.87383	0.028359
14	0.9396	0.93471	0.005204
15	0.81208	0.79469	0.021415
…	…	…	…
160	0.75258	0.72724	0.033671
161	0.86598	0.8581	0.009105
162	0.74227	0.7096	0.044007
163	0.8866	0.89151	0.005535
164	0.73196	0.68805	0.059996
165	0.7732	0.72722	0.059471
166	0.75258	0.71576	0.048929
167	0.82474	0.82683	0.00253
168	0.83505	0.82845	0.007907

Table 9. The predicted yield based on BPNN.

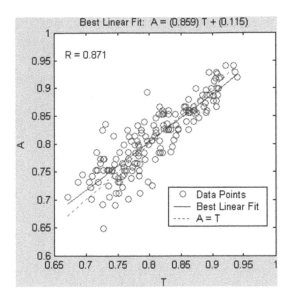

Figure 11. The linear regression analysis of the output of BPNN.

4.2.5. Results discussion

Aiming to assess the performance the proposed FNN methods, experiment with three contrast method was conducted for comparison. The lineal correlation analyses between the actual wafer yield and the prediction value of four methods are shown in **Figure 12**, which indicates that the FNN method outperforms other three methods from the view of convergence. The

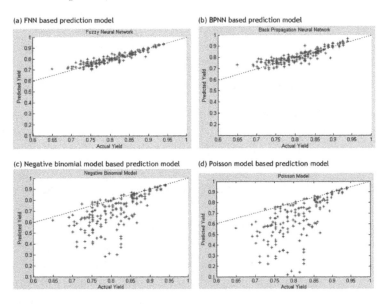

Figure 12. The relationship between the actual yields and predicted yields based on the FNN, BPNN and Poisson model and negative binomial model approach.

results of four methods in the RMSE and correlation coefficient R is presented in Table 10. The RMSE of the FNN method is 0.017, which is the smallest value above the four methods, and the R of the FNN-based model is 0.941, which is larger than other three methods. It indicates that the proposed FNN-based approach is more accurate and effective than other three methods, which are widely used in the yield predicting.

Yield prediction model	The actual yield		The predicted yield		RMSE	R
	Average	SD	Average	SD		
Poisson model	0.80864	0.06168	0.65394	0.18694	0.0169	0.637
Negative binomial model			0.70047	0.14789	0.0123	0.693
BPNN			0.80691	0.05736	0.0024	0.886
FNN			0.80838	0.05711	0.0017	0.941

Table 10. The comparisons of RMSE and correlation coefficients among the FNN, BPNN, Poisson model and negative binomial model.

5. Conclusion

The artificial neural networks (ANN) have a wide range of applications. For example, in complex discrete event manufacturing systems, they can be used to control, make decision and predict. SWFS is exactly such a complex manufacturing system. It has many characteristics, such as a mix of different process types, re-entrant flows, very expensive equipment and sequence dependent setup times and so on. In order to get more applications of ANN used in quality analysis and production scheduling in the semiconductor wafer fabrication system, this chapter implements two novel fuzzy neural networks that are used in the yield prediction of SWFS and rescheduling decision separately.

In the respect of rescheduling decision, this chapter puts forward a new method using a FNN model with which a system can make itself adapted to the current states and disturbances. In uncertain dynamic environments, current states and disturbances of the system are mathematically characterized. Rescheduling decision model, which assuming FNN builds the relationship between the inputs (i.e. disturbance, system state parameters) and the outputs (i.e. disturbance, system state parameters) of FNN. According to the current system disturbances, an optimal rescheduling method which can be used to schedule the semiconductor wafer fabrication lines is chosen by the make-decision model. We do experiment studies in Shanghai, which are based on 6-in. SWFS. The proposed rescheduling decision mechanism is proved to be effective by the linear regression between ideal targets and output of FNN. The rescheduling decision-making method which is proposed is demonstrated to be accurate by comparing with regression and traditional BPNN. We also do the comparison between the layered rescheduling method which is on the basis of FNN rescheduling decision mechanism and the two methods that are FCFS approach and the rescheduling approach based on the monolayer. The results indicate that, in respect of machine utilization and daily movement, layered rescheduling method, which is on the basis of FNN rescheduling decision mechanism, is superior to the other two approaches.

A yield prediction method for semiconductor manufacturing systems which is on the basis of new fuzzy neural networks is proposed for the yield prediction. This method builds the yield prediction model based on FNN by using the following parameters as input variables, which are the number of defects in each wafer, mean number of defects in each chip, mean number of defects in each unit area, clustering parameter, chip size and five critical electrical test parameters.

According to the data from the experiment studies in Shanghai which are based on 6-in. SWFS. The proposed rescheduling decision mechanism is proved to be effective by the linear regression between ideal targets and output of FNN. The rescheduling decision-making method which is proposed is demonstrated to be accurate by comparing with regression and traditional BPNN. The approach proposed in this paper has the advantage that it considers more variables' influences than other model such as negative binomial yield model, BPNN model and Poisson yield model. The variables here include physical parameters of wafer, key attributed parameters of defects and wafer electrical test parameters on wafer yield and so on. In a word, the model proposed in this paper is more accurate than the other traditional yield prediction approaches.

Acknowledgements

This work was supported by the State Key Program of the National Natural Science Foundation of China under Grant No. 51435009.

Author details

Jie Zhang*, Junliang Wang and Wei Qin

*Address all correspondence to: zhangjie_cims@hotmail.com

School of Mechanical Engineering, Shanghai Jiao Tong University, Shanghai, China

References

[1] Uzsoy, R., et al., A review of production planning and scheduling models in the semiconductor industry. Part II: shop-floor control IIE Transactions, 1994, 26(5): 44–55.

[2] Leachman, R.C., The competitive semiconductor manufacturing survey. IEEE international symposium on semiconductor manufacturing conference, 20–21 September 1993, Austin, Texas, USA. Piscataway, NJ: IEEE, 1993: 359–381.

[3] Uzsoy, R., et al., A review of production planning and scheduling models in the semiconductor industry. Part I: system characteristics, performance evaluation and production planning, IIE Transactions, 1992, 24(4): 47–60.

[4] Cheng, M., Sugi, M., Ota, J., Yamamoto, M., Ito, H., and Inoue, K., A fast rescheduling method in semiconductor manufacturing allowing for tardiness and scheduling stability. Proceeding of the 2006 IEEE, international conference on automation science and engineering, Shanghai, China, October, 2006: 7–10.

[5] Huang, H.P. and Chen, T.Y., A new approach to on-line rescheduling for a semiconductor foundry Fab. 2006 IEEE international conference on systems, man, and cybernetics, Taipei, China, October, 2006: 8–11.

[6] Kumar, R., Tiwari, M.K., and Allada, V., Modelling and rescheduling of a re-entrant wafer fabrication line involving machine unreliability, International Journal of Production Research, 2004, 42(21): 4431–4455.

[7] Maosn, S.J., Jin, S., and Wessels, M., Rescheduling strategies for minimizing total weighted tardiness in complex job shops, International Journal of Production Research, 2004, 42(3): 613–628.

[8] Toba, H., Segment-based approach for real-time reactive rescheduling for automatic manufacturing control, IEEE Transactions on Semiconductor Manufacturing, 2000, 13(3): 264–272.

[9] Tsai, C.J., and Huang, H.P., A real-time scheduling and rescheduling system based on RFID for semiconductor foundry fabs, Journal of the Chinese Institute of Industrial Engineers, 2007, 24(6): 437–444.

[10] Kumar, P.R., Scheduling semiconductor manufacturing plants, IEEE Control Systems Magazine, 1994, 14(6): 33–40.

[11] Kumar, N., et al., A review of yield modeling techniques for semiconductor manufacturing, International Journal of Production Research, 2006, 44(23): 5019–5036.

[12] Cunningham, S.P. and Spanos, C.J., Semiconductor yield improvement: results and best practices, IEEE Transactions on Semiconductor Manufacturing, 1995, 8(2): 103–109.

[13] Tong, L.-I. and Chao, L.-C., Novel yield model for integrated circuit with clustered defects, Expert Systems with Applications, 2008, 34: 2334–2341.

[14] Zhang, J., Qin, W., Wu, L.H., et al., Fuzzy neural network-based rescheduling decision mechanism for semiconductor manufacturing, Computers in Industry, 2014, 65(8): 1115–1125.

[15] Wu, L.H., Zhang, J., Fuzzy neural network based yield prediction model for semiconductor manufacturing system, International Journal of Production Research, 2010, 48(48): 3225–3243.

[16] Li, X.L., Yao, Y.X., and Yuan, Z.J., On-line tool condition monitoring system with wavelet fuzzy neural network, Journal of Intelligent Manufacturing, 1997, 8(4): 271–276.

[17] Zhou, Y.F., Li, S.J., Jin, R.C., A new fuzzy neural network with fast learning algorithm and guaranteed stability for manufacturing process control, Fuzzy Sets and Systems, 2002, 132(2): 201–216.

[18] Chang, P.C., Wang, Y.W., and Ting, C.J., A fuzzy neural network for the flow time estimation in a semiconductor manufacturing factory, International Journal of Production Research, 2008, 46(4): 1017–1029.

[19] Xu, D.M., and Yan, H.S., An intelligent estimation method for product design time, International Journal of Advanced Manufacturing Technology, 2006, 30(7–8): 601–613.

[20] Chang, Y.J., Kang, Y., Kang, Y., Hsu, C.L., Chang, C.T., and Chan, T.Y., Virtual metrology technique for semiconductor manufacturing. IEEE international conference on neural networks-conference proceedings, international joint conference on neural networks, Vancouver, BC, Canada, July, 2006: 5289–5293.

[21] Tong, L.-I., Lee, W.-I., and Su, C.-T., Using a neural network-based approach to predict the wafer yield in integrated circuit manufacturing, IEEE Transactions on Components, Packaging, and Manufacturing Technology – Part C, 1997, 20(4): 288–294.

[22] Tong, L.-I. and Chao, L.-C., Novel yield model for integrated circuit with clustered defects. Expert Systems with Applications, 2008, 34: 2334–2341.

[23] Chen, T. and Wang, M.J., A fuzzy set approach for yield learning modeling in wafer manufacturing, IEEE Transactions on Semiconductor Manufacturing, 1999, 12(2): 252–258.

[24] Chen, T. and Lin, Y.C., A fuzzy-neural system incorporating unequally important expert opinions for semiconductor yield forecasting, International Journal of Uncertainty, Fuzziness and Knowledge-Based Systems, 2008, 16(1): 35–58.

[25] Chung, K.S. and Sang, C.P., A machine learning approach to yield management in semiconductor manufacturing, International Journal of Production Research, 2000, 38(17): 4261–4271.

[26] Kim, T.S., et al., Yield prediction models for optimisation of high-speed micro-processor manufacturing processes. 26th IEEE/CPMT international electronics manufacturing technology symposium, 2–3 October 2000, Santa Clara, CA, USA. Piscataway, NJ: IEEE, 2000: 368–373.

[27] Kim, T.S., Intelligent yield and speed prediction models for high-speed microprocessors. IEEE electronic components and technology conference, 28–31 May 2002, San Diego, CA, USA. Piscataway, NJ: IEEE, 2002: 1158–1162.

[28] Zhai, W.B., Chu, X.N., Zhang, J., Ma, D., Jin, Y., and Yan, J.Q., Research of combination auction based short-term scheduling technology of semiconductor fabrication line, Journal of Mechanical Engineering, 2004, 40(9): 95–99.

[29] Zhai, W.B., Zhang, J., Yan, J.Q., and Ma, D., Research of ETAEMS/GPGP-CN based on dynamic scheduling technology of semiconductor fabrication, Journal of Mechanical Engineering, 2005, 46(3): 53–58.

[30] Wang, J., and Malakooti, B., Feed-forward neural network for multiple criteria decision making, Computer & Operations Research, 1992, 19(2): 151–167.

[31] Malhotra, M.K., Sharma, S., and Nair, S.S., Decision making using multiple models, European Journal of Operational Research, 1999, 114(1): 1–14.

[32] Wong, A.Y., A statistical parametric and probe yield analysis methodology. Proceedings of IEEE international symposium on defect and fault tolerance in VLSI systems, 6–8 November 1996, Boston, MA, USA. Los Alamitos, CA: IEEE Comput. Soc. Press, 1996, 131–139.

[33] Jun, C.-H., et al., A simulation-based semiconductor chip yield model incorporating a new defect cluster index, Microelectronics Reliability, 1999, 39: 451–456.

[34] Cunningham, J.A., The use and evaluation of yield models in integrated circuit manufacturing, IEEE Transactions on Semiconductor Manufacturing, 1990, 3(2): 60–71.

[35] Aakash, T. and Bayoumi, M.A., Defect clustering viewed through generalised Poisson distribution, IEEE Transactions on Semiconductor Manufacturing, 1992, 5(3): 196–206.

[36] Koren, I., Koren, Z., and Stepper, C.H., A unified negative binomial distribution for yield analysis of defect-tolerant circuits. IEEE Transactions on Computers, 1993, 42: 724–734.

3

Advanced Methods in Neural Networks-Based Sensitivity Analysis with their Applications in Civil Engineering

Maosen Cao, Nizar F. Alkayem, Lixia Pan and
Drahomír Novák

Additional information is available at the end of the chapter

Abstract

Artificial neural networks (ANNs) are powerful tools that are used in various engineering fields. Their characteristics enable them to solve prediction, regression, and classification problems. Nevertheless, the ANN is usually thought of as a black box, in which it is difficult to determine the effect of each explicative variable (input) on the dependent variables (outputs) in any problem. To investigate such effects, sensitivity analysis is usually applied on the optimal pre-trained ANN. Existing sensitivity analysis techniques suffer from drawbacks. Their basis on a single optimal pre-trained ANN model produces instability in parameter sensitivity analysis because of the uncertainty in neural network modeling. To overcome this deficiency, two successful sensitivity analysis paradigms, the neural network committee (NNC)-based sensitivity analysis and the neural network ensemble (NNE)-based parameter sensitivity analysis, are illustrated in this chapter. An NNC is applied in a case study of geotechnical engineering involving strata movement. An NNE is implemented for sensitivity analysis of two classic problems in civil engineering: (i) the fracture failure of notched concrete beams and (ii) the lateral deformation of deep-foundation pits. Results demonstrate good ability to analyze the sensitivity of the most influential parameters, illustrating the underlying mechanisms of such engineering systems.

Keywords: civil engineering, neural networks, sensitivity analysis, NNC-based sensitivity analysis, NNE-based sensitivity analysis

1. Introduction

In solving complex civil engineering problems, conventional analytical and empirical method-ologies suffer from many difficulties. This is mainly because of the limitations of such methods in handling large, complex structures that may require time-consuming and exhausting tasks. In such situations, soft-computing techniques come into the picture. They are effective estimation tools that reduce the cost and time of design and analysis. Neural networks are useful soft-computing tools that can be used for classification and prediction in complex civil engineering problems [1–3].

Sensitivity analysis is a necessary approach for understanding the relationship and the influence of each input parameter on the outputs of a problem. The key point behind sensitivity analysis is that by slightly varying each explicative input parameter and registering the response in the output, the explicative parameters with the highest sensitivity values gain the greatest importance. Sensitivity analysis of the most significant parameters can be very useful for analyzing complex engineering problems.

Neural network-based parameter sensitivity analysis in civil engineering systems is gaining more importance due to the remarkable ability of neural networks to explain the nonlinear relationships between the explicative and response variables of a problem [1, 4]. Commonly, a specific training technique is used to develop one optimal neural network to be a system model, and this model is then used for sensitivity analysis [5–10]. Yet, it is relatively difficult to determine the most optimal neural network model, for reasons such as random initialization of the underlying connection weights in the neural network model, different features of various learning techniques used to train the neural network, the absence of a reliable technique for defining the optimal structure in neural network modeling, etc. To overcome these difficulties, two potential techniques, namely neural network committee (NNC)-based sensitivity analy-sis [1] and neural network ensemble (NNE)-based sensitivity analysis [11], are illustrated. These two paradigms utilize a group of pre-trained optimal neural networks to handle the neural network modeling, thereafter implementing parameter sensitivity analysis individually and lastly defining the sensitivity of parameters. This chapter is organized as follows. A complete explanation is given of some traditional neural network-based sensitivity analysis. Thereafter, the NNC-based parameter sensitivity analysis method is presented, followed by a geotechnical engineering case study of strata movement and two case studies related to classical civil engineering. Then, the NNE-based sensitivity analysis paradigm is described, followed by two illustrative case studies. Finally, a complete summary of the chapter is presented.

2. Typical neural networks-based sensitivity analysis algorithms

Many studies have been concerned with improving existing neural network-based sensitivity analysis methods [9]. Among the different techniques, the partial derivative algorithm [5] and the input perturbation algorithm [10] have superior performance compared to other techniques based on the magnitude of weights [6, 7]. Therefore, these two algorithms are explored in detail in this chapter, along with some other techniques.

2.1. Partial derivative algorithm

The partial derivative algorithm is a famous neural network-based sensitivity analysis technique [5, 11]. Its characteristics enable it to deal with neural networks that apply first-derivative activation functions, such as back-propagation neural networks (BPNNs) and radial basis function neural networks (RBFNNs) [1, 8]. By implementing the partial derivative algorithm, it is possible to identify the variations of output parameters of neural networks with respect to small changes in each input parameter, thereby defining the contribution of each such input on the output parameters. This can be done by deriving the output parameters of the neural network with respect to input parameters, in other words, by calculating the Jacobian matrix that contains the partial derivatives of outputs with respect to inputs [5, 11].

For a successful BPNN model having input x_i with n_i as the total number of inputs and output y_k with n_k as the total number of outputs, the Jacobian matrix $\frac{\partial y_k}{\partial x_i}$ can be defined by using the chain rule as [1]

$$\frac{\partial y_k}{\partial x_i} = \frac{\partial y_k}{\partial O_k}\frac{\partial O_k}{\partial y_{h_n}}......\frac{\partial y_{h_i}}{\partial O_{h_i}}\frac{\partial O_{h_i}}{\partial x_i} = \sum_{h_i}\sum_{h_{i-1}}\sum_{h_i}\left[\begin{array}{c}W_{h_n k}f'(O_k)W_{h_{n-1}h_n}\\ f'(O_{h_n})......W_{ih_1}f'(O_{h_1})\end{array}\right] \quad (1)$$

where x_i is the ith input variable $h_n, h_{n-1},...,$ and h_i are the hidden neurons from the nth to the first hidden layer, respectively; $y_k, y_{h_n},$ and y_{h_n} are the output values for output neuron k, hidden neurons h_n, and n_1 in the respective nth and the first hidden layer; $W_{h_n k}$ is the connection weight between the kth output neuron and the hidden neuron h_n; $W_{h_{n-1}h_n}$ is the connection weight between the hidden neurons h_{n-1} and h_n and W_{ih_1} is the connection weight between the ith input neuron and the hidden neuron h_1; $O_k, O_{h_n}^1,$ and O_{h_n} are the weighted sums of kth output neuron, the hidden neuron h_n, and h_1, respectively; f^1 denotes the derivative of the activation function f. $y_k, y_{h_n},$ and y_{h_1} can be given as

$$\left\{\begin{array}{l} y_k = f(O_k), O_k = \sum_{h_n} y_{h_n}W_{h_n,k} + b_k \\ y_{h_n} = f(O_{h_n}), O_{h_n} = \sum_{h_n} y_{h_{n-1}}W_{h_{n-1},k} + b_{h_n} \\ \qquad\qquad \vdots \\ y_{h_1} = f(O_{h_1}), O_{h_1} = \sum_{h_n} x_i W_{i,h_1} + b_{h_1} \end{array}\right. \quad (2)$$

where $b_k, b_{h_{n}}$, and b_{h_1} are the biases of the kth output neuron, the hidden neuron h_n, and, h_1, respectively.

For p training samples of each input x_i on the output y_k of the neural network, c_{ik} can be calculated as

$$c_{ik} = \sum_p \left| \left(\frac{\partial y_k}{\partial x_i} \right)_p \right| \tag{3}$$

For each input parameter, the value of c can be used as a factor for classification of the influence of total inputs on the outputs of the neural network model. The most important or crucial input parameter may have the highest c value [1].

2.2. Input perturbation algorithm

The input perturbation algorithm is another common method for neural-network-based sensitivity analysis [6, 9]. It implements a small perturbation on each input of the neural network model and measures the corresponding change in the outputs. This perturbation is applied on one input individually at a time while all other inputs are fixed, and the response for perturbation of each output is registered. Sensitivity analysis is performed by giving a rank for each response of the output generated by the same perturbation in every input parameter. The input that has the highest effect on the outputs after perturbation is considered the most influential or important [1].

In essence, when a larger amount of perturbation is added to the selected input parameter, the mean square error (MSE) of the neural network increases. The variance of the input parameter can be represented as $x_i = x_i + \Delta x_i$, where x_i is the current selected input variable and Δx_i is the perturbation. The perturbation can be varied from 0 to 50% by steps of 5% of the input value. Depending on the increasing value of the MSE corresponding to each perturbed input, outputs can be ranked and thus sensitivity analyses are performed [1, 8].

2.3. Weights method

This method was proposed by Garson [12] and Goh [13]. In this method, for each hidden neuron, the connection weights are divided into components related to each input neuron. This method was simplified by Gevrey et al. [8] to give the same results as the initial method. For the purpose of illustration, a multilayer neural network with a single hidden layer is considered; thereafter, for each hidden neuron the following calculations are used:

For $i = 1$ to n_i

    For $j = 1$ to n_j

$$D_{ij} = \frac{|W_{ij}|}{\sum_{i=1}^{n_i} |W_{ij}|} \quad (4)$$

End

End

where n_i and n_j are the number of input and hidden neurons, respectively; W_{ij} is the weight corresponding to input neuron i and hidden neuron j. The percentage relative contribution of all inputs RC_i is then calculated as

For $i = 1$ to n_i

$$RC_i = \frac{\sum_{j=1}^{n_j} D_{ij}}{\sum_{j=1}^{n_j} \sum_{i=1}^{n_i} D_{ij}} \quad (5)$$

End

2.4. Profile method

This method was proposed by Lek et al. [14–16], and further explained by Gevrey et al. [8]. The key point behind this method is to analyze one particular input at a time while fixing the values of all other inputs. The procedure starts by dividing the value of each input parameter into equal subintervals, whereas all other inputs are set prior to minimum, quarter, half, three quarters of the maximum and maximum, respectively. At the end of this task, patterns of five values corresponding to different input parameters result and the median value for each pattern is calculated. The median values are plotted with respect to the subintervals to form a profile that explains the contribution of the input parameter. Finally, for all inputs, a set of curves explaining the relative importance for all input parameters is obtained [8].

2.5. Stepwise method

In this method, one input parameter is blocked and the responses of the outputs are recorded. This process is performed step by step for all input parameters and the responses of the outputs are recorded by means of the MSE. Depending on the MSE, the relative importance of each input variable is ranked correspondingly. There are two main strategies for the stepwise method. The first is to construct a number of neural network models by evolving the input parameters one by one. This strategy is called forward stepwise, while the backward stepwise strategy can be implemented in the reverse way, that is, constructing neural network models by first using all input parameters and then blocking each input parameter [8, 17].

This method can be improved to reduce the difficulty of producing many neural network models by using a single model. In this model, one input parameter is blocked and the MSE is calculated. The parameter with the maximum MSE value is ranked as the most important and can then be either removed from the model or fixed at its mean value so that the contribution of other parameters can be found, and so on.

3. Neural network committee-based sensitivity analysis

Consider a neural network model with a sensitivity analysis-ranking vector $R = [r_1, r_2, ..., r_n]$ and the actual sensitivity analysis-ranking vector $R_0 = [a_1, a_2, ..., a_n]$, where r_i and a_i are the calculated and actual ranks of ith input parameter, respectively, and n is the number of input parameters. To reduce the difference between R and R_0 to minimum, it is not efficient to use single neural network model to perform sensitivity analysis. The reason is the absence of persistence in sensitivity analysis of one neural network model even when a major sensitivity analysis strategy is implemented. In recognition of this fact, it is more effective to utilize a set of good pre-trained neural network models instead of using a single optimal model for sensitivity analysis. This procedure is well used in neural network committee (NNC)-based sensitivity analysis [1].

The mathematical foundation of NNC-based sensitivity analysis starts from the weak law of large numbers in probability. Having $x_1, x_2, ...$ infinite set of random variables with no correlation between any two of them, each having the exact value of μ and variance σ^2, the sample average convergence in probability can be written as [18]

$$\bar{x}_n = \frac{(x_1 + x_2 + ... + x)}{n} \tag{6}$$

or, in other words, for a small number ε, the following can be expressed:

$$\lim_{n \to \infty} P(|\bar{x}_n| - \mu < \varepsilon) = 1 \tag{7}$$

By considering single neural network sensitivity analysis-ranking vector R, the elements $r_1, r_2, ...$ can be defined as random variables; in other words, R is composed of n random variables. In the case of neural network ensemble-based sensitivity analysis, a set of random variables $r_i^1, r_i^2, ..., r_i^m$ related to r_i are obtained. Depending on the weak law of large numbers, for a large number m, the mean of $r_i^1, r_i^2, ..., r_i^m$ can converge to the actual ranking values a_i in R_0. Therefore, in NNC-based sensitivity analysis, it is possible to find a ranking vector R that is close to the actual ranking vector R_0.

As the number of input variables is specified and the input variables are not completely random, due to the many specifications that appear during neural network model training, the condition of the weak law of large numbers that is applied on an infinite number of random variables is not satisfied. For this reason, optimization strategy can be an efficient tool to select a number of good pre-trained neural network models and skip those with weak performance. By electing the best neural network elements and eliminating the bad ones, optimization can generate good predictions of sensitivity analysis-ranking vectors [1].

Depending on the above principles, we can summarize NNC-based sensitivity analysis in three basic procedures. First, groups (seeds) of successful neural network models are prepared using neural network-training techniques such as back propagation (BP) or radial basis functions, etc. Then, a set of best-performance models are chosen to compose the optimal NNC that is used in performing ensemble neural network sensitivity analysis by individual applications of sensitivity analysis, giving large numbers of R. Finally, the mean of R is calculated to find the accurate approximation of R_0. A schematic diagram of NNC-based sensitivity analysis strategy is given in **Figure 1**.

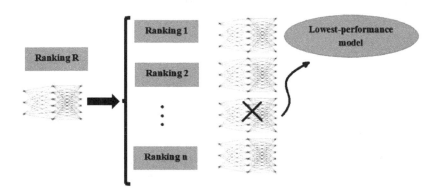

Figure 1. A schematic diagram of NNC-based sensitivity analysis strategy.

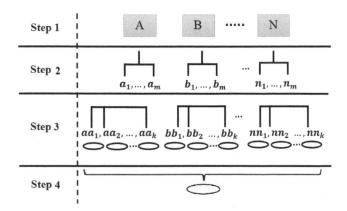

Figure 2. NNC-based sensitivity analysis strategy stepwise procedure: A–N, the neural network model seeds; $a_1 - a_m$, $b_1 - b_m$, and $n_1 - n_m$, the candidate groups of neural network models; $a_1 - aa_k$, $bb_1 - bb_k$, and $nn_1 - nn_k$, the superior neural network models; ellipse refers to a sensitivity analysis ranking of an input parameter.

The basic steps for the NNC-based sensitivity analysis algorithm are shown in **Figure 2** and can be explained as follows:

1. Select the best available types of neural network model empirically. These are called "seeds" for NNC-based sensitivity analysis.

2. Each seed involves a set of neural network models. These models are varied by means of a number of hidden neurons or hidden layers to produce a candidate group of neural network models.

3. Depending on the MSE, a subset k of superior neural network models is picked up, where $k = \frac{3}{10}m$ has been experimentally specified and m is the number of neural network models in the candidate group. Thereafter, sensitivity analysis is employed on each model to generate a group of sensitivity analysis-ranking vectors R.

4. For each input parameter, the mean of the related ranking number in the sensitivity analysis-ranking vector R is calculated to form a predicted ranking vector close to the actual ranking vector R_0, which is calculated as

$$a_i \approx \hat{a}_i = \frac{1}{NK}\sum\nolimits_{s=1}^{N}\sum\nolimits_{t=1}^{K} r_i^{st}, i = 1,2,\ldots,l \tag{8}$$

where $\hat{a}_i$ is the predicted value of a_i in R_0 for variable x_i in R, K is the number of elements in the candidate group of neural network models (committee), N is the number of neural network seeds, and l is the number of input parameters.

4. NNC-based sensitivity analysis of strata movement

Strata movement is a critical problem in geotechnical engineering because of the complex highly nonlinear properties involved. It is necessary to define the most significant factors involved in strata movement. Therefore, NNC-based sensitivity analysis strategy is used. The dataset of strata movement is composed of 168 samples taken from multiple typical observation stations of earth surface movement above underground metal mines. The dataset has six input parameters and three output parameters as shown in **Table 1**. These parameters characterize the working operation of strata movement of underground metal mines.

In NNC-based sensitivity analysis, four scenarios are chosen, depending on the output variables (**Table 1**): scenario (1) all output parameters, (2) only MAU, (3) only MAL, and (4) only AA. At the beginning, radial basis function and BP neural networks are selected as seeds, because of their proven ability to handle nonlinear features. Then, 50 neural network models are generated by each seed to construct two candidate sets of neural network models. Thereafter, 15 superior neural network models are chosen from each set to form a committee containing the best-performed neural network models. After that, sensitivity analysis is applied to each model by utilizing both a perturbation algorithm and a partial derivative algorithm to produce a group of ranking vectors R. Next, the sum of corresponding ranking numbers that is considered as a score for input parameters is calculated. The score is a reflection of the near actual ranking R_0. The sum is used instead of the mean to prevent the repetition of the identical values for different parameters, in order to have fewer neural network models from which to decide the final ranking. The best-performed neural networks and the input parameter ranking for scenario (1) are illustrated in **Table 2**.

Parameter	Characteristics	Parameter type
MCU	Mean consistency of upper wall rock	Input
LCL	Mean consistency of lower wall rock	Input
SAO	Slope angle of ore body	Input
TO	Thickness of ore body	Input
LO	Length of ore body	Input
DE	Depth of excavation	Input
MAU	Movement angle of upper wall rock	Output
MAL	Movement angle of lower wall rock	Output
AA	Avalanche angle	Output

Table 1. Measured parameters of strata movement [1].

Best-performed neural network model	MCU	LCL	SAO	TO	LO	DE
RBF1	5	6	1	4	3	2
RBF2	2	1	6	5	4	3
RBF3	3	6	5	2	4	1
RBF4	5	6	3	1	4	2
RBF5	4	6	3	2	5	1
RBF6	5	4	2	3	6	1
RBF7	4	6	5	2	3	1
RBF8	2	6	3	5	4	1
RBF9	4	6	5	2	3	1
RBF10	2	5	6	3	4	1
RBF11	3	4	1	6	5	2
RBF12	3	4	2	6	5	1
RBF13	2	4	3	6	5	1
RBF14	2	4	3	6	5	1
RBF15	4	2	3	5	6	1
BP1	1	4	3	6	5	2

Best-performed neural network model	MCU	LCL	SAO	TO	LO	DE
BP2	2	4	3	6	5	1
BP3	4	2	3	5	6	1
BP4	4	3	2	6	5	1
BP5	2	3	4	6	5	1
BP6	4	2	1	5	6	3
BP7	5	3	2	6	4	1
BP8	4	3	1	5	6	2
BP9	4	3	2	6	5	1
BP10	4	3	1	5	6	2
BP11	3	4	2	5	6	1
BP12	3	5	1	4	6	2
BP13	4	3	2	5	6	1
BP14	4	3	1	6	5	2
BP15	3	5	1	4	6	2

Table 2. Sensitivity analysis rankings produced by best-performed neural network model groups [1].

Scenarios	Score and ranking	MCU	LCL	SAO	TO	LO	DE
(1)	Score	101	120	80	138	148	43
	Ranking	3	4	2	5	6	1
(2)	Score	96	114	64	162	145	49
	Ranking	3	4	2	6	5	1
(3)	Score	96	81	87	75	155	136
	Ranking	4	2	3	1	6	5
(4)	Score	109	121	113	103	86	98
	Ranking	4	6	5	3	1	2

Table 3. NNC-based sensitivity analysis results for strata movement.

The outcome sensitivity analysis for the four scenarios is illustrated in **Table 3**. It is clear from the table that for scenario (1), *DE* has the highest importance, followed by *SAO, MCU, LCL, TO*, and *LO*, respectively. In scenario (2), the degree of importance is the same as in scenario (1), but *LO* is more significant than *TO*. Nevertheless, in scenario (3), *TO* has the highest significance, above that of *LCL, SAO*, and *MCU*, which have approximately similar significance, and then *DE* and *LO* have the least significance. Finally, in scenario (4) *LO* has the highest contribution followed by *DE, TO, MCU, SAO,* and *LCL,* respectively. However, the contributions of *DE* and *TO* are very close to those of *MCU, SAO,* and *LCL.*

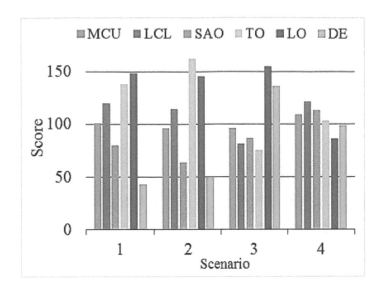

Figure 3. Activity analysis of dependent variables for strata movement based on NNC-based sensitivity analysis results [1].

The working condition of strata movement is defined by the predictability of response parameter (output parameters). For this reason, the scores of the input variables after sensitivity analysis for three scenarios (*MAU, MAL,* and *AA*) that are related to the response variables are plotted in **Figure 3**. The response variable with the highest sensitivity against explicative variables has the highest predictability, and this can be calculated by finding the variance of the score vector of the explicative variables. The result of that procedure is 1965.6, 1068.4, and 150, corresponding to the response variables *MAU, MAL,* and *AA,* respectively. It is obvious that *MAU* has the highest predictability, followed by *MAL* and *AA*. Therefore, we can consider the angles of the upper wall rocks as the most significant feature, ahead of the lower wall rocks and the avalanche angle that are less important.

5. NNE-based parameter sensitivity analysis

The NNE-based parameter sensitivity analysis technique is a modified version of the NNC-based sensitivity analysis. It reduces the time-consuming procedure of using different neural network types as seeds by using just one preferred neural network type as the seed [4]. NNE-based parameter sensitivity analysis incorporates the following steps: (1) one preferred type of neural network is considered as the seed, (2) a set of k-neural network models that are varied with regard to the number of hidden neurons and hidden layers is defined, (3) from k-neural network models, a group of n best-performed models ($n < k$) is picked up and the other poorly performed models are eliminated to form an NNE model, and (4) a sophisticated sensitivity analysis algorithm is performed on the NNE model to obtain a sensitivity ranking of all input variables of the engineering problem under consideration. A schematic diagram of NNE-based parameter sensitivity analysis is shown in **Figure 4**.

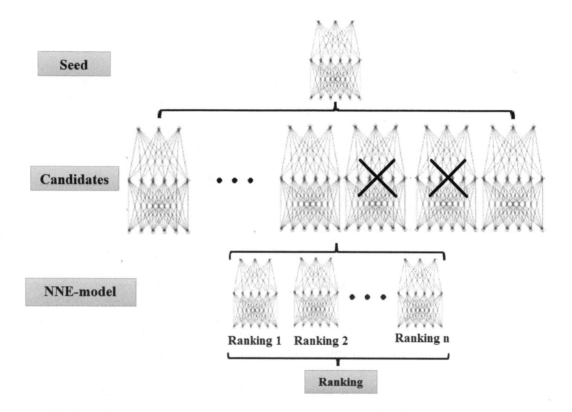

Figure 4. A schematic representation of NNE-based parameter sensitivity analysis.

6. Illustrative case studies

To highlight the application of NNE-based parameter sensitivity analysis technique, two civil engineering case studies are explained. The first is the determination of the importance of material properties in the fracture failure of a notched concrete beam and the second is the specification of significant parameters in the lateral deformation of a deep-foundation pit [4].

6.1. Fracture failure of notched concrete beam

Fracture failure is the most common problem facing engineers in the analysis and usage of concrete structures [19,20]. Good knowledge of appropriate material properties is necessary during modeling of the fracture behavior of concrete structures. Such material properties are defined by a three-point bending of a notched concrete specimen. Therefore, the NNE-based parameter sensitivity analysis strategy is used to find the most crucial material properties in the fracture failure of a notched concrete beam. The geometry of the notched concrete beam is shown in **Figure 5**, with experimentally determined mean values of material properties [21]: modulus of elasticity $E_c = 35$ GPa, tensile strength $f_t = 3$ MPa, compressive strength $f_c = 65$ MPa, fracture energy $G_f = 100$ N/m, and compressive strain at compressive strength in the uniaxial compressive test $e_c = 0.003$. A group of 20 notched concrete beam samples is prepared depending on a stratified Monte Carlo-type simulation called Latin hypercube sampling (LHS) [22], using FReET software [23] with a correlation control procedure [24].

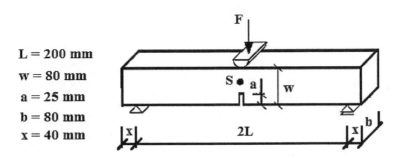

Figure 5. Notched concrete beam under three-point bending [4].

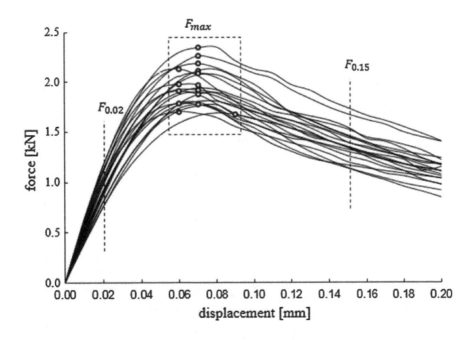

Figure 6. Force-displacement curves at the notch tip S from 20 simulated realizations of notched concrete beams [4].

The 20 notched concrete beam samples are determined by employing the following steps: (1) material properties are considered as random variables and mean values are obtained by experiments; (2) for each property, the LHS stochastic simulation is utilized to produce 20 random realizations of $\{E_c, f_t, f_c, G_f, e_c\}$ that feature variation of 0.15 and that obey a rectangular probability distribution, to impose variability for the creation of the training set. Each random realization determines a numerical nonlinear fracture mechanic calculation of a notched concrete beam; and (3) the finite element method (FEM) software ATENA [25] is applied to each realization to simulate the tensile fracture of the corresponding notched concrete beam. The fracture failure is described by a force-displacement curve at the notch tip S (**Figure 5**). A set of 20 force-displacement curves is illustrated in **Figure 6**. This set can be used as input data for the NNE-based sensitivity analysis. These curves describe the correlation between material fracture-mechanical properties and the nonlinear response of the beam. The sensitivity of the material properties to tensile fracture is studied depending on three forces: $F_{0.02}$, the force corresponding to 0.02-mm displacement; F_{max} the maximum force; and $F_{0.15}$ the force corresponding to 0.15-mm displacement. For each force, NNE-based parameter sensitivity analysis is applied to determine the significance of the material properties.

Parameter	Characteristics	Parameter type
E_c	Modulus of elasticity	Input
f_t	Tensile strength	Input
f_c	Compressive strength	Input
G_f	Fracture energy	Input
ε_c	Compressive strain	Input
$F_{0.02}$	Force at 0.02-mm displacement	Output
F_{max}	Maximum force	Output
$F_{0.15}$	Force at 0.15-mm displacement	Output

Table 4. Material properties in fracture failure of notched concrete beam [4].

Force	Ranking				
	E_c	f_t	f_c	G_f	ε_c
$F_{0.02}$	1	2	3	4	5
F_{max}	2	1	4	3	5
$F_{0.15}$	4	2	3	1	5

Table 5. Sensitivity analysis results of material parameters in fracture failure [4].

In NNE-based sensitivity analysis paradigm, a BP neural network with five input neurons and one output neuron (**Table 4**) is used as the seed to create a set of k-candidate neural network models. These models correlate the relationship between the material properties and the fracture failure. Depending on the performance of these models, the three best-performed neural network models are selected in the NNE model and the input perturbation algorithm is used for parameter sensitivity analysis. The result of the sensitivity analysis in this case is shown in **Table 5**. It is obvious from the table that f_t, followed by E_c and G_f, are the most important parameters in the fracture failure of the notched concrete beam.

6.2. Lateral deformation of deep-foundation pit

The construction of underground structures such as subway system tunnels, etc. requires deep-foundation pits. The working condition of a deep-foundation pit is usually defined by means of lateral deformation [26]. This lateral deformation usually involves a group of variables (**Table 6**), namely surface load q, deformation modulus of soil E, Poisson's ratio λ, soil cohesion C, and internal friction angle of soil φ. To analyze the working process of the deep-foundation pit, it is essential to study the sensitivity of these variables in order. Therefore, NNE-based parameter sensitivity analysis is applied to determine the importance of parameters in the lateral deformation of deep-foundation pits. For such analysis, a deep polygon-shaped foundation pit, as in [27], is utilized, having an excavation depth of 9.71 m, a width of earth-retaining wall of 8.7 m, and a length of reinforcement piles of 19.0 m, with the insertion ratio about 1.0. For testing cases, an orthogonal design of experiments is used to generate 25 testing cases, as shown in **Table 7** [27]. The testing cases are employed within the NNE-based sensitivity analysis paradigm to finally specify the contribution of each parameter to the lateral deformation y of the deep-foundation pits.

Parameter	Characteristics	Parameter type
q	Surface load	Input
E	Deformation modulus of soil	Input
ε	Poisson's ratio	Input
C	Soil cohesion	Input
φ	Internal friction angle of soil	Input
y	Lateral deformation of deep-foundation pit	Output

Table 6. Properties in lateral deformation of deep-foundation pit [4].

No.	q (kPa)	E (kPa)	ε	C (kPa)	φ (rad)	y (cm)
1	1 (5.0)	1 (3855)	1 (0.325)	1 (5.63)	1 (0.1386)	63.7
2	1	2 (6168)	2 (0.376)	2 (7.44)	2 (0.1834)	35.3
3	1	3 (7710)	3 (0.410)	3 (8.65)	3 (0.2133)	26.7
4	1	4 (9252)	4 (0.444)	4 (9.86)	4 (0.2432)	20.9
5	1	5 (11,565)	5 (0.478)	5 (11.68)	5 (0.2731)	12.5
6	2 (8.0)	1	2	3	4	55.8
7	2	2	3	4	5	32.1

No.	q (kPa)	E (kPa)	ε	C (kPa)	φ (rad)	y (cm)
8	2	3	4	5	1	21.9
9	2	4	5	1	2	16.3
10	2	5	1	2	3	25.2
11	3 (10.0)	1	3	5	2	47.8
12	3	2	4	1	3	26.1
13	3	3	5	2	4	16.2
14	3	4	1	3	5	30.4
15	3	5	2	4	1	22.1
16	4 (12.0)	1	4	2	5	37.1
17	4	2	5	3	1	18.0
18	4	3	1	4	2	34.9
19	4	4	2	5	3	25.8
20	4	5	3	1	4	18.9
21	5 (15.0)	1	5	4	3	25.2
22	5	2	1	5	4	42.4
23	5	3	2	1	5	30.1
24	5	4	3	2	1	22.4
25	5	5	4	3	2	15.6

Table 7. Orthogonal experimental design for producing testing samples [27].

Model	Ranking				
	q	E	λ	C	φ
NNM1	5	1	2	3	4
NNM2	5	1	2	3	4
NNM3	5	1	2	3	4

Table 8. Sensitivity analysis results in lateral deformation of deep-foundation pit [4].

As in the previous case study, a BP neural network is chosen as the seed in NNE-based sensitivity analysis to generate a set of k-candidate neural network models having five inputs and one output as listed in **Table 6**. By selecting three superior neural network models, namely NNM1, NNM2, and NNM3, and implementing input perturbation algorithm for sensitivity analysis, the ranking of each input parameter corresponding to each neural network model is shown in **Table 8**. It is clear that E is the most important parameter, followed by λ, C, ϕ, and q, respectively.

7. Summary

A short review of traditional neural network sensitivity analysis techniques was illustrated, followed by the presentation of two advanced techniques, NNC-based sensitivity analysis and NNE-based sensitivity analysis. These two techniques utilized selective superior neural network models along with some mathematical concepts to analyze the sensitivity of significant explicative variables. The efficiency of NNC-based sensitivity analysis paradigm was verified by studying the underlying influential parameters in strata movement. The effectiveness of NNE-based sensitivity analysis paradigm was proved by two case studies in civil engineering, the fracture failure of notched concrete beams and the lateral deformation of deep-foundation pits. These paradigms are essential for understanding the neural-network-based sensitivity analysis of critical engineering problems, due to their ability to determine the most and least important parameters, thereby reducing the inputs of neural network models to generate better predictability. They are good tools for analyzing the mechanism of engineering problems that black-box neural network models cannot explain.

Author details

Maosen Cao[1*], Nizar F. Alkayem[1], Lixia Pan[1] and Drahomír Novák[2]

*Address all correspondence to: cmszhy@hhu.edu.cn

1 Department of Engineering Mechanics, Hohai University, Nanjing, People's Republic of China

2 Faculty of Civil Engineering, Institute of Structural Mechanics, Brno University of Technology, Brno, Czech Republic

References

[1] Cao MS, Qiao P. Neural network committee-based sensitivity analysis strategy for geotechnical engineering problems. Neural Computing & Applications. 2008;17(5): 509–519. DOI: 10.1007/s00521-007-0143-5

[2] Cao M, Qiao P, Ren Q. Improved hybrid wavelet neural network methodology for time-varying behavior prediction of engineering structures. Neural Computing and Applications. 2009;18(7):821–832. DOI: 10.1007/s00521-009-0240-8

[3] Waszczyszyn Z, Ziemiański L. Neural networks in mechanics of structures and materials—new results and prospects of applications. Computers & Structures. 2001;79(22-25):2261–2276. DOI: 10.1016/S0045-7949(01)00083-9

[4] Cao MS, Pan LX, Gao YF, Novák D, Ding ZC, Lehký D, Li XL. Neural network ensemble-based parameter sensitivity analysis in civil engineering systems. Neural Computing & Applications. Forthcoming. DOI: 10.1007/s00521-015-2132-4

[5] Dimopoulos Y, Bourret P, Lek S. Use of some sensitivity criteria for choosing networks with good generalization ability. Neural Processing Letters. 1995;2(6):1–4. DOI: 10.1007/BF02309007

[6] Gedeon TD. Data mining of inputs: analysing magnitude and functional measures. International Journal of Neural Systems. 1997;8(2):209–218. DOI: 10.1142/S0129065797000227

[7] Wang W, Jones P, Partridge D. Assessing the impact of input features in a feedforward neural network. Neural Computing & Applications. 2000;9(2):101–112. DOI: 10.1007/PL00009895

[8] Gevrey M, Dimopoulos I, Lek S. Review and comparison of methods to study the contribution of variables in artificial neural network models. Ecological Modelling. 2003;160(3):249–264. DOI: 10.1016/S0304-3800(02)00257-0

[9] Montaño JJ, Palmer A. Numeric sensitivity analysis applied to feedforward neural networks. Neural Computing & Applications. 2003;12(2):119–125. DOI: 10.1007/s00521-003-0377-9

[10] Zeng X, Yeung DS. A quantified sensitivity measure for multilayer perceptron to input perturbation. Neural Computation. 2003;15(1):183–212. DOI: 10.1162/089976603321043757

[11] Yang Y, Zhang Q. A hierarchical analysis for rock engineering using artificial neural networks. Rock Mechanics and Rock Engineering. 1997;30(4):207–222. DOI: 10.1007/BF01045717

[12] Garson GD. Interpreting neural network connection weights. AI Expert. 1991;6(4):46–51.

[13] Goh ATC. Back-propagation neural networks for modelling complex systems. Artificial Intelligence in Engineering. 1995;9(3):143–151. DOI: 10.1016/0954-1810(94)00011-S

[14] Lek S, Belaud A, Baran P, Dimopoulos I, Delacoste M. Role of some environmental variables in trout abundance models using neural networks. Aquatic Living Resources. 1996;9(1):23–29.

[15] Lek S, Delacosteb M, Baranb P, Dimopoulosa I, Laugaa J, Aulagnierc S. Application of neural networks to modelling nonlinear relationships in ecology. Ecological Modelling. 1996;90(1):39–52. DOI: 10.1016/0304-3800(95)00142-5

[16] Lek S, Belaud A, Dimopoulos I, Lauga J, Moreau J. Improved estimation, using neural networks, of the food consumption of fish populations. Marine and Freshwater Research. 1995;46(8):1229–1236 . DOI: 10.1071/MF9951229

[17] Sung AH. Ranking importance of input parameters of neural networks. Expert Systems with Applications. 1998;15(3-4): 405–411. DOI: 10.1016/S0957-4174(98)00041-4

[18] Durrett R. Probability: Theory and Example, 3rd ed. Pacific Grove, CA: Duxbury; 2004. 521 p.

[19] Carpinteri A, Ferro G. Size effects on tensile fracture properties: a unified explanation based on disorder and fractality of concrete microstructure. Materials and Structures. 1994;27(10):563–571. DOI: 10.1007/BF02473124

[20] Rott JG. Computational modelling of concrete fracture [dissertation]. Delft: Technische Hogeschool Delft; 1988.

[21] Novák D, Lehký D. ANN inverse analysis based on stochastic small-sample training set simulation. Engineering Applications of Artificial Intelligence. 2006;19(7):731–740. DOI: 10.1016/j.engappai.2006.05.003

[22] Stein M. Large sample properties of simulations using Latin hypercube sampling. Technometrics. 1987;29(2):143–151 . DOI: 10.2307/1269769

[23] Novák D, Vořechovský M, Teplý B. FReET: software for the statistical and reliability analysis of engineering problems and FReET-D: degradation module. Advances in Engineering Software. 2014;72:179–192. DOI: 10.1016/j.advengsoft.2013.06.011

[24] Vořechovský M, Novák D. Correlation control in small-sample Monte Carlo type simulations I: a simulated annealing approach. Probabilistic Engineering Mechanics. 2009;24(3):452–462. DOI: 10.1016/j.probengmech.2009.01.004

[25] Červenka V, Jendele L, Červenka J. ATENA Program Documentation, Part 1: Theory. Prague: Červenka Consulting; 2009. 94 p.

[26] Feng S, Wu Y, Li J, Li P, Zhang Z, Wang D. The analysis of spatial effect of deep foundation pit in soft soil areas. Procedia Earth and Planetary Science. 2012;5:309–313. DOI: 10.1016/j.proeps.2012.01.052

[27] XU C, YE GB. Parameter sensitivity analysis of numerical model by cross test design technique. Hydrogeology and Engineering Geology. 2004;1:95–97.

4

Thunderstorm Predictions Using Artificial Neural Networks

Waylon G. Collins and Philippe Tissot

Additional information is available at the end of the chapter

Abstract

Artificial neural network (ANN) model classifiers were developed to generate $\leq$ 15 h predictions of thunderstorms within three 400-km^2 domains. The feed-forward, multi-layer perceptron and single hidden layer network topology, scaled conjugate gradient learning algorithm, and the sigmoid (linear) transfer function in the hidden (output) layer were used. The optimal number of neurons in the hidden layer was determined iteratively based on training set performance. Three sets of nine ANN models were developed: two sets based on predictors chosen from feature selection (FS) techniques and one set with all 36 predictors. The predictors were based on output from a numerical weather prediction (NWP) model. This study amends an earlier study and involves the increase in available training data by two orders of magnitude. ANN model performance was compared to corresponding performances of operational forecasters and multi-linear regression (MLR) models. Results revealed improvement relative to ANN models from the previous study. Comparative results between the three sets of classifiers, NDFD, and MLR models for this study were mixed—the best performers were a function of prediction hour, domain, and FS technique. Boosting the fraction of total positive target data (lightning strikes) in the training set did not improve generalization.

Keywords: thunderstorm prediction, artificial neural networks, correlation-based feature selection, minimum redundancy maximum relevance, multi-linear regression

1. Introduction

A *thunderstorm or convective storm* is a cumulonimbus cloud that produces the electric discharge known as lightning (which produces thunder) and typically generates heavy rainfall, gusty surface wind, and possibly hail [1]. Meteorologists use the term convection/convective to refer to the vertical component of convective heat transfer owing to buoyancy [2–4]. The term *deep moist convection* (DMC), which refers to the overturning of approximately the entire troposphere due to convective motions and involving condensation of water vapor associated with rising parcels [5], is part of the literature and includes both thunderstorms and moist convection not involving thunder [4]. The terms *thunderstorm, convective storm*, and *convection* are used interchangeably in this chapter to refer to thunderstorms. Thunderstorms adversely affect humans and infrastructure. An estimated 24,000 deaths and 240,000 injuries worldwide are attributable to lightning [6, 7]. In the USA, lightning is the third leading cause of storm-related deaths based on averages during the period 1985–2014 [8]. Additional hazards that can occur include large hail, flash flooding associated with heavy rainfall, and damage from wind from tornadoes and/or non-rotational (straight-line) wind. During the period 1980–2014, 70 severe thunderstorm events each totaling ≥ 1 billion US dollar damage occurred in the USA, which totaled to 156.3 billion US dollars (adjusted for inflation to 2014 dollars) [9]. Further, convection exacts an economic cost on aviation in terms of delays [10]. Given the adverse socioeconomic impact associated with thunderstorms, there is motivation to predict thunderstorm occurrence and location to inform the public with sufficient lead time.

However, the complexity of thunderstorm generation (hereafter *convective initiation*, or CI), given the myriad of processes (operating on different scales) that influence the vertical thermodynamic structure of the atmosphere (that directly influences the thunderstorm development) and the CI itself [11], the characteristic Eulerian (with respect to a fixed point at the surface) time and linear space scales of individual thunderstorms [12], and the inherent predictability limitations of atmospheric phenomena on the scale of individual thunderstorms [13, 14], renders the skillful prediction of thunderstorm occurrence, timing, and location very difficult. This chapter begins by explaining the thunderstorm development process in order to help the reader understand the predictor variables used in the artificial neural network (ANN) models. Next, the variety of methods used to predict thunderstorms are presented in order to acquaint the reader with the relative utility of the ANN model option. The main section starts with an account of the previous methods developed by the authors and presents a new approach to the development of ANN models to predict thunderstorms with high temporal and spatial resolution. Finally, concluding remarks, including a discussion of future research.

2. Thunderstorm development

To properly understand the process of thunderstorm development, it is essential to define the terms *parcel* and *environment*. The environment refers to the ambient atmospheric conditions. In general, a parcel is an imaginary volume of air that can be assigned various properties [1]. A parcel in this discussion is infinitesimal in dimension and is assumed to be thermally insulated from the surrounding environment which allows for adiabatic temperature changes owing to vertical displacement, and it has a pressure that immediately adjusts to the environmental pressure [15]. One method used by meteorologists to assess the potential for the development of thunderstorms is the *parcel method* [3]. This method is used to assess atmospheric stability and involves the finite vertical displacement of a parcel from hydrostatic equilibrium (balance between vertical pressure force and gravity) while the environment remains unchanged. After the displacement, the temperature contrast between the parcel and the environment at the same level results in buoyancy forces that determine stability.

Consider an environment of depth H with a temperature lapse rate (decrease in temperature with height) Γ satisfying the condition $\Gamma_m < \Gamma < \Gamma_d$, where $\Gamma_d = 9.8°\text{Ckm}^{-1}$ and $\Gamma_m = 6.5°\text{Ckm}^{-1}$ are the dry and moist adiabatic/pseudoadiabatic lapse rates, respectively. Now consider a *surface-based parcel*, defined as a parcel originating in the convective *planetary boundary layer* (PBL) (also called *mixing layer*) that eventually contribute to the primary thunderstorm updraft if thunderstorms develop [16]. The convective PBL refers to the bottom layer of the atmosphere in contact with the earth surface with a diurnal depth varying between tens of meters (near sunrise) to 1–4 km (near sunset) [1]. Let us begin with an unsaturated parcel located at a particular position $(x, y, z = h)$ within the PBL and at the same temperature, density, and pressure as the environment (hydrostatic equilibrium.) Consider an upward vertical displacement of this parcel and apply the parcel method. Since the parcel is unsaturated, it will initially cool at the dry adiabatic lapse rate. Since $\Gamma < \Gamma_d$, the parcel will become cooler than its surrounding environment. Applying the ideal gas law and the assumption that the parcel's pressure instantly adjusts to the environmental pressure, the parcel's density becomes greater than environmental air density. Thus, the parcel is negatively buoyant, a condition known as *positive static stability* [15]. If this parcel is released, it will return to its original height h with negative buoyancy acting as the restoring force. However, let us assume that the parcel overcomes this negative buoyancy via certain upward-directed external force. The parcel eventually reaches the *lifted condensation level* (LCL), whereby the parcel becomes saturated followed by condensation. (The condensation of parcels is manifested by the development of cumulus clouds.) Due to the associated latent heat release, the parcel cools at the pseudoadiabatic rate during subsequent lift. Since $\Gamma_m < \Gamma$, the parcel now cools at a lesser rate than the environmental rate and (with the help of the external force) will eventually reach the environmental temperature at the level referred to as the *level of free convection*. Afterward, the parcel becomes warmer than the environment and thus positively buoyant. If the parcel is released, it will continue to rise without the aid of an external force, a condition known as *static instability*. Thus, a parcel with sufficient vertical displacement within an environment with lapse rates following the $\Gamma_m < \Gamma < \Gamma_d$ constraint may become positively buoyant. This condition is known as *conditional instability*.

The parcel will remain positively buoyant until it reaches the *equilibrium level* (EL). The magnitude of the energy available to a given parcel for convection is the *convective available potential energy* (CAPE) [3] which is the integrated effect of the parcel's positive buoyancy between its original height h and the EL:

$$CAPE_h = \int_{P_{EL}}^{P_h} R_d \left(T_{vp} - T_{ve} \right) d\ln p \tag{1}$$

The variables T_{vp}, T_{ve}, R_d, and p refer to the virtual temperatures of the parcel and environment, specific gas constant for dry air, and air pressure, respectively. Recall that before the surface-based parcel reached the LFC, an external force was needed. The amount of energy required of the external force to lift the parcel to its LFC is known as *convective inhibition* (CIN) [1], represented as follows:

$$CIN_h = - \int_{p_h}^{p_{LFC}} R_d \left(T_{vp} - T_{ve} \right) d\ln p \qquad (2)$$

Now, consider a separate case whereby the environment is *absolutely stable* with respect to a surface-based parcel ($\Gamma_m > \Gamma$). This condition is characterized by negative buoyancy during the parcel's entire vertical path of depth H within the troposphere. Hence, the parcel method would suggest that convection is not possible. However, consider a layer of depth $l \le H$ within this environment where water vapor content decreases rapidly with height. Owing to this moisture profile, if the entire layer l is lifted, parcels at the bottom of the layer will reach their LCL before parcels at the top of the layer. The differential lapse rates within this layer resulting from continued lifting will transform the layer from absolutely stable to conditionally unstable. This condition is known as *convectively (or potential) instability* [3, 15]. A convectively unstable layer is identified as one that satisfies:

$$\frac{\partial \theta_e}{\partial z} < 0 \qquad (3)$$

The symbols θ_e and z refer to *equivalent potential temperature* and geometric height, respectively. It must be emphasized that CAPE is necessary for the potential for convection [3]. Recall that a convectively unstable layer is not necessarily unstable. In this example, the environment is absolutely unstable, devoid of positive buoyancy, and thus CAPE = 0. A mechanism is required to lift the convectively unstable layer to one characterized by conditional instability.

Air parcels extending above the LFC accelerate upward owing to positive buoyancy and draw energy for acceleration from CAPE. The relationship between maximum updraft velocity (w_{max}) and CAPE (parcel theory) is as follows:

$$w_{max} = \left(2CAPE \right)^{1/2} \qquad (4)$$

The moist updraft is integral to the development of a supersaturated condition that results in excess water vapor that (with the aid of hygroscopic aerosols that serve as cloud condensation nuclei or CNN) condenses to form water in liquid and solid form (condensate) manifested as the development of a *cumulus cloud*, followed by the transition to *cumulus congestus*, then ultimately to *cumulonimbus*. With respect to the production of rain during convection, the stochastic *collision-coalescence* mechanism is likely the predominant process that transforms cloud droplets (with broad drop-size distribution) to liquid hydrometeors large enough (diameter 500 μm) to combine with gravity and fall as rain on convective time scales [17].

As saturated parcels rise to the region with environmental temperatures colder than −4°C, the likelihood that ice crystals will develop within the cloud increases. Further, a fraction of water remains in liquid form (supercooled water) until around −35°C [15]. Thus, a region character-ized by water in all three phases (vapor, liquid, and solid) develops. The development of the solid hydrometeors known as *ice crystals* and *graupel* within this mixed phase region contribute to the development of lightning. In particular, ice-graupel collisions contribute to the transfer of negative (positive) charge to the larger graupel (smaller ice crystal) particles with charge separation caused by gravity, resulting in a large-scale positive dipole within the cumulonim-bus [18]. A smaller positively charged region exists near the cloud base. *Intracloud* (IC) lightning occurs in response to the foregoing dipole, *cloud-to-ground* (CTG) lightning involves a transfer of negative charge from the dipole to the earth surface, and the less common *cloud-to-air* (CTA) lightning variety links the large-scale negative charge with the smaller positive charge near cloud base [18]. The temperatures in the air channel through which lightning occurs exceed the surface of the sun and result in a shockwave followed by a series of sound waves recognized as thunder that is heard generally 25 km away from the lightning occurrence [1, 15].

Straight-line thunderstorm surface winds develop as negative buoyancy (owing to cooling associated with evaporation of water/melting of ice), condensate loading (weight of precipi-tation dragging air initially downward before negative buoyancy effects commence), and/or downward-directed pressure gradient force (associated with convection developing within strong environmental vertical wind shear) contribute to the generation of the *convective downdrafts* which are manifested as *gust fronts* (also called *outflow boundaries*) after contact with the earth surface [19]. Hail associated with a thunderstorm involves a complex process whereby graupel and frozen raindrops serve as pre-existing hail embryos and transition to hailstones by traveling along optimal trajectories favorable for rapid growth within the region of the cumulonimbus composed of supercooled water [20].

Given the foregoing thunderstorm development process, the simultaneous occurrence of three conditions are necessary for CI: sufficient atmospheric moisture, CAPE, and a lifting/triggering mechanism. Moisture is necessary for the development of the cumulonimbus cloud condensate which serves as a source material for the development of hydrometeors rain, ice crystals, graupel, and hail. The environmental moisture profile contributes to the development conditional and convective instability. CAPE provides the energy for updraft to heights necessary for the development of the cumulonimbus cloud and the associated mixed phase region that contributes to lightning via charge separation. A mechanism is necessary to lift surface-based parcels through the energy barrier to their LFC, and to lift convectively unstable layers necessary for the development of conditional instability. A myriad of phenomena can provide lift, including fronts, dry lines, sea breezes, gravity waves, PBL horizontal convective rolls, orography, and circulations associated with local soil moisture/vegetation gradients [11, 21].

A myriad of synoptic scale [12] patterns/processes can alter the thermodynamic structure of the environment at a particular location to one favorable for the development of CAPE or convective instability [22]. One scenario in the USA involves the advection of lower-level moist air toward the north across the Southern Plains from the Gulf of Mexico in advance of an upper-level disturbance approaching from the west and advecting midtropospheric dry air originating from the desserts of northern Mexico. The thermodynamic profile over a location influenced by those air masses (e.g., Oklahoma City, Oklahoma) would become one characterized by both conditional and convective instabilities owing to the dry air mass moving over the moist air mass [3].

The foregoing discussion is not exhaustive with respect to thunderstorms. The transition to *severe* convective storms (defined as thunderstorms which generate large hail, damaging straight-line wind, and/or tornadoes), flash flooding, and convective storm mode (squall lines, single cells, multi-cells, supercells, etc.) are not relevant to the development of *non-severe* (also called *ordinary*) thunderstorms in general and are not discussed. Further, *slantwise convection* owing to *conditional symmetric instability* due to the combination of gravitational and centrifugal forces [1] is not considered.

3. Thunderstorm prediction methods

We classify thunderstorm prediction based on the following methods: (1) numerical weather prediction (NWP) models, (2) post-processing of NWP model ensemble output, (3) the post-processing of single deterministic NWP model output via statistical and artificial intelligence (AI)/machine learning (ML), and (4) classical statistical, AI/ML techniques.

3.1. Secondary output variables/parameters from Numerical Weather Prediction (NWP) models

NWP models are based on the concept of determinism which posits that future states of a system evolve from earlier states in accordance with physical laws [23]. Meteorologists describe atmospheric motion by a set of nonlinear partial differential conservation equations — derived from Newton's second law of motion for a fluid, the continuity equation, the equation of state, and the thermodynamic energy equation — that describe atmospheric heat, momentum, water, and mass referred to as *primitive equations, Euler equations,* or *equations of motion* [24–26]. These equations cannot be solved analytically and are thus solved numerically. Further, the earth's atmosphere is a continuous fluid with 10^{44} molecules (Appendix A) which the state-of-the-art NWP models cannot resolve. Thus, NWP model developers undertake the process known as *discretization*, which involves the representation of the atmosphere as a three-dimensional (3D) spatial grid (which divides the atmosphere into volumes or grid cells), the representation of time as finite increments, and the substitution of the primitive equations with corresponding numerical approximations known as *finite difference equations* solved at the grid points [26]. Atmospheric processes resolved by the NWP equations are termed *model dynamics* while unresolved processes are *parameterized* via a series of equations collectively known as *model physics* [25]. Parameterization involves using a set of equations on the resolved scale to implicitly represent the unresolved process. These unresolved (sub-grid-scale) processes include solar/infrared radiation and microphysics (which occur on the molecular scale), cumulus convection, earth surface/atmosphere interactions, and planetary boundary layer/turbulence [27]. If these primary unresolved processes are not taken into account, the quality of NWP output would deteriorate in less than 1 h when simulating the atmosphere at horizontal grid scales of 1–10 km [25]. The NWP model prediction process is an *initial value problem*. A process known as *data assimilation* is used to provide the requisite initial values. A predominate data assimilation technique involves the use of balanced (theoretical and observed winds in phase) short-term output from an earlier NWP model run to serve as a first guess, followed by the incorporation of meteorological observations to create a balanced *analysis* which serve as the initial condition for the NWP model [26]. Next, the finite difference equations are solved forward in time. The primary output variables include temperature, wind, pressure/height, mixing ratio, and precipitation. At the completion of the NWP model run, *post-processing* is performed which includes the calculation of secondary variables/parameters (CAPE, relative humidity, etc.) and the development of techniques to remove model biases [25, 26, 28].

The state-of-the-art high-resolution NWP models have the ability to explicitly predict/simulate individual thunderstorm cells rather than parameterize the effects of sub-grid-scale convection [29]. NWP output identified as thunderstorm activity involves assessment of NWP output parameter/secondary variable known as *radar reflectivity* defined as the efficiency of a radar target to intercept and return of energy from radio waves [1]. Operational meteorologists in the NWS use radar technology to diagnose/analyze thunderstorms. With respect to hydrometeor targets (rain, snow, sleet, hail, graupel, etc.), radar reflectivity is a function of hydrometeor size, number per volume, phase, shape, and is proportional to six times the effective diameter of the hydrometeor [1]. Radar reflectivity magnitudes ≥ 35dB at the $-10°C$ level are generally regarded as a proxy for CI and for the initial CG lightning flash [30, 31]. Further, the increase in the reflectivity within the mixed-phase region of cumulonimbus clouds correlates strongly with lightning rate [32]. An example of a high-resolution (≤ 4-km) NWP model that can simulate/predict *radar reflectivity* is version 1.0.4 of the 3-km High-Resolution Rapid Refresh (HRRR) Model, developed by National Oceanic and Atmospheric Administration (NOAA)/Oceanic and Atmospheric Research (OAR)/Earth Systems Research Laboratory implemented by the National Weather Service (NWS) National Centers for Environmental Prediction (NCEP) Environmental Modeling Center (EMC) on 30 September 2014 to support NWS operations [33]. The specific model dynamical core, physics, and other components are detailed in Appendix B. Yet, we emphasize here that the HRRR does not incorporate cumulus/convective parameterization (CP), thus allowing for the explicit prediction of thunderstorm activity. One of the output parameters relevant to thunderstorm prediction is *simulated radar reflectivity 1-km (dBZ)*, which is an estimate of the *radar reflectivity* at the constant 1-km level.

Despite the utility of NWP models, there exist fundamental limitations. In particular, the atmosphere is chaotic—a property of the class of deterministic systems characterized by sensitive dependence on the system's initial condition [13, 14, 23]. Thus, minor errors between the initial atmospheric state and the NWP model representation of the initial state can result in a future NWP solution divergent from the future true atmospheric state. Unfortunately, a true, exact, and complete representation of the initial state of the atmosphere using the state-of-the-art NWP models is not possible. Even if the NWP model could perfectly represent the initial atmospheric state, errors associated with imperfections inherent in model formulation and time integration would grow. Model discretization and physics parameterizations introduce errors. Further, the gradient terms in the finite difference equations are approximated using a Taylor series expansion of only a few orders [26, 34], thus introducing *truncation* error. Errors associated with the initial condition, discretization, truncation, and parameterization limits predictability; an intrinsic finite range of predictability exists that is positively correlated to spatial scale [14]. A high-resolution NWP simulation of a tornadic thunderstorm can result in inherent predictability with lead times as short as 3–6 h [35].

Accurately predicting the exact *time* and *location* of individual convective storms is extremely difficult [36]. High-resolution (≤4-km) NWP models can accurately simulate/predict the *occurrence* and *mode* of convection (e.g., whether a less common left-moving and devastating *supercell thunderstorm* will develop), yet have difficulty with regard to the *time* and *location* (exactly when and where will the *supercell* occur) [37, 38]. Even very high-resolution (≤1-km) NWP models that can resolve and predict individual convective cells [29] will not necessarily provide greater accuracy and skill relative to coarser resolution NWP models [39].

3.2. Post processing of NWP model ensembles

Methods exist to generate more optimal or skillful thunderstorm predictions/forecasts when using NWP models. One such method is known as ensemble forecasting [40], which is essentially a Monte Carlo approximation to *stochastic dynamical forecasting* [28, 41]. Stochastic dynamical forecasting is an attempt to account for the uncertainty regarding the true initial atmospheric state. The idea is to run an NWP model on a probability distribution (PD) that describes initial atmospheric state uncertainty. Due to the impracticability of this technique, a technique was proposed whereby the modeler chooses a small random sample of the PD describing initial state uncertainty [41]; the members are collectively referred to as ensemble of initial conditions. The modeler then conducts an NWP model run on each member of the ensemble, hence the term ensemble forecasting [28]. In practice, each member of the ensemble represents a unique combination of model initial condition, dynamics, and/or physics [27, 42]. An advantage of ensemble forecasting over prediction with single deterministic NWP output is the ability to assess the level of forecast uncertainty. One method to assess this uncertainty is to assume a positive correlation between uncertainty and the divergence/spread in the ensemble members [28]. Prediction probabilities can be generated by post-processing the ensemble. Applying ensembles to thunderstorm forecasting, the NWS Environmental Modeling Center developed the *short-range ensemble forecast (SREF)*, a collection of selected output from an ensemble of 21 mesoscale (16-km) NWP model runs. The NWS Storm Prediction Center (SPC) post-processes SREF output to create a quasi-real-time suite of products that includes the *calibrated probabilistic prediction of thunderstorms* [42]. There exist utility in the use of ensembles in thunderstorm forecasting. According to [16], the timing of CI within selected mesoscale regions can be predicted accurately using an ensemble-based approach.

One limitation of NWP ensembles to support operational forecasters is the tremendous computational cost necessary to run since each ensemble member is a separate NWP model run. Another limitation is the realization that the true PD of the initial condition uncertainty is unknown and changes daily [28].

3.3. Post-processing of single deterministic NWP model output using other statistical and artificial intelligence/machine learning techniques

Statistical methods can be utilized to post-process NWP output to correct for certain systematic NWP model biases and to quantify the level of uncertainty in single NWP deterministic output [28, 43]. Statistical post-processing methods include *model output statistics* (MOS) [44] and *logistic regression* [28].

MOS involves the development of data-driven models to predict the future state of a target based on a data set of past NWP output (features/predictors) and the corresponding target/predictand. Following [28], a regression function f_{MOS} is developed to fit target Y at future time t to a set of predictors/features (from NWP output known at $t = 0$) represented by vector x. The development and implementation is as follows:

$$Y_t = f_{MOS}(x_t)$$ (5)

One limitation of the MOS technique involves NWP model changes made by the developers. If NWP model adjustments alter *systematic errors*, new MOS equations should be formulated [28]. Model changes can occur somewhat frequently. Consider the North American Mesoscale (NAM), which is the placeholder for the official NWS operational mesoscale NWP model for the North American domain. On 20 June 2006, the NAM representative model switched from the *hydrostatic Eta* to the *Weather Research and Forecasting (WRF)-Non-hydrostatic Mesoscale Model (NMM)*, a change in both the model dynamical formulation and modeling framework. Then, on 1 October 2011, the NAM representative model switched to *NOAA Environmental Modeling System Non-hydrostatic Multiscale Model on the B-grid (NEMS-NMMB)* resulting in changes to the model framework (WRF to NEMS) and model discretization (change from Arakawa E to B grid) (Appendix C).

The NWS uses multiple linear regression (MLR) (with forward selection) applied to operational NWP model predictors and corresponding weather observations (target) to derive MOS equations to support forecast operations [43]. The NWS provides high-resolution gridded MOS products which include a 3-h probability of thunderstorms [45] and thunderstorm probability forecasts as part of the NWS *Localized Aviation Model Output Statistics Program* (LAMP) [46].

Logistic regression is a method to relate the predicted probability p_j of one member of a binary target to the jth set of n predictors/features $(x_1, x_2, ..., x_n)$ to the following nonlinear equation:

$$p_j = \frac{1}{1 + exp\left(-b_0 - b_1 x_1 - b_2 x_2 - ... - b_n x_n\right)} \qquad (6)$$

The regression parameters are determined via the method of *maximum likelihood* [28].

Logistic regression models were used by [47] to develop MOS equations to generate probability of thunderstorms and the conditional probability of severe thunderstorms in twelve 7200 km² regions at 6-h projections out to 48-h in the Netherlands. The NWP output was provided by both the High-Resolution Limited-Area Model (HIRLAM) and the European Centre for Medium-Range Weather Forecasts (ECMWF) NWP model. The Surveillance et d'Alerte Foudre par Interférométrie Radioélectrique (SAFIR) lightning network provided the target data. Verification results suggest that the prediction system possessed good skills.

Artificial intelligence (AI) involves the use of computer software to reproduce human cognitive processes such as learning and decision making [1, 48]. More recently, the term *machine learning* (ML) is used to describe the development of computer systems that improve with experience [1, 49]. Specific AI/ML techniques involving the post-processing of NWP output include *expert systems* [50], *adaptive boosting* [51], *artificial neural networks* [52, 53], and *random forests* [31].

A random forest [54] is a classifier resulting from an ensemble/forest of tree-structured classifiers, whereby each tree is developed from independent random subsamples of the data set (including a random selection of features from which the optimum individual tree predictors are selected) drawn from the original training set. The generalization error (which depends on individual tree strength and tree-tree correlations) convergences to a minimum as the number of trees becomes large, yet overfitting does not occur owing to the law of large numbers. After training, the classifier prediction is the result of a synthesis of the votes of each tree.

In one study, selected thermodynamic and kinematic output from an Australian NWP model served as input for an expert system using the decision tree method to assess the likelihood of thunderstorms and severe thunderstorms [50]. Further, an artificial neural network model to predict significant thunderstorms that require the issuance of the Convective SIGMET product (called WST), issued by the National Weather Service's Aviation Weather Center, for the 3–7 h period after 1800 UTC; the model demonstrated skill, including the ability to narrow the WST outlook region while still capturing the subsequent WST issuance region [52]. Logistic regression and random forests were used to develop models to predict convective initiation (CI) ≤1 h in advance. The features/predictors included NWP output and selected Geostationary Operational Environmental Satellite (GOES)-R data. The performance of these models was an improvement of an earlier model developed based on GOES-R data alone [31].

3.4. Classical statistical and artificial intelligence/machine learning techniques

Statistical methods not involving the use of NWP model output (classical statistical) that have been used to predict thunderstorm occurrence include *multiple discriminate analysis (MDA)*, *scatter diagrams*, and *multiple regression*. Corresponding AI/ML techniques include *expert systems, artificial neural networks*, and *logistic regression*.

MDA is essentially a form of multiple linear regression used to predict an event. In particular, a discriminant function relates a nonnumerical predictand to a set of predictors; the value of the function that distinguishes between event groups [1, 55]. An MDA was used to obtain 12 h prediction functions to distinguish between the following two or three member groups within selected domains in portions of the Central and Eastern USA: thunderstorm/no-thunderstorm, thunderstorm/severe thunderstorm, and thunderstorm/severe thunderstorm/no-thunderstorm. The verification domains were within 1° latitude radius relative to the position of the data source that provided the predictor variables. The MDA prediction system provided skill in the 0-12 h period [55].

In one study, the utility of both a graphical method and multiple regression was tested to predict thunderstorms [56]. The graphical method involved scatter diagrams that were used to analyze multiple pairs of atmospheric stability index parameters in order to discover any diagram(s) whereby the majority of thunderstorm occurrence cases were clustered within a zone while the majority of the non-thunderstorm occurrence cases were outside of the zone. Two such diagrams were found—scatter diagrams of Showalter index versus Total Totals index, and Jefferson's modified index versus the George index. The multiple regression technique involved the stepwise screening of 274 potential predictors to 9 remaining. Both prediction models provided thunderstorm predictions in probabilistic terms. Objective techniques were used to convert probabilistic predictions to binary predictions for the purpose of verification. Results indicate that the multiple regression model performed better.

An expert system is a form of artificial intelligence that attempts to mimic the performance of a human expert when making decisions. The expert system includes a knowledge base and an inference engine. The knowledge base contains the combination of human knowledge and experience. Once the system is developed, questions are given to the system and the inference engine uses the knowledge base and renders a decision [57]. An expert system was developed using the decision tree method to forecast the development of thunderstorms and severe thunderstorms [58]; the tree was based on physical reasoning using the observation of meteorological parameters considered essential for convective development. An expert system named *Thunderstorm Intelligence Prediction System (TIPS)* was developed to predict thunderstorm occurrence [59]. Selected thermodynamic sounding data from 1200 UTC and forecaster assessment of likely convective triggering mechanisms were used to forecast thunderstorm occurrence for the subsequent 1500–0300 UTC period. Critical values of five (5) separate atmospheric stability parameters for thunderstorm occurrence and corresponding consensus rules served as the knowledge base. The forecaster answer regarding trigger mechanism and the values of the stability parameters served as input to the inference engine, which interrogated the knowledge base and provided an answer regarding future thunder-storm occurrence. Verification of TIPS revealed utility.

The artificial neural network (ANN) has been used to predict thunderstorms. Thermodynamic data from Udine Italy rawinsondes, surface observations, and lightning data were used to train/optimize an ANN model to predict thunderstorms 6 h in advance over a 5000-km^2 domain in the Friuli Venezia Giulia region [60]. An ANN model was developed (also using thermo-dynamic data) to predict severe thunderstorms over Kolkata India during the pre-monsoon season (April–May) [61].

Logistic regression was used to develop a binary classifier to predict thunderstorms 6–12 h in advance within a 6825–km^2 region in Spain. A total of 15 predictors (combination of stability indices and other parameters) were chosen to adequately describe the pre-convective environment. The classifier generated satisfactory results on the novel data set [62].

A limitation of classical statistics to weather prediction is that utility is bimodal in time; confined to very short time periods (less than a few hours) or long time periods (10 days) [28]. The utility of AI/ML techniques without NWP may not be as restrictive. Convective storm prediction accuracies associated with expert systems may be similar to that of NWP models [36].

4. The utility of post-processing NWP model output with artificial neural networks to predict thunderstorm occurrence, timing, and location

The rapid drop in prediction/forecast accuracy per unit time for classical statistical techniques renders it less than optimal for thunderstorm predictions over time scales greater than nowcasting (≤ 3 h).

Predicting thunderstorms with the use of deterministic NWP models allows for the prediction of atmospheric variables/parameters in the ambient environment that directly influence thunderstorm development. As discussed previously, limitations of NWP models include predictability limitations owing to a chaotic atmosphere and inherent model error growth [13, 14, 23]. NWP model ensembles attempt to account for the uncertainty in the NWP model's initial condition which contributes to predictability limitations in NWP models [40]. The post-processing of NWP model ensembles can generate useful probabilistic thunderstorm output [42]. However, there is a much greater computational cost to generate an ensemble of deter-ministic runs relative to a single run. The post-processing of output from a single deterministic NWP model can improve skill by minimizing certain systematic model biases, yet predicta-bility limitations associated with single deterministic NWP model output remain.

The authors explored the use of the artificial neural network (ANN) to post-process output from a single deterministic NWP model in an effort to improve thunderstorm predictive skill, based on an adjustment to the author's previous research [53]. As mentioned earlier, this approach involves a much lower computational cost relative to model ensembles. In particular, the single NWP model used in the development of the thunderstorm ANN (TANN) models discussed in this chapter is the 12-km NAM (North American Mesoscale), which refers to either the Eta, NEMS-NMMB, or WRF-NMM model (only one model used at a time; see Appendix C). The model integration cost to run the 21-member SREF ensemble would be of the order of 20 times the cost required to run the 12-km NAM (Israel Jirak 2016, personal communication.)

Given that ANN was developed to capture the parallel distributed processing thought to occur in the human brain and has tremendous pattern recognition capabilities [63–65], we posit that the ANN will learn the limitations/errors associated with a single NWP deterministic model solution to generate skillful forecasts, notwithstanding NWP predictability limitations. Thus, AI/ML rather than NWP model ensembles would be utilized to deal with atmospheric chaos. The remainder of this chapter focuses on the development of ANN models to predict thunderstorms (TANN) that are part of the ongoing research.

5. Artificial neural network models to predict thunderstorms within three South Texas 400-km² domains based solely on a data set within the same domain of each

In an earlier study [53], a thunderstorm ANN (TANN) was developed to predict thunderstorm occurrence in three separate 400-km² square (box) domains in South Texas (USA), 9, 12, and 15 h (+/−2 h) in advance, by post-processing 12-km NWP model output from a single deterministic NWP model (Appendix C) and 4-km sub-grid-scale output from soil moisture magnitude and heterogeneity estimates. A framework was established to predict thunderstorms in 286 box domains (**Figure 1**), yet predictions were only performed for three. The three box regions were strategically located to access model performance within the *Western Gulf Coastal Plain* region (boxes 103 and 238), the more arid *Southern Texas Plains* region (box 73), and within the region with the greatest amount of positive target data/thunderstorm occurrences based on CTG lightning density (box 238.) A skillful model was envisioned based on the combination of the deterministic future state of ambient meteorological variables/parameters related to thunderstorm development and sub-grid-scale data related to CI. TANN models were trained with the foregoing NWP model output and sub-grid data as predictors and corresponding CTG lightning data as the target. Each TANN model was trained using the feed-forward multi-layer perceptron topology with one hidden layer, the log-sigmoid and linear transfer functions in the hidden and output layers, respectively, and the scaled conjugate gradient (SCG) learning algorithm. The SCG algorithm makes implicit use of the second-order terms of the Hessian, searches the weight space/error surface in conjugate directions, avoids problems associated with line searches, and converges more efficiently than gradient descent [66]. The nomenclature X-Y-Z was used to describe the topology, where X, Y, and Z are the number of neurons in the input, hidden, and output layers, respectively. The data set consisted of a training/validation set (2004–2006; 2009–2012) and a testing set (2007–2008) for final performance and comparison with human forecasters and MLR. For each TANN model variant, the number of neurons in the hidden layer was determined iteratively For Y hidden layers, where $Y = \{1 - 10, 12, 15, 17, 20, 25, 30, 35, 40, 45, 50, 60, 70, 80, 90, 100\}$, the TANN model was trained 50 times. After each training, receiver operating characteristic (ROC) curves were generated to determine the optimal threshold, defined as the case where the Peirce Skill Score (PSS) was greatest [67]. The trained ANN with optimal threshold was then used to make predictions on the testing set (2007–2008); the corresponding performance results were calculated. The mean PSS of the 50 results from both the training and testing sets, for each Y, was archived. The chosen Y corresponded to the least number of hidden layer neurons with a PSS standard error which overlaps the standard error associated with the maximum PSS. Once Y is chosen, the performance results of the TANN are simply the mean of the 50 runs previously archived that corresponds to the chosen Y.

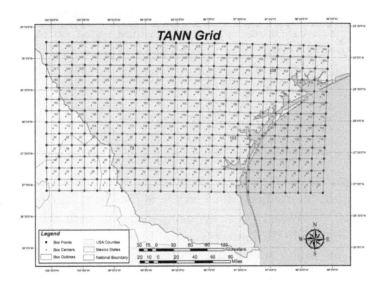

Figure 1. TANN and TANN2 grid domain. This grid is represented as 286 20 km× 20 km regions (boxes). The label inside each box is the identification number (ID). The boxes with ID values in larger font (73, 103, and 238) are the subject of this study. Image from Collins and Tissot [53].

Eighteen (18) TANN classifiers were developed with half based on a reduced set of predictors/ features due to feature selection (FS) and the other half using the full set of 43 potential predictors. FS involves a determination of the subset of potential predictors that describes much of the variability of the target/predictand. This is very important for very large dimensional models which may suffer from the *curse of dimensionality*, which posits that the amount of data needed to develop a skillful data-driven model increases exponentially as model dimension increases linearly [68]. When the features in the subset generated by the FS method are used to train an ANN model, it is important that such features are both relevant and nonredundant. Irrelevant features can adversely affect ANN model learning by introducing noise, and redundant features can result in reduced ANN model predictive skill by increasing the likelihood of convergence on local minima on the error surface during training [69]. The FS technique used was *correlation-based feature selection* (CFS) [70–72]. CFS is a filtering-based FS technique, meaning that statistical associations between the features and the target are assessed outside of the model. Specifically, CFS uses an information theory-based heuristic known as *symmetric uncertainty* to assess feature-target and feature-feature correlations to assess relevance and redundancy, respectively. The search strategy is the *Best First search* with a stopping criterion of five consecutive non-improving feature subsets.

The optimized TANN binary classifiers were evaluated on a novel data set (2007–2008), and performance was compared to MLR-based binary classifiers, and to operational forecasts from the NWS (National Digital Forecast Database, NDFD, Appendix D).

The MLR models were developed via stepwise forward linear regression (SFLR). For each MLR model, the SFLR process began with an empty set of features (constant value $y = \beta_0$. At each subsequent forward step, a predictor is added (from the list of 36 predictors in **Tables 2** and **3**, less the predictors already chosen) based on the change in the value of the Akaike information criterion (AIC) [73], while also considering removal of previously selected predictors based on the same criterion. The optimal MLR model chosen has the smallest AIC which is essentially a trade-off between model size and accuracy based on the training data. The MATLAB® function *stepwiselm* was used to perform SFLR to determine the regression equation coefficients. The resultant MLR models in this study are of the form:

$$y_i = \beta_0 + \sum_{j=1}^{k} \beta_j x_{ij} + \varepsilon_i \tag{7}$$

where y_i is the ith predictand response, β_j is the jth regression coefficient, β_0 is a constant, x_{ij} is the ith observation for the jth predictor, for $j = 1, \ldots, k$. Finally, ε_i represents error. Each MLR model was transformed into a binary classifier using the same method used in ANN classifier development, except that each MLR model was calibrated on the entire training sample to determine the coefficients, unlike ANN calibration which involved the splitting of the training sample into training and validation data sets. (However, one could argue that the ANN is also using the entire training sample as the validation set is inherently necessary to properly calibrate a model.)

The results were mixed—the TANN, MLR, and human forecasters performed better than the other two depending on the domain, prediction hour, and performance metric used. Results revealed the utility of an automated TANN model to support forecast operations with the limitation that a larger number of individual ANNs must be calibrated in order to generate operational predictions over a large area. Further, the utility of sub-grid-scale soil moisture data appeared limited given the fact that only 1/9 of the TANN models with reduced features retained any of the sub-grid parameters as a feature. The NWP model convective precipitation (CP) feature was retained in all the nine feature selection TANN models, suggesting that CP adequately accounted for the initiation of sub-grid-scale convection. This result is consistent with another study [47] which found that model CP was the most relevant predictor of thunderstorm activity.

6. Artificial neural network models to predict thunderstorms within three South Texas 400-km² domains based on data set from two-hundred and eighty-six 400-km² domains

With respect to TANN skill, the endeavor to predict thunderstorms in a small domain relative to domains used in other studies restricted the amount of CG lightning cases. A large number of thunderstorm cases would be beneficial to the model calibration and verification process; the amount of target data in [53] may have been insufficient to train this data-driven model with sufficient skill owing to the curse of dimensionality [67]. Further, the method of training/ optimizing TANN models for each 400-km² domain limits operational applicability since it would require the development of literally thousands of TANN models at a country scale. In order to retain thunderstorm predictions in 400-km² domains while increasing predictive skill, a new approach was developed (TANN2), whereby for each prediction hour (9, 12, 15), a single TANN model is trained over all two-hundred and eighty six 400-km² continuous domains. This approach dramatically increased the amount of positive target data (thunderstorm cases) and total cases/instances. **Table 1** depicts the quantity of data utilized in this project. The total number of cases over the study period was 1,148,576 with 939,510 cases used for model calibration and 209,066 cases contained in the 2007–2008 testing set.

Prediction hour	Total instances (training sample)	Positive target data	Percent positive target
9	663,519	22,139	3.3
12	646,073	16,904	2.6
15	659,801	12,682	1.9

Table 1. Quantity of data available to train TANN2 models.

Relative to the previous study [53], only the NWP model and Julian date predictor variables (features) were retained (resulting in 36 potential features used in this study; see **Tables 2** and **3**.) Given that in [53], only one sub-grid parameter was chosen for only 1/9 of the box/prediction hour combinations, and that the model including this sub-grid-scale parameter did not result in classifier performance improvement, the utility of the sub-grid-scale data appeared very limited. As mentioned in [53], the NWP model CP parameter was a ubiquitous output of the FS technique and thus considered a skillful predictor of convection. Physically, it was surmised that CP adequately accounted for the effects of sub-grid-scale convection. The use of FS was retained in order to eliminate irrelevant and redundant features to improve model skill and to reduce model size. The reduction in model size/dimension (owing to FS) and the increase in both the training data set and the amount of target CG lightning cases are expected to result in a more accurate/skillful model when considering the curse of dimensionality.

Abbreviation	Description (Units)	Justification as thunderstorm predictor
PWAT	Total precipitable water (mm)	Atmospheric moisture proxy
MR_{850}	Mixing ratio at 850 hPa ($g\ kg^{-1}$)	Lower level moisture necessary for convective cell to reach horizontal scale ≥4 km in order to overcome dissipative effects [84]
RH_{850}	Relative humidity at 850 hPa (%)	When combined with CAPE, predictor of subsequent thunderstorm location independent of synoptic pattern [85]
CAPE	Surface-based convective available potential energy ($J\ kg^{-1}$)	Instability proxy; the quantity $(2CAPE)^{0.5}$ is the theoretical limit of thunderstorm updraft velocity [11]

Abbreviation	Description (Units)	Justification as thunderstorm predictor
CIN	Convective inhibition (J kg^{-1})	Surface-based convective updraft magnitude must exceed $(CIN)^{0.5}$ for parcels to reach level of free convection [11]
LI	Lifted index (K)	Atmospheric instability proxy; utility in thunderstorm prediction [86]
U_{LEVEL}, V_{LEVEL}	U, V wind components at surface, 850 hPa (LEVEL = surface, 850 hPa) (ms^{-1})	Strong wind can modulate or preclude surface heterogeneity induced mesoscale circulations [87, 88]
VV_{LEVEL}	Vertical velocity at 925, 700, and 500 hPa (LEVEL = 925, 700, 500 hPa) (Pa s^{-1})	Account for mesoscale and synoptic scale thunderstorm triggering mechanisms (sea breezes, fronts, upper level disturbances) that are resolved by the NAM
$DROPOFF_{PROXY}$	Potential temperature dropoff proxy (K)	Atmospheric instability proxy; highly sensitive to CI [89]
LCL	Lifted condensation level (m)	Proxy for cloud base height; positive correlation between cloud base height and CAPE to convective updraft conversion efficiency [90]
T_LCL	Temperature at the LCL (K)	T_LCL $\geq -10°$C essential for presence of supercooled water in convective cloud essential for lightning via graupel-ice crystal collision mechanism [91]
CP	Convective precipitation (kg m^{-2})	By-product of the *Betts-Miller-Janjic* convective parameterization scheme [92] when triggered; proxy for when the NAM anticipates existence of sub-grid-scale convection
VSHEARS8	Vertical wind shear: 10 m to 800 hPa layer ($\times 10^{-3}$ s^{-1})	The combination of horizontal vorticity (associated with ambient 0–2 km vertical shear), and density current (e.g., gust front) generated horizontal vorticity (associated with 0–2 km vertical shear of opposite sign than that of ambient shear can trigger new convection [93]
VSHEAR86	Vertical wind shear: 800–600 hPa layer ($\times 10^{-3}$ s^{-1})	Convective updraft must exceed vertical shear immediately above the boundary layer for successful thunderstorm development [58, 89]

Table 2. Description of NAM predictor variables/parameters used in TANN and TANN2 (from [53]).

Abbreviation	Description (units)	Justification as thunderstorm predictor
U_{LEVEL}, V_{LEVEL}	U, V wind at the surface, 900, 800, 700, 600, 500 hPa levels (LEVEL= surface, 900, 800, 700, 600, 500) (ms^{-1})	Thermodynamic profile modification owing to veering of wind (warming) or backing of wind (cooling); backing (veering) of wind in the lowest 300 hPa can suppress (enhance) convective development [94]
HI_{LOW}	Humidity index (°C)	Both a constraint on afternoon convection and an atmospheric control on the interaction between soil

Abbreviation	Description (units)	Justification as thunderstorm predictor
		moisture and convection [94]
CTP Proxy	Proxy for convective triggering potential (dimensionless)	Both a constraint on afternoon convection and an atmospheric control on the interaction between soil moisture and convection [95]
VSHEARS7	Vertical wind shear: surface to 700 hPa layer ($\times 10^{-3}$ s^{-1})	Strong vertical shear in the lowest 300 hPa can suppress convective development [94]
VSHEAR75	Vertical wind shear: 700 to 500 hPa layer ($\times 10^{-3}$ s^{-1})	Convective updraft must exceed vertical shear immediately above the boundary layer for successful thunderstorm development [58, 89]

Table 3. Description of NAM initialization variables/parameters used in TANN and TANN2 (from [53]).

With respect to model training, validating, optimizing, and testing, the same strategy was utilized as in [53], with two differences. First, when determining the optimal number of hidden layer neurons, the range of neurons was extended to $Y = \{1-10, 12, 15, 17, 20, 25, 30, 35, 40, 45, 50, 60, 70, 80, 90, 100, 125, 150, 200\}$. Second, before each split of the training sample into training and validation components, a training set of the same size of the total training data available was drawn randomly from the training set with replacement. This technique allows for an exploration of training data set variability.

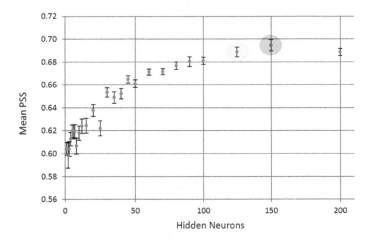

Figure 2. Determination of the optimal number of hidden layer neurons (Y) for the 12 h TANN2 36-Y-1 model (all 36 potential predictors used). Each point and corresponding error bar represents the mean Peirce Skill Score (PSS) and standard error resulting from 50 iterations with results computed based on the training portions of the training sample including the generation of ROC curves based on the same data; the selected thresholds/models correspond to the maximum PSS along the respective ROC curve. The number of hidden layer neurons chosen is the least number of hidden layer neurons with a PSS standard error which overlaps the standard error corresponding to the maximum PSS. Thus, in this example, 150 hidden layer neurons corresponds to the maximum mean PSS = 0.694 ± 0.005 (within the red circle.) The performance of the TANN2 model with 125 hidden neurons, PSS = 0.689 ± 0.005, overlapped with the 150 hidden neuron confidence interval and hence was selected as the optimum number of hidden neurons, thus TANN 36-125-1.

Figure 2 depicts an example of how the optimal Y is chosen. The light red highlight identifies the number of hidden neurons leading to the largest mean PSS while the green highlight indicates the number of hidden neurons selected as the two cases standard errors overlap. **Table 4** depicts the optimal topologies for the TANN2 X-Y-1 and 36-Y-1 models.

With respect to FS, an exhaustive search involving the 36 potential features, although ideal, would have been computationally unrealistic. The FS methods used for this work were filter based, information theoretic, and designed to choose feature subsets relevant to the corresponding target while non-redundant to each feature in the subset. The methods used were multi-variate in the sense that feature-feature relationships were also considered, rather than the univariate strategy of assessing only feature-target relationships sequentially. The methods used are CFS (described earlier) and *minimum Redundancy Maximum Relevance* (mRMR) [74]. The *mRMR classic* function from the **mRMRe** package as part of the **R** programming language [75] was used to calculate mRMR. The following is an explanation of the mRMR technique in the context of mRMR classic as described in [76]: Consider $r(x, y)$ the correlation coefficient between features x and y. The mRMR technique uses the information-theoretic parameter known as *mutual information* (MI), defined as

$$1 - r(x,y)^2 \ MI(x,y) = \frac{-1}{2} ln \tag{8}$$

Let t be the target/predictand and $X = \{x_1, ..., x_n\}$ represent the set of n features. We desire to rank X such that we maximize relevance (maximize MI with t) and minimize redundancy (minimize mean MI with all previously selected features.) First, we selected x_i, the feature with the greatest MI with t:

$$x_i = arg \ max_{x_i \in X} MI(x_i, t) \tag{9}$$

Thus, we initialize the set of selected features S with x_i. For each subsequent step j, features are added to S by choosing the feature with the greatest relevance with t and lowest redundancy with previously selected features to maximize score Q:

$$Q_j = MI(x_j, t) - \frac{1}{|S|} \sum_{x_k \in S} MI(x_j, x_k) \tag{10}$$

The mRMR classic function requires the user to select the size of S, which we chose to equal the maximum number of features. We then choose the subset by choosing only those features corresponding to $Q_j > 0$.

Table 4 depicts the reduced set of features chosen via CFS and mRMR. **Table 5** summarizes the resulting TANN2 topologies.

Prediction hour	CFS	mRMR
9 h	PWAT,	$U_{800}(0)$, HI_{LOW}, CP, VV_{925}, VV_{500} RH_{850}, CIN, LCL, T_LCL, CAPE,
	CP	VSHEAR86, $V_{600}(0)$, PWAT, CTP_PROXY, VSHEAR75(0)
12 h	CP	CP, VV_{500}, VV_{925}, PWAT, RH_{850}, CTP_PROXY, CAPE, VSHEAR86,
		HI_{LOW}, $DROPOFF_{PROXY}$, $U_{800}(0)$, VV_{700}
15 h	CP	CP, LI, CAPE, VV_{925}, PWAT,
		RH_{850}, CTP_PROXY, VV_{700} $V_{500}(0)$, $U_{SFC}(0)$, VV_{500}, HI_{LOW}

Table 4. Variables/parameters chosen by the CFS and mRMR feature selection techniques; variables followed by zero depict NAM initialization variables.

Prediction hour	Optimal 36-Y-1 topology	Optimal X-Y-1 topology (CFS)	Optimal X-Y-1 topology (mRMR)
9	36-150-1	2-60-1	15-100-1
12	36-125-1	1-1-1	12-90-1
15	36-70-1	1-1-1	12-90-1

Table 5. Optimal TANN2 topologies based on iterative method to determine the optimal number of hidden layer neurons.

Forecast	Observed		Total
	Yes	No	
Yes	a (hit)	b(false alarm)	$a + b$
No	c(miss)	d(correct rejection)	$c + d$
Total	$a + c$	$b + d$	$a + b + c + d = n$

Table 6. Contingency Matrix from which scalar performance metrics (**Table 7**) were derived (from [53]).

Performance metric (value range)	Symbol	Equation
Probability of detection [0,1]	POD	$a/(a + c)$
False alarm rate [0,1]	F	$b/(b + d)$
False alarm ratio [0,1]	FAR	$b/(a + b)$
Critical success index [0,1]	CSI	$a/(a + b + c)$
Peirce skill score [−1,1]	PSS	$(ad - bc)/(b + d)(a + c)$
Heidke skill score [−1,1]	HSS	$2(ad - bc)/[(a + c)(c + d) + (a + b)(b + d)]$
Yule's Q (odds ratio skill score) [−1,1]	ORSS	$(ad - bc)/(ad + bc)$
Clayton skill score [−1,1]	CSS	$(ad - bc)/(a + b)(c + d)$
Gilbert skill score [−1/3,1]	GSS	$(a - a_r)/(a + b + c - a_r);\ a_r = (a + b)(a + c)/n$

Table 7. Relevant scalar performance metrics for binary classifiers used to evaluate TANN2 and MLR Models and NDFD (from [53]).

Tables 6 and **7** depict the contingency matrix and the corresponding performance metrics for binary classifiers used in this study.

Tables 8–11 depict the performance results of the TANN2 models, trained over all 286 boxes, and applied to boxes 73, 103, 238, and 1–286 (all boxes.) For each skill-based performance metric (PSS, CSI, HSS, ORSS, CSS, GSS), the *Wilcoxon Sign Rank* Test was used to determine whether TANN2 median performance (based on the 50 runs on the 2007–2008 testing set corresponding to the optimal number of hidden neurons) was statistically significantly different (5% level) than the corresponding MLR model and human forecaster performances. The relevant human forecasters were operational forecasters from the National Weather Service (NWS) (Appendix D). A summary of the results follow.

There is a significant improvement in the value of selected performance metrics for TANN2 over TANN in absolute terms. For example, with respect to the TANN models developed without FS, the PSS metric for the TANN2 models increased over the corresponding TANN models, by approximately 10–70%, 55–74%, and 10–120%, respectively, for boxes 238, 103, and 73.

When comparing TANN2 model performance relative to the operational forecasters (NDFD), and defining superior performance as statistically significant superior performance with respect to at least one skill-based performance metric (PSS, CSI, HSS, ORSS, CSS, and GSS), the results are as follows: For *box 238*, at least one of the TANN2 model performances exceeded that of the forecasters (NDFD), for all three prediction hours; all three TANN2 models (TANN 36-150-1, TANN 2-60-1 CFS, and TANN 15-100-1 mRMR) performed superior to NDFD for prediction hour 9, both TANN 36-150-1 and TANN 2-60-1 CFS performed better for prediction hour 12, and only TANN 2-6-1 CFS performed better for prediction hour 15. With respect to *box 103*, results were mixed. None of the TANN2 models performance was superior to NDFD for prediction hour 9, the TANN 36-125-1 and TANN 12-90-1 mRMR performed better for prediction hour 12, and only the TANN 1-1-1 CFS performed superior to the forecasters for prediction hour 15. Results were again mixed with regard to *box 73*. TANN 36-150-1 and TANN 15-100-1 mRMR performed superior to NDFD for prediction hour 9, none of the TANN2 models performed better than NDFD for prediction hour 12, and only TANN 36-70-1 performed superior to NDFD for prediction hour 15.

Conducting the same analysis with respect to TANN2 model compared to MLR, namely assessing statistically significant superior performance with respect to at least one skill-based performance metric, the results are as follows: For *box 238*, all three TANN2 models performed better than MLR at 9 h, none of the TANN2 models performed better at 12 h, and only the TANN 1-1-1 CFS model performed superior to MLR at 15 h. Regarding *box 103*, the TANN 36-125-1 and TANN 15-100-1 mRMR performed better than MLR for both 9 h and 12 h, while TANN 36-70-1 and TANN 1-1-1 CFS performed better than MLR for 15 h. For *box 73*, only TANN 36-150-1 performs better than MLR at 9 h, only TANN 1-1-1 CFS performs better at both 12 h and 15 h.

	POD	FAR	F	PSS	CSI	HSS	ORSS	CSS	GSS
9 h Model predictions									
TANN 36-150-1	0.94	0.80	0.30	0.63	0.20	0.24	0.94	0.19	0.13
TANN 2-60-1 CFS	0.98	0.81	0.33	0.65	0.19	0.22	0.98	0.19	0.13
TANN 15-100-1 mRMR	0.91	0.80	0.30	0.63	0.20	0.23	0.93	0.19	0.13
MLR	0.96	0.80	0.32	0.64	0.19	0.23	0.96	0.19	0.13
9 h Operational public forecasts									
NDFD	0.94	0.81	0.35	0.59	0.19	0.21	0.93	0.18	0.12
12 h Model predictions									
TANN 36-125-1	0.81	0.93	0.28	0.53	0.07	0.09	0.83	0.06	0.04
TANN 1-1-1 CFS	0.56	0.93	0.20	0.36	0.06	0.08	0.67	0.05	0.04
TANN 12-90-1 mRMR	0.75	0.94	0.32	0.42	0.05	0.06	0.71	0.05	0.03
MLR	0.88	0.93	0.30	0.57	0.07	0.09	0.88	0.07	0.05
12 h Operational public forecasts									
NDFD	0.67	0.92	0.28	0.39	0.07	0.08	0.67	0.06	0.04
15 h Model predictions									
TANN 36-70-1	0.64	0.95	0.23	0.41	0.05	0.06	0.71	0.04	0.03
TANN 1-1-1 CFS	0.45	0.91	0.08	0.37	0.08	0.13	0.81	0.08	0.07
TANN 12-90-1 mRMR	0.64	0.96	0.28	0.36	0.04	0.04	0.63	0.03	0.02
MLR	0.73	0.95	0.27	0.46	0.05	0.06	0.76	0.04	0.03
15 h Operational public forecasts									
NDFD	0.92	0.92	0.23	0.69	0.08	0.11	0.95	0.07	0.06

Values corresponding to each TANN X-Y-Z model represent the median of 50 separate trial runs of the model. Yellow (blue) denotes TANN X-Y-Z median values of skill-based metrics (PSS, CSI, HSS, ORSS, CSS, and GSS only) NOT statistically significantly different (based on the Wilcoxon Sign Rank Tests, 2 sided, 1 sample, 5% significant level) from the NDFD (MLR) values.

Table 8. Performance results of TANN X-Y-Z models for box 238 for the 2007–2008 independent data set and corresponding comparisons to the WFO CRP forecasters (NDFD), multi-linear regression (MLR) models.

	POD	FAR	F	PSS	CSI	HSS	ORSS	CSS	GSS
9 h Model predictions									
TANN 36-150-1	0.93	0.87	0.31	0.62	0.13	0.15	0.93	0.12	0.08
TANN 2-60-1 CFS	0.90	0.88	0.33	0.57	0.12	0.14	0.89	0.11	0.07
TANN 15-100-1 mRMR	0.87	0.87	0.29	0.56	0.13	0.15	0.87	0.12	0.08
MLR	0.97	0.88	0.36	0.61	0.12	0.14	0.96	0.12	0.08
9 h Operational public forecasts									
NDFD	1.00	0.85	0.31	0.69	0.15	0.19	1.00	0.15	0.10

	POD	FAR	F	PSS	CSI	HSS	ORSS	CSS	GSS
12 h Model predictions									
TANN 36-125-1	0.80	0.95	0.23	0.58	0.05	0.07	0.87	0.05	0.04
TANN 1-1-1 CFS	0.50	0.96	0.18	0.32	0.04	0.05	0.64	0.03	0.03
TANN 12-90-1 mRMR	0.90	0.95	0.27	0.63	0.05	0.07	0.92	0.05	0.04
MLR	0.80	0.95	0.25	0.55	0.05	0.06	0.85	0.05	0.03
12 h Operational public forecasts									
NDFD	0.80	0.94	0.24	0.56	0.06	0.08	0.86	0.06	0.04
15 h Model predictions									
TANN 36-70-1	0.83	0.96	0.21	0.62	0.04	0.05	0.90	0.03	0.03
TANN 1-1-1 CFS	0.50	0.92	0.06	0.44	0.07	0.12	0.89	0.07	0.06
TANN 12-90-1 mRMR	0.83	0.97	0.29	0.55	0.03	0.04	0.86	0.03	0.02
MLR	0.83	0.97	0.24	0.60	0.03	0.05	0.88	0.03	0.02
15 h Operational public forecasts									
NDFD	1.00	0.97	0.19	0.81	0.04	0.07	1.00	0.04	0.04

Values corresponding to each TANN X–Y–Z model represent the median of 50 separate trial runs of the model. Yellow (blue) denote TANN X–Y–Z median values of skill-based metrics (PSS, CSI, HSS, ORSS, CSS, and GSS only) NOT statistically significantly different (based on the Wilcoxon Sign Rank Tests, 2 sided, 1 sample, 5% significant level) from the corresponding NDFD (MLR).

Table 9. Performance results of TANN X-Y-Z models for box 103 for the 2007–2008 independent data set and corresponding comparisons to the WFO CRP forecasters (NDFD), multi-linear regression (MLR) models.

	POD	FAR	F	PSS	CSI	HSS	ORSS	CSS	GSS
9 h Model predictions									
TANN 36-150-1	0.94	0.81	0.22	0.71	0.19	0.25	0.96	0.19	0.14
TANN 2-60-1 CFS	0.94	0.85	0.30	0.64	0.14	0.18	0.95	0.14	0.10
TANN 15-100-1 mRMR	0.97	0.83	0.26	0.70	0.17	0.22	0.98	0.17	0.12
MLR	0.97	0.82	0.25	0.72	0.18	0.23	0.98	0.17	0.13
9 h Operational public forecasts									
NDFD	0.91	0.83	0.26	0.65	0.16	0.21	0.93	0.16	0.12
12 h Model predictions									
TANN 36-125-1	0.86	0.90	0.29	0.57	0.10	0.12	0.88	0.09	0.07
TANN 1-1-1 CFS	0.77	0.88	0.21	0.56	0.11	0.15	0.85	0.11	0.08
TANN 12-90-1 mRMR	0.91	0.91	0.35	0.56	0.08	0.10	0.90	0.08	0.05
MLR				0.68	0.10	0.13	1.00	0.10	0.07

	POD	FAR	F	PSS	CSI	HSS	ORSS	CSS	GSS
12 h Operational public forecasts									
NDFD	0.91	0.86	0.23	0.68	0.14	0.19	0.94	0.14	0.11
15 h Model predictions									
TANN 36-70-1	0.92	0.93	0.25	0.68	0.07	0.10	0.95	0.07	0.05
TANN 1-1-1 CFS	0.33	0.96	0.15	0.18	0.04	0.04	0.47	0.03	0.02
TANN 12-90-1 mRMR	0.83	0.96	0.34	0.47	0.04	0.05	0.79	0.04	0.02
MLR	0.92	0.94	0.30	0.62	0.06	0.07	0.93	0.05	0.04
15 h Operational public forecasts									
NDFD	0.85	0.93	0.24	0.61	0.07	0.10	0.89	0.07	0.05

Values corresponding to each TANN X-Y-Z model represent the median of 50 separate trial runs of the model. Yellow (blue) denote TANN X-Y-Z median values of skill-based metrics (PSS, CSI, HSS, ORSS, CSS, and GSS only) NOT statistically significantly different (based on the Wilcoxon Sign Rank Tests, 2 sided, 1 sample, 5% significant level) from the corresponding NDFD (MLR) value.

Table 10. Performance results of TANN X–Y–Z models for box 73 for the 2007–2008 independent data set and corresponding comparisons to the WFO CRP forecasters (NDFD), multi-linear regression (MLR) models.

	POD	FAR	F	PSS	CSI	HSS	ORSS	CSS	GSS
9 h Model predictions									
TANN 36-150-1	0.92	0.86	0.24	0.68	0.14	0.18	0.95	0.13	0.10
TANN 2-60-1 CFS	0.93	0.89	0.31	0.62	0.11	0.14	0.93	0.11	0.07
TANN 15-100-1 mRMR	0.93	0.87	0.27	0.66	0.13	0.17	0.94	0.12	0.09
MLR	0.92	0.87	0.27	0.65	0.13	0.16	0.94	0.12	0.09
12 h Model predictions									
TANN 36-125-1	0.85	0.93	0.26	0.59	0.07	0.10	0.89	0.07	0.05
TANN 1-1-1 CFS	0.68	0.92	0.19	0.49	0.07	0.10	0.80	0.07	0.05
TANN 12-90-1 mRMR	0.88	0.94	0.31	0.58	0.06	0.08	0.89	0.06	0.04
MLR	0.88	0.93	0.27	0.61	0.07	0.09	0.90	0.07	0.05
15 h Model predictions									
TANN 36-70-1	0.83	0.94	0.24	0.59	0.06	0.08	0.88	0.06	0.04
TANN 1-1-1 CFS	0.53	0.92	0.11	0.42	0.08	0.11	0.80	0.07	0.06
TANN 12-90-1 mRMR	0.81	0.95	0.30	0.51	0.05	0.06	0.82	0.04	0.03
MLR	0.88	0.95	0.28	0.59	0.05	0.07	0.89	0.05	0.04

Table 11. Performance results of TANN X–Y–Z models for all 286 boxes for the 2007–2008 independent data set and corresponding comparisons to the NWS forecasters (NDFD), multi-linear regression (MLR) models.

	9-h Prediction	12-h Prediction	15-h Prediction
ORSS			
Box 73		NDFD	TANN 36-70-1
Box 103	NDFD		NDFD
Box 238	TANN 2-60-1	TANN 36-125-1	NDFD
PSS			
Box 73	TANN 36-150-1	NDFD	TANN 36-70-1
Box 103	NDFD		NDFD
Box 238	TANN 2-60-1	TANN 36-125-1	NDFD
HSS			
Box 73	36-150-1	NDFD	NDFD
Box 103	NDFD	NDFD	TANN 1-1-1
Box 238			TANN 1-1-1

Gray boxes indicate that a single performer did not distinguish itself.

Table 12. Best performers (based on the equitable ORSS, PSS, and HSS performance metrics) between the TANN2 models and NWS forecasters (NDFD) using the combination of Wilcoxon Sign Rank Tests (2 sided, 1 sample, 5% significant level) to compare each TANN model to NDFD, and the Nemenyi post-hoc analyses of pairwise combination of TANN2 models (5% significance level).

An alternative analysis was performed to determine the single best-performing classifiers for each box and prediction hour based only on performance metrics PSS, HSS, and ORSS. HSS and PSS are truly equitable and ORSS is asymptotically equitable (approaches equitability as size of the data set approaches infinity) and truly equitable for the condition $\frac{(a+c)}{n} = 0.5$ (see contingency matrix.) [77]. Equitability includes the desirable condition whereby the performance metric is zero for random or constant forecasts. For each of the three performance metrics and for each box and prediction hour combination, comparisons were made between the TANN2 models and NDFD. Such a comparison was performed separately between the TANN2 models and MLR. The best performers were determined in the following manner: First, the output from the *Wilcoxon sign rank test* was used to determine statistically significant differences between the TANN2 models and NDFD or MLR (**Tables 8–10**). Next, the *Friedman rank sum test* was used to determine whether significant differences existed only between the three TANN2 models. If differences existed, the *Nemenyi post-hoc test* [78] was performed to determine statistical significance between pairwise combinations of TANN2 models. The best performer was based on a synthesis of the Wilcoxon and Friedman/Nemenyi results (see Appendix E). The Friedman and Nemenyi post-hoc tests were performed using the *friedman.test* and *posthoc.friedman.nemenyi.test* functions from the Pairwise Multiple Comparison of Mean Rank (*PMCMR*) package in the **R** programming language [74]. Results are depicted in **Tables 12** and **13**. The results are mixed. With respect to comparisons between the TANN2 models and NDFD, the best performer is a function of the performance metric, box number, and prediction hour. The same is true for the TANN2 model-MLR comparisons. However, it is noteworthy to mention that none of the TANN2 models based on the mRMR FS method were determined to be the single best performer for 15 h (**Tables 12** and **13**).

	9-h Prediction	*12-h Prediction*	*15-h Prediction*
ORSS			
Box 73	MLR	MLR	TANN 36-70-1
Box 103	MLR		
Box 238	TANN 2-60-1	MLR	TANN 1-1-1
PSS			
Box 73		MLR	TANN 36-70-1
Box 103			
Box 238	TANN 2-60-1	MLR	MLR
HSS			
Box 73	TANN 36-150-1	TAN 1-1-1	TAN 36-70-1
Box 103			TANN 1-1-1
Box 238			TANN 1-1-1

Gray boxes indicate that a single performer did not distinguish itself.

Table 13. Best performers (based on the equitable ORSS, PSS, and HSS performance metrics) between the TANN2 models and MLR using the combination of Wilcoxon Sign Rank Tests (2 sided, 1 sample, 5% significant level) to compare each TANN model to MLR, and the Nemenyi post-hoc analyses of pairwise combination of TANN2 models (5% significance level).

The increase in data as compared to the previous study [53] likely contributed to performance enhancements. **Figure 3** depicts the change in performance of the 36-Y-1 12 h model as a function of training data used. Note that performance improvement was positively correlated with the quantity of training data. This adds credence to the argument that the amount of data in [53] may have been insufficient. Further, note that for ≤1% of available data (~6000 instances), performance decreased after the number of neurons in the hidden layer (Y) exceeded 100, possibly due to the curse of dimensionality. **Figure 4** depicts the relationship between an overfitting metric, defined as $\left(AUC_{val} - AUC_{train}\right)/AUC_{train}$, and the number of hidden layer neurons. Note that overfitting generally increases with the number of hidden layer neurons when the training set is reduced to ≤ 10 of the total available training data, and particularly apparent when only 1 of available, or about 6000 cases. In [53], only a few thousand cases were available. This partially explains why the original TANN models are relatively smaller ($Y \le 35$) than the TANN2 models. The ability to obtain similar performance while training on a smaller portion of the data set would have allowed substantial gains in computational efficiency. ANNs were trained using MATLAB® R2015b on several multi-core personal computers (PCs) and on a computer cluster with compute nodes with two Xeon E5 with 10 core processors each and

256 gigabytes (GB) of memory. For the full data set (**Table 1**), training times varied from less than 1 h to more than two days per batch of 50 ANNs when increasing the number of hidden layer neurons from 1 to 200. When reducing the size of the training set to 1%, training times decreased to less than 3 min for each Y case (not shown.) evaluated. Reducing the size of the training set to 10% of the full set decreased training times by about one order of magnitude for each Y case.

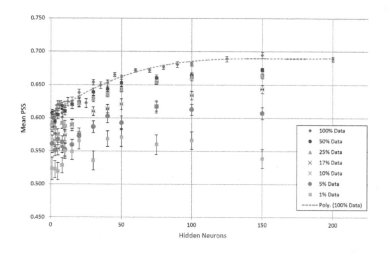

Figure 3. 12 h 36-Y-1 TANN performance versus hidden layer neuron quantity (Y) as a function of the percentage of total training data available.

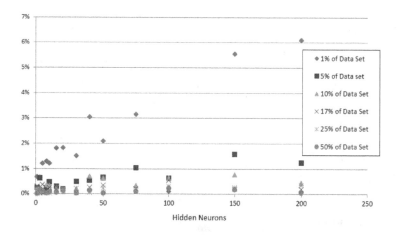

Figure 4. 12 h 36-Y-1 TANN overfitting index versus hidden layer neuron quantity (see text).

With regard to data set size and composition, it was hypothesized that performance gains may be obtained when artificially increasing the proportion of positive targets (CTG lightning strikes) in the training set. All possible inputs were included and the total number of training cases was maintained constant with positive and negative cases randomly selected (with replacement) to create target vectors with 5, 10, 25, and 50% of CTG lightning strikes. Substantial increases in performance were obtained for the training sets for all prediction lead times; **Figure 5** depicts the 12 h prediction example. Maximum PSS increased progressively while increasing proportion of lightning strikes in the data set. However, as the percent of positive targets was raised, the performance over the 2007–2008 independent testing decreased. Efforts are continuing to further modify the training of the TANN to improve performance.

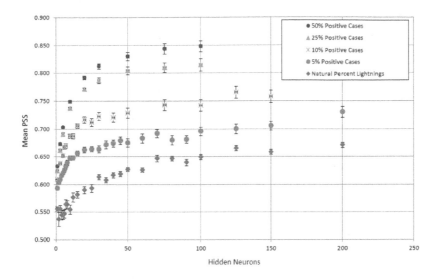

Figure 5. 12 h 36-Y-1 TANN performance versus hidden neuron quantity (Y) as a function of the proportion of positive target (CG lightning) data in the training set.

7. Conclusion

We presented here the results of an ANN approach to the post processing of single deterministic NWP model output for the prediction of thunderstorms at high spatial resolution, 9, 12, and 15 h in advance (TANN2.) ANNs were selected to take advantage of a large data set of over 1 million cases with multiple predictors and attempt to capture the complex relationships between the predictors and the generation of thunderstorms. This study represents an adjustment to a previous ANN model framework, resulting in the generation of a significantly larger data set. The larger data set allowed for more complex ANN models (by increasing the number of neurons in the hidden layer). Three groups of TANN2 model variants were generated based on two filtering-based feature selection methods (designed to retain only relevant and non-redundant features) and one group based on models calibrated with all predictors.

The skills of these TANN2 models within each of the three 400-km² boxes were substantially improved over previous work with the improvements attributed to the increase of the size of the data set. TANN2 model performance was compared to that of NWS operational forecasters and to MLR models. Results regarding the best-performing classifiers per prediction hour and box were mixed. Several attempts were made to further improve model performance or decrease training time. Training the models using a small fraction of the data set reduced model calibration time yet resulted in lower performance skill. Altering the target by artificially boosting the proportion of positive outcomes (lightning strikes) resulted in substantial performance improvements over the training sets but did not lead to substantial improvements of performance on the independent 2007–2008 cases.

Given that the atmosphere is chaotic, or deterministic with highly sensitive dependence on the initial condition, one future research plan includes the prediction of thunderstorms by the post-processing of single deterministic NWP model output using ANN models that account for chaotic systems [79]. Such a strategy would be an alternative to the state of the art practice of using NWP model ensembles to account for the sensitive dependence on the initial condition. In addition, another plan involves the development of ensemble ANN models [80]. Specifically, an optimal TANN prediction can be developed by integrating output from 50 unique TANN models.

Appendix A

The total mean mass of the atmosphere: 5.1480×10^{21}g [81]

Total mol of dry air: $5.1480 \times 10^{21}\text{g} \times \dfrac{1}{28.97\text{gmol}^{-1}} = 1.777 \times 10^{20}\text{mol}$

Total molecules of dry air: $1.777 \times 10^{20}\text{mol} \times 6.02214 \times 10^{23}\text{mol}^{-1} = 1.0701 \times 10^{44}\text{molecules}$

(Mass of dry air: 28.97gmol^{-1}; Avogadro's number: $6.02214 \times 10^{23}\text{mol}^{-1}$)

Appendix B

Version 1.04 of the HRRR uses the Advanced Research WRF (ARW) dynamic core within the WRF modeling framework (version 3.4.1 WRF-ARW). The HRRR uses GSI 3D-VAR data assimilation. With respect to parameterizations, the RRTM longwave radiation, Goddard shortwave radiation, Thompson microphysics (version 3.4.1), no cumulus/convective parameterization, MYNN planetary boundary layer, and the rapid update cycle (RUC) land surface model [33].

Appendix C

At any given time, only one NWP model was utilized in the TANN. Yet, three different modeling systems were used, each during a unique time period—the hydrostatic Eta model [82] (1 March 2004 to 19 June 2006), the Weather Research and Forecasting Non-hydrostatic

Mesoscale Model (WRF-NMM) [83] (20 June 2006 to 30 September 2011), and the NOAA Environmental Modeling System Non-hydrostatic Multiscale Model (NEMS-NMMB) (October 2011 to December 2013.)

Appendix D

NWS operational forecasts were obtained from the NWS *National Digital Forecast Database* [96] (NDFD) [96], a database of archived NWS forecasts; the forecasts are written to a 5-km coterminous USA (CONUS) grid (or to 16 pre-defined grid sub-sectors) and provided to the general public in Gridded Binary Version 2 (GRIB2) format [97]. The forecasts for most of the 286 boxes (**Figure 1**) originated from the NWS Weather Forecast Office (WFO) in Corpus Christi, Texas (CRP) in the USA.

Appendix E

The following are three examples to explain how the "best performers" where determined in **Tables 12** and **13**.

Example 1: Table 12 (Determining the best performers between the three TANN model variants and NDFD) Box 238 Prediction Hour 9 ORSS: Step 1: Based on the Wilcoxon Sign Rank Test, the performer with the largest ORSS value was TANN 2-60-1, and that value (0.98) was statistically significantly larger than the corresponding NDFD value (0.93) (**Table 8**). Step 2: Based on the Nemenyi post-hoc analysis of the pairwise combination of the three TANN model variants, the TANN 2-60-1 ORSS value was statistically significantly different than the corresponding ORSS values from the TANN 36-150-1 and TANN 15-100-1 models. *Thus, the best performer is TANN 2-60-1.*

Example 2: Table 12 (Determining the best performers between the three TANN model variants and NDFD) Box 103 Prediction Hour 12 PSS: Step 1: Based on the Wilcoxon Sign Rank test, the performer with the largest PSS value was TANN 12-90-1, and that value (0.63) was statistically significantly larger than the corresponding NDFD value (0.56) (**Table 9**). Step 2: Based on the Nemenyi post-hoc analysis of the pairwise combination of the three TANN model variants, there was no statistically significant difference between the PSS values for TANN 12-90-1 (0.63) and TANN 36-125-1 (0.58). *Thus, there is no single best performer.*

Example 3: Table 13 (Determining the best performers between the three TANN model variants and MLR) Box 73 Prediction Hour 12 PSS: Step 1: Based on the Wilcoxon Sign Rank Test, the performer with the largest PSS value was MLR, and that value (0.68) was statistically significantly greater than the corresponding PSS values from each of the three TANN variants (**Table 10**.) *Thus, the best performer is MLR. No additional steps are required.*

Author details

Waylon G. Collins[1*] and Philippe Tissot[2]

*Address all correspondence to: Waylon.Collins@noaa.gov

1 National Weather Service, Weather Forecast Office Corpus Christi, TX, USA

2 Texas A&M University—Corpus Christi, Conrad Blucher Institute, Corpus Christi, TX, USA

References

[1]   Glickman TS. Glossary of Meteorology. 2nd ed. Boston: American Meteorological Society; 2011. 1132 p.

[2]   Byers HR. General Meteorology, 3rd ed. New York: McGraw Hill Book Company; 1959. 540 p.

[3]   Emanuel KA. Atmospheric Convection. New York: Oxford University Press; 1994. 580 p.

[4]   Doswell CA, editor. Severe Convective Storms (Meteorological Monographs, Volume 28, Number 50). Boston: American Meteorological Society; 2001. 561 p.

[5]   Groenemeijer, P. Sounding-derived parameters associated with severe convective storms in the Netherlands [thesis]. Utrecht: Utrecht University; 2005.

[6]   Holle RL. Annual rates of lightning fatalities by country. In: 20th International Lightning Detection Conference; 21–23 April 2008; Tucson.

[7]   Holle RL, Lopez RE. A comparison of current lightning death rates in the U.S. with other locations and times. In: International Conference on Lightning and Static Electricity; 2003; Blackpool. p. 103–134.

[8]   NWS. Natural Hazards Statistics National Weather Service Office of Climate, Water, and Weather Services [Internet]. 2015. Available from: http://www.nws.noaa.gov/om/hazstats.shtml [Accessed 2015-10-26].

[9]   NOAA. Billion-Dollar Weather and Climate Disasters: Summary Stats, National Oceanic and Atmospheric Administration (NOAA) National Centers for Environmental Information [Internet]. 2016. Available from: https://www.ncdc.noaa.gov/billions/summary-stats [Accessed 2016-01-28].

[10] Wolfson MM, Clark DA. Advanced Aviation Weather Forecasts. Lincoln Lab. J. 2006; 16: 31–58.

[11] Trier SB. Convective storms – Convective Initiation. In: Holton Jr, editor. Encyclopedia of Atmospheric Sciences. New York: Oxford University Press; 2003. p. 560–570.

[12] Orlanski I. A Rational Subdivision of Scales for Atmospheric Processes. Bull. Am. Meteorol. Soc. 1975; 56: 527–530.

[13] Lorenz EN. Deterministic nonperiodic flow. J. Atmos. Sci. 1963; 20: 130–141.

[14] Lorenz EN. The predictability of a flow which possesses many scales of motion. Tellus. 1969; 3: 1–19.

[15] Wallace JM, Hobbs PV. Atmospheric Science: An Introductory Survey. New York: Academic Press; 1977. 466 p.

[16] Kain JS, Coniglio MC, Correia J, Clark AJ, Marsh PT, Ziegler CL, Lakshmanan V, Miller SD, Dembek SR, Weiss SJ, Kong F, Xue M, Sobash RA, Dean AR, Jirak IL, CJ Melick. A feasibility study for probabilistic convection initiation forecasts based on explicit numerical guidance. Bull. Amer. Meteor. Soc. 2013; 94: 1213–1225.

[17] Lamb D. Rain Production in Convective Storms. In: Doswell CA, editor. Severe Convective Storms. Boston: American Meteorological Society; 2001. p. 299–321.

[18] Williams ER. The Electrification of Severe Storms. In: Doswell CA, editor. Severe Convective Storms. Boston: American Meteorological Society; 2001. p. 527–561.

[19] Wakimoto RM. Convectively Driven High Wind Events. In: Doswell CA, editor. Severe Convective Storms. Boston: American Meteorological Society; 2001. p. 255–298.

[20] Knight CA, Knight NC. Hailstorms. In: Doswell CA, editor. Severe Convective Storms. Boston: American Meteorological Society; 2001. p. 223–254.

[21] Taylor CM, Gounou A, Guichard F, Harris PP, Ellis RJ, Couvreux F. Frequency of Sahelian storm initiation enhanced over mesoscale soil-moisture patterns. Nat. Geosci. 2011; 4: 430–433.

[22] Doswell CA, Bosart LF. 2001. Extratropical synoptic-scale processes and severe convection. In: Doswell CA, editor. Severe Convective Storms. Boston: American Meteorological Society; 2001. p. 27–70.

[23] Lorenz, EN. The Essence of Chaos. Seattle: University of Washington Press; 1993. 227 p.

[24] Bjerknes V. Das Problem der Wettervorhersage, betrachtet vom Stanpunkt der Mechanik und der Physik. Meteor. Zeits. 1904; 21: 1–7.

[25] Kalnay E. Atmospheric Modeling, Data Assimilation and Predictability. Cambridge: Cambridge University Press; 2003.

[26] Stull R. Meteorology for Scientists and Engineers. 3rd ed. Pacific Grove: Brooks Cole; 2015.

[27] Stensrud DJ. Parameterization Schemes, Keys to Understanding Numerical Weather Prediction Models. New York: Cambridge University Press; 2007. 459 p.

[28] Wilks DS. Statistical Methods in the Atmospheric Sciences. 2nd ed. Oxford: Elsevier; 2006.

[29] Bryan GH, Wyngaard JC, Fritsch JM. Resolution Requirements for the Simulation of Deep Moist Convection. Mon. Wea. Rev. 2003; 131: 2394–2416.

[30] Hodanish S, Holle RL, Lindsey DT. A Small Updraft Producing a Fatal Lightning Flash. Wea. Forecasting. 2004; 19: 627–632.

[31] Mecikalski JR., Williams JK, Jewett CP, Ahijevych D, LeRoy A, Walker JR. Probabilistic 0–1-h convective initiation nowcasts that combine geostationary satellite observations and numerical weather prediction model data. J. Appl. Meteor. Climatol. 2015; 54: 1039–1059.

[32] Pessi AT, Businger S. Relationships among lightning, precipitation, and hydrometeor characteristic over the North Pacific Ocean. J. Appl. Meteorol. Climatol. 2009; 48: 833–848.

[33] Earth System Research Laboratory. The High-Resolution Rapid Refresh [Internet]. 2016. Available from: http://rapidrefresh.noaa.gov/hrrr [Accessed: 2016-01-14]

[34] Pielke RA. Mesoscale Meteorological Modeling. International Geophysics Series. San Diego: Academic Press; 2002. 676 p.

[35] Zhang Y, Zhang R, Stensrud DJ, Zhiyong M. Intrinsic Predictability of the 20 May 2013 Tornadic Thunderstorm Event in Oklahoma at Storm Scales. Mon. Wea. Rev. 2016; 144: 1273–1298

[36] Wilson JW, Crook NA, Mueller CK, Sun J, Dixon M. Nowcasting Thunderstorms: A Status Report. Bull. Am. Meteorol. Soc. 1998; 79: 2079–2099.

[37] Fowle MA, Roebber PJ. Short-range (0–48 h) Numerical predictions of convective occurrence, model and location. Wea. Forecasting. 2003; 18: 782–794.

[38] Weisman ML, Davis C, Wang W, Manning KW, Klemp JB. Experiences with 0-36-h explicit convective forecasts with the WRF-ARW model. Wea. Forecasting. 2008; 23: 407–437.

[39] Elmore KL, Stensrud DJ, Crawford KC. Explicit cloud-scale models for operational forecasts: a note of caution. Wea. Forecasting. 2002; 17: 873–884.

[40] Leith C.E. Theoretical skill of Monte Carlo forecasts. Mon. Wea. Rev. 1974; 102: 409–418.

[41] Epstein ES. Stochastic dynamic prediction. Tellus. 1969; 21: 739–759.

[42] Storm Prediction Center. Short Range Ensemble Forecast (SREF) Products [Internet]. 2015. Available from: URL http://www.spc.noaa.gov/exper/sref [Accessed: 2015-10-23].

[43] Meteorological Development Laboratory. Model Output Statistics (MOS) [Internet.]. 2016. Available from http://www.weather.gov/mdl/mos_home [Accessed: 2016-03-01].

[44] Glahn HR, Lowry DA. The use of model output statistics (MOS) in objective weather forecasting. J. Appl. Meteorol. 1972; 11: 1203–1211.

[45] Glahn B, Gilbert K, Cosgrove R, Ruth DP, Sheets K. The gridding of MOS. Wea. Forecast. 2009; 24: 520–529.

[46] Ghirardelli JE, Glahn B. The Meteorological Development Laboratory's aviation weather prediction system. Wea. Forecast. 2010; 25: 1027–1051.

[47] Schmeits MJ, Kok KJ, Vogelezang DHP. Probabilistic forecasting of (severe) thunderstorms in the Netherlands using model output statistics. Wea. Forecast. 2005; 20: 134–148.

[48] Costello RB. Random House Webster's College Dictionary. New York: Random House; 1992.

[49] Mitchell, T. The discipline of machine learning. Carnegie Mellon University Technical Report, CMU-ML-06-108, 2006.

[50] Mills GA, Colquhoun JR. Objective prediction of severe thunderstorm environments: preliminary results linking a decision tree with an operational regional NWP model. Wea. Forecast. 1998; 13: 1078–1092.

[51] Perler D, Marchand O. A study in weather model output postprocessing: using the boosting method for thunderstorm detection. Wea. Forecast. 2009; 24: 211–222.

[52] McCann DW. A neural network short-term forecast of significant thunderstorms. Wea. Forecast. 1992; 7: 525–534.

[53] Collins W, Tissot P. An artificial neural network model to predict thunderstorms within 400km^2 South Texas domains Meteorol. Appl. 2015; 22: 650–665.

[54] Breiman L. Random forests. Machine Learn. 2001; 45: 5–32.

[55] McNulty RP. A statistical approach to short-term thunderstorm outlooks. J. Appl. Meteorol. 1981; 20: 765–771.

[56] Ravi N. Forecasting of thunderstorms in the pre-monsoon season at Delhi. Meteorol. Appl. 1999; 6: 29–38.

[57] de Silva CW. Intelligent Machines: Myths and Realities. Boca Raton: CRC Press LLC; 2000.

[58] Colquhoun JR. A decision true method of forecasting thunderstorms serve a thunderstorms and tornados. Wea. Forecast. 1987; 2: 337–345.

[59] Lee RR, Passner JE. The development and verification of TIPS: an expert system to forecast thunderstorm occurrence. Wea. Forecast. 1993; 8: 271–280.

[60] Manzato A. The use of sounding-derived indices for a neural network short-term thunderstorm forecast. Wea. Forecast. 2005; 20: 896–917.

[61] Chaudhuri S. Convective energies in forecasting severe thunderstorms with one hidden layer neural net and variable learning rate back propagation algorithm. Asia Pac. J. Atmos. Sci. 2010; 46: 173–183.

[62] Sanchez JL, Ortega EG, Marcos JL. Construction and assessment of a logistic regression model applied to short-term forecasting of thunderstorms in Leon (Spain). Atmos. Res. 2001; 56: 57–71.

[63] Rumelhart DE, McClelland JL. Parallel Distributed Processing: Explorations in the Microstructure of Cognition: Foundations. Vol 1. Cambridge: MIT Press; 1986.

[64] Haykin S. Neural Networks, A Comprehensive Foundation. 2nd ed. New Jersey: Prentice Hall; 1999.

[65] Bishop CM. Neural Networks for Pattern Recognition. New York: Oxford University Press; 2005.

[66] Moller M. A scaled conjugate gradient algorithm for fast supervised learning. Neural Netw. 1993; 6: 525–533.

[67] Manzato A. A note on the maximum peirce skill score. Wea. Forecast. 2007; 22: 1148–1154.

[68] Bellman R. Adaptive Control Processes: A Guided Tour. Princeton: Princeton University Press; 1961.

[69] May R., Dandy G, Maier H. Review of input variable selection methods for artificial neural networks. In: Suzuki K, editor. Artificial Neural Networks- Methodological Advances and Biomedical Applications. Rijeka: InTech Europe; 2011. P. 19–44.

[70] Hall MA. Correlation-based feature selection for machine learning [thesis]. Hamilton: University of Waikato; 1999.

[71] Hall MA, Smith LA. Feature selection for machine learning: comparing a correlation-based filter approach to the wrapper. In: Proceedings of the Twelfth International Florida Artificial Intelligence Research Society Conference; 1–5 May 1999; Orlando.

[72] Arizona State University. Feature Selection at Arizona State University [Internet]. 2016. Available from: http://featureselection.asu.edu/index.php# [Accessed: 2016-02-16].

[73] Akaike H. Information theory and an extension of the maximum likelihood principle. In: 2nd International Symposium on Information Theory; 1973; Budapest: Akademiai Kiado. p. 267–281.

[74] Ding C, Peng H. Minimum redundancy feature selection from microarray gene expression data. J. Bioinform. Comput. Biol. 2005; 3: 185–205.

[75] A Language and Environment for Statistical Computing. R Foundation for Statistical Computing [Internet]. Available from: https://www.r-project.org [Accessed: 2005-12-14].

[76] De Jay N, Papillon-Cavanagh S, Olsen C, El-Hachem N, Bontempi G, Haibe-Kains. mRMRe: An R package for parallelized mrmr ensemble feature selection. Bioinformatics. 2013; 29: 2365–2368.

[77] Hogan RJ, Ferro CAT, Jolliffe IT, Stephenson DB. Equitability revisited: why the "equitable threat score" is not equitable. Wea. Forecast. 2010; 25: 710–726.

[78] Nemenyi P. Distribution-free multiple comparisons [thesis]. Princeton: Princeton University; 1963.

[79] Pan S-T, Lai C-C. Identification of chaotic systems by neural network with hybrid learning algorithm. Chaos Soliton Fract. 2008; 37: 233–244.

[80] Maqsood I, Khan MR, Abraham A. An ensemble of neural networks for weather forecasting. Neural Comput. Appl. 2004; 13: 112–122.

[81] Trenberth KE, Smith L. The Mass of the Atmosphere: A Constraint on Global Analyses. J. Climate. 2005; 18: 864–875.

[82] Rogers E, Black TL, Deaven DG, DiMego GJ. Changes to the operational "early" eta analysis/forecast system at the National Centers for Environmental Prediction. Wea. Forecast. 1996; 11: 391–413.

[83] Janjic ZI, Gerrity JP, Nickovic S. An alternative approach to nonhydrostatic modeling. Mon. Wea. Rev. 2001; 129: 1164–1178.

[84] Khairoutdinov M, Randall D. High-resolution simulation of shallow-to-deep convection transition over land. J. Atmos. Sci. 2006; 63: 3421–3436.

[85] Ducrocq V, Tzanos D, Sénési S. Diagnostic tools using a mesoscale NWP model for the early warning of convection. Meteorol. Appl. 1998; 5: 329–349.

[86] Haklander AJ, Van Delden A. Thunderstorm predictors and their forecast skill for the Netherlands. Atmos. Res. 2003; 67–68: 273–299.

[87] Dalu GA, Pielke RA, Baldi M, Zeng X. Heat and momentum fluxes induced by thermal inhomogeneities with and without large-scale flow. J. Atmos. Sci. 1996; 53: 3286–3302.

[88] Wang JR, Bras L, Eltahir EAB. A stochastic linear theory of mesoscale circulation induced by thermal heterogeneity of the land surface. J. Atmos. Sci. 1996; 53: 3349–3366.

[89] Crook NA. Sensitivity of moist convection forced by boundary layer processes to low-level thermodynamic fields. Mon. Wea. Rev. 1996; 124: 1767–1785.

[90] Williams ER, Mushtak V, Rosenfeld D, Goodman S, Boccippio D. Thermodynamic conditions favorable to superlative thunderstorm updraft, mixed phase microphysics and lightning flash rate. Atmos. Res. 2005; 76: 288–306.

[91] Saunders CPR. A review of thunderstorm electrification processes. J. Appl. Meteorol. 1993; 32: 642–655.

[92] Janji´c ZI. The step-mountain eta coordinate model: further developments of the convection, viscous sublayer, and turbulence closure schemes. Mon. Weather Rev. 1994; 122: 927–945.

[93] Rotunno RJ, Klemp B, Weisman ML. A theory for strong, long-lived squall lines. J. Atmos. Sci. 1998; 45: 464–485.

[94] Findell KL, Eltahir EAB. Atmospheric controls on soil moisture-boundary layer interactions: three-dimensional wind effects. J. Geophys. Res. 2003b; 108 (D8), 8385.

[95] Findell KL, Eltahir EAB. Atmospheric controls on soil moisture-boundary layer interactions: Part I: Framework development. J. Hydrometeorol. 2003a; 4: 552–569.

[96] National Weather Service National Digital Forecast Database [Internet]. 2016. Available from: http://www.nws.noaa.gov/ndfd/ [Accessed: 2016-03-23]

[97] World Meteorological Organization. WMO Manual on Codes, WMO Publication No. 306, Vol. 1, Part B. Geneva: WMO; 2001.

5

Application of Neural Networks (NNs) for Fabric Defect Classification

H. İbrahim Çelik, L. Canan Dülger and
Mehmet Topalbekiroğlu

Additional information is available at the end of the chapter

Abstract

The defect classification is as important as the defect detection in fabric inspection process. The detected defects are classified according to their types and recorded with their names during manual fabric inspection process. The material is selected as *"undyed raw denim"* fabric in this study. Four commonly occurring defect types, hole, warp lacking, weft lacking and soiled yarn, were classified by using artificial neural network (ANN) method. The defects were automatically classified according to their texture features. Texture feature extraction algorithm was developed to acquire the required values from the defective fabric samples. The texture features were assessed as the network input values and the defect classification is obtained as the output. The defective images were classified with an average accuracy rate of 96.3%. As the hole defect was recognized with 100% accuracy rate, the others were recognized with a rate of 95%.

Keywords: artificial neural network (ANN), fabric defect classification, pattern recognition, texture feature extraction, denim fabric

1. Introduction

The woven fabric is formed by interlacing warp and weft yarns at right angles. The fabric has a unique pattern construction along length (warp direction) and width (weft direction). The deformations that damage the appearance and performance of the fabric are called as *"fabric defect."* In the literature, it is stated that there are 235 different fabric defect types [1]. The defects are evaluated as "major" and "minor" in relation to their size and types. After the weaving process is achieved, the fabric defects are inspected by a quality-control worker (**Figure 1**). As the fabric is wound by passing over an illuminated surface, the quality-control worker scans approximately 2 m width. She/he then records the type and location of the defects. The quality of the detected fabric is evaluated by means of the 4-point system, either Graniteville or a 10-point system. The main concept of all these systems is that the operator calculates the number of major and minor defects. This is taken as the point values in meter square, and then the fabric quality is considered as "first" and "second" quality. Defect detection procedure is time consuming and tiring. Thus, many different attempts are seen to replace the traditional inspection system by automated visual systems.

Figure 1. Traditional fabric inspection.

Artificial intelligence methods, such as fuzzy logic (FL), neural network (NN), or genetic algorithm (GA), are generally preferred for fabric defect classification problems. Neural network is most frequently used method for defect classification. The input parameters of the neural network are obtained by using different types of feature extraction methods (FEMs). Different textile problems considered from fiber classification, color grading, and yarn and fabric property prediction can be given as examples. Hybrid modeling applications include neuro-fuzzy, Sugeno-Takagi fuzzy system, neuro-genetic, and neuro-fuzzy-genetic methods. Better results are obtained when they are used in combination [2]. The artificial intelligence system is based on learning the texture features and distinguishing them into the categories. Thus, the defect classification process is carried out as a solution of pattern recognition problem. The spatial filtering methods, morphological operations, noise-removing filters, and artificial intelligence methods must be used together. They can be combined properly for a robust defect detection and classification algorithm [2].

In the present study, Artificial Neural Network (ANN) method has been applied for a fabric defect classification problem. A texture feature extraction (TFE) algorithm was developed to acquire the required values from the defective fabric samples. The defects were automatically classified according to their texture features by using ANN method. The texture features were assessed as the network input values and the defect classification is obtained as the output. Four most common fabric defects, such as hole, warp lacking, weft lacking, and soiled yarn, are classified. Success in defect classification was given by using statistical measures at the end.

2. Previous studies

Artificial Neural Network methods are used from fiber to fabric in all textile product studies. Fiber identification is made by using ANN. Fiber properties according to the process parameters are also predicted by means of ANN. As far as yarns are concerned, the thrust of research is certainly on yarn property prediction particularly on the tensile properties. Researchers have tried to model the structure of a yarn with the ultimate aim of being able to predict its properties before the yarn is actually spun. In the area of fabric property prediction, traditionally subjective areas such as handle and drape have received considerable attention. Also some physical properties of the fabric; strength, elongation, air permeability, stiffness etc. are tried to predict before the fabric production. Most of the studies on fabric property prediction are performed for the identification and classification of faults in fabrics and carpets. These processes are attempted to automate. As far as dyeing is concerned, the prediction of dye concentration in the dye bath and dye recipes has been attempted [3].

In the literature survey, it is seen that Artificial intelligence techniques such as Artificial Neural Network, fuzzy logic, and genetic algorithm are especially preferred for fabric defect detection and also for classification. The texture features of the fabric samples are extracted by using different methods and these features are used as input. The artificial intelligence system learns the texture features and distinguishes them into categories [2, 3].

Huang and Chen have proposed a neuro-fuzzy system by combining FL and NN methods [4]. Nine categories were classified as normal fabrics and eight kinds of fabric defects. The results of the neuro-fuzzy system and NN systems were compared and it is concluded that better results are obtained with neuro-fuzzy system.

Tilocca et al. have presented a method using a different optical image acquisition system and ANN to analyze the acquired data [5]. The different light sources were used to illuminate the sample in order to acquire the different features. A three-layered Feed-Forward Neural Network (FFNN) with sigmoidal activation function and back propagation (BP) was used in this work. Four different types of defects, large knot, slub, broken thread, and knot, were classified by the given system. The percentage of correctly classified patterns was found as 92%.

Kumar has presented an approach for the segmentation of local textile defects using FFNN and fast-web inspection method using linear neural network (LNN) [6]. A twill-weave fabric sample with defect miss pick was tested by using FFNN method. Fabric inspection image with the defects slack end, dirty yarn, miss pick, and thin bar were tested. Linear neural network method is used. Plain-weave fabric samples with defect types, double weft, thin bar, broken ends, and slack pick, were used for real-time defect detection.

Islam et al. have developed an automated textile defect detection system based on adaptive NN [7]. The study was mainly based on to combine thresholding techniques and ANN for defect classification. In this system, defect types such as hole, scratch, stretch, fly yarn, dirty spot, slub, cracked point, color bleeding, etc. would be immediately recognized. Then, the system was triggered with the laser beams in order to display the upper offset and the lower offset of the faulty portion. The performance of recognition was stated as 72% in identifying hole-classified faults, 65% in identifying scratch-classified faults, 86% in identifying other classified faults, and 83% identifying no fault defects. The total performance of the system was found as 77%.

Liu et al. have presented an article about fabric defect classification [8]. Particle Swarm Optimization (PSO) was applied in BP-NN training. PSO-BP Neural Network was applied to the classification of fabric defect. PSO algorithm was introduced into BP-NN training to determine neural network connection weight and threshold values reasonably. Three types of fabric defects such as broken warp, broken weft, and oil stain were used in this article. As a result, it was stated that PSO-BP-NN had less hidden unit numbers, a shorter training period, and a higher accuracy of classification.

Suyi et al. have presented a study [9]. The fabric image was decomposed into sub-images by using DB3 wavelet transform function. The energy, entropy, and variance features of both horizontal and vertical detail coefficients are extracted. These features were used as inputs to PSO-BP-NN for classification. There were five types of defects such as warp direction, weft direction, particle, hole, and oil stain in this study.

Suyi et al. have proposed a defect detection algorithm by combining cellular automata theory and fuzzy theory [10]. Edge detection method was used to mark the boundary of the defective area. Broken warp, double weft, broken weft, and broken-filling type defects were chosen in this study.

Jianli and Baoqi have proposed a method consisting of Gray Level Co-occurrence Matrix (GLCM), Principle Component Analysis (PCA), and NN [11]. Denoising operation was applied to the fabric image by using wavelet thresholding. Then, Laplacian operation was applied to smooth the image. GLCM of the image was obtained and 13 different features of the matrix were extracted by using Haralick method. The feature vectors were prepared for NN input. Principle component analysis method was used to reduce the dimension of the input vector. The NN was trained for four types of fabric defects: warp lacking, weft lacking, oil stain, and hole. The defects were classified successfully by using a three-layer BP-NN.

Kuo and Su have made fabric defect classification by using GLCM and NN methods [12]. The GLCM of the fabric sample images was obtained and then the features such as energy, entropy, contrast, and dissimilarity were extracted. The features were used as input vector and the defect types were introduced to the NN. After the NN was trained, it was tested by using different fabric defect images. The NN was trained for four types of fabric defects: warp lacking, weft lacking, oil stain, and hole.

Kuo and Lee have classified the warp lacking, weft lacking, hole, and oil stain defects by training a three-layer BP-NN [13]. Plain-weave white fabric was used as the material. The images of the fabric sample were acquired via an area scan camera. The image was transmitted to a computer for filtering and thresholding. After thresholding operation, the maximum length, maximum width, and gray level of the detected region were extracted as inputs for NN. The classification was achieved with high recognition for all types of defects.

Celik et al. have developed a machine vision system. Five types of fabric defects, such as warp lacking, weft lacking, hole, soiled yarn, and yarn flow or knot, have been detected by using different image analysis approaches: Linear filtering (LF), Gabor filter (GF), and Wavelet analysis (WA) [14–18]. The defect types have then been classified automatically by using ANN method.

3. Description and fundamentals of ANN method

An artificial neuron is a computational model inspired in the natural neurons. A neuron system consists of dendrites, cell body, axon, and synapses (output dendrites) connected to the dendrites of other neurons. The cell body is taken at the center of neuron. Dendrites and axon branch establish the connection between other neurons. Activity such as remember, think, and actions as a response to the environmental states passes from one neuron to another in terms of electrical triggers. This certainty is considered as an electrochemical process of voltage-gated ion exchange.

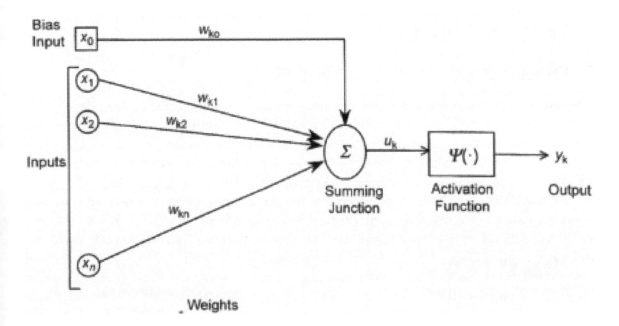

Figure 2. ANN architecture [3].

Synapses are the branches of the axon interface with the dendrites of other neurons through certain specialized structures. The input is taken by the triggering signal coming from the other neurons to the cell body of the dendrites. The cell body response is transmitted along the axon [3, 14, 19].

ANN is a simple analog of the neural structure of the human brain. The basic element of the brain is taken as a natural neuron. The basic element of every neural network is considered as an artificial neuron. ANN is then built by putting the neurons in layers and connecting the outputs of neurons from one layer to the inputs of the neurons from the next layer (**Figure 2**). There are three distinct functional operations happening in ANN architecture. First, the inputs from x_1 to x_n are multiplied by the corresponding weight $(w_{k1}, w_{k2} \ldots \ldots w_{kn})$ in the layer to from the product of **wp**. The second operation, the weighted input **wp**, is added to the bias w_{k0} to form the input n. The bias can then be considered as a weight having a constant value of 1. The weighed inputs are summed to form the parameter of u_k (Eq. (1)):

$$u_k = \sum_{J=0}^{n} w_{kj} x_j \tag{1}$$

Finally, the output y_k is produced by passing the parameter u_k through the activation function [19–21]. The activation functions modify the signal input according to its nature. The most commonly used activation functions are given as *"Linear transfer function," "Log-sigmoid function,"* and *"Tangent-sigmoid function."* The activation functions are determined according to the problem by trial and error method.

3.1. The architecture of artificial neural network (ANN)

The neurons are combined in a layer. The network may consist of one or more layers. The neurons in different layers are connected to each other with a particular pattern. The connections between the neurons and the number of layers are generally called as architecture of the neural network [20]. The networks are categorized into two main groups according to their architecture: feed-forward and feedback networks. Feed-forward networks have no loops and feedback networks have loops because of feedback connections. The networks are also classified into subgroups according to the layer connections: single layer network and multilayer network with hidden layers [22]. The network establishes a relation between input and output values. The network is untrained when it is first built. The weight and the bias values are selected randomly, and so the output pattern totally mismatches the desired pattern. The network first uses the input pattern to produce its own output pattern. The actual output pattern is compared with the desired output pattern (target) and the weights are changed according to the difference. The procedure continues until the pattern matching occurs or the desired amount of matching error is obtained. This process is called as *"training network."* When the training is achieved, the network is able to not only recall the input-output patterns but also interpolate and extrapolate them. This network is then called as *"trained"* or *"learned"* [3,

19]. After the network is trained, the network parameters such as the number of hidden layers, the number of units in the hidden layer, the learning rate, and the number of training cycles that is known as epochs must be optimized.

4. Texture feature extraction (TFE)

The surface or structure property of an object is defined as texture [23]. A fabric has got a regular pattern property in all regions. This uniform pattern provides a regular texture to the fabric. Due to the defective regions, the uniform texture property is deformed and a difference arises between them. Since every defect type causes a different change on the fabric texture, the fabric defects can be distinguished and classified by applying texture analysis and pattern recognition methods.

Two main approaches, *"statistical"* and *"spatial approaches,"* are used for measuring the texture properties. The statistical approach most frequently used one for texture analyzing and classification is based on the statistical properties of the intensity histogram. The spectral approach is based on the Fourier spectrum and suited for describing directionality of periodic patterns in an image [24]. The feature vector of a fabric image is composed of the first- and second-order statistical properties of the texture. The feature vectors of whole fabric images used for the application are extracted separately. The first- and second-order statistics are given in the following sections.

4.1. First-order statistics

The first-order statistical properties consist of average gray level (m), average contrast (σ), smoothness (R), third moment (μ_3), uniformity (U), and entropy (e) (**Table 1**). These properties are derived from the intensity histogram of the gray-level image [25]. The statistical moments are used to measure some statistical properties. The expression for the nth moment is given by Eq. (2):

$$\mu_n = \sum_{i=0}^{L-1} (z_i - m)^n \cdot p(z_i) \tag{2}$$

where z_i is a random variable indicating the pixel intensity, $p(z)$ is the histogram of the intensity levels in a region, and L is the number of possible intensity levels [25].

4.2. Second-order statistics

The second-order statistical properties include energy (f_1), contrast (f_2), correlation (f_3), variance (f_4), inverse difference moment (f_5), sum average (f_6), sum variance (f_7), sum entropy (f_8), entropy (f_9), difference variance (f_{10}), difference entropy (f_{11}), and Information Measure of Correlation (IMC) 1 (f_{12}) and 2 (f_{13}) (**Table 2**) [26–28].

Statistical property	Formula
Average gray level (mean)	$$m = \sum_{i=0}^{L-1} z_i p(z_i)$$
Average contrast (standard deviation)	$$\sigma = \sqrt{\mu_2(z)} = \sqrt{\sigma^2}$$
Smoothness	$$R = 1 - 1/(1 + \sigma^2)$$
Third moment	$$\mu_3 = \sum_{i=0}^{L-1} (z_i - m)^3 \cdot p(z_i)$$
Uniformity	$$U = \sum_{i=0}^{L-1} p^2(z_i)$$
Entropy	$$e = -\sum_{i=0}^{L-1} p(z_i)\log_2 p(z_i)$$

Table 1. First-order statistics [14].

Statistical property	Formula
Energy (angular second moment)	$$f_1 = \sum_i \sum_j p(i,j)^2$$
Contrast	$$f_2 = \sum_{n=0}^{N-1} n^2 p_{x-y}(n)$$
Correlation	$$f_3 = \frac{\sum_i \sum_j (ij)p(i,j) - \mu_x \mu_y}{\sigma_x \sigma_y}$$
Variance (sums of squares)	$$f_4 = \sum_i \sum_j (i-\mu)^2$$
Inverse difference moment	$$f_5 = \sum_i \sum_j \frac{1}{1+(i-j)^2} p(i,j)$$

Statistical property	Formula
Sum average	$$f_6 = \sum i = 22Nip_{x+y}(i)$$
Sum variance	$$f_7 = \sum_{i=2}^{2N} (i - f_6)^2 p_{x+y}(i)$$
Sum entropy	$$f_8 = -\sum_{i=2}^{2N} p_{x+y}(i)\log(p_{x+y}(i))$$
Entropy	$$f_9 = -\sum_i \sum_j p(i,j)\log(p(i,j))$$
Difference variance	$$f_{10} = -\sum_{i=0}^{N-1} \left(i - \mu_{x-y}\right)^2 p_{x-y}(i)$$
Difference entropy	$$f_{11} = -\sum_{i=0}^{N-1} p_{x-y}(i)\log(p_{x-y}(i))$$
Information measure of correlation 1	$$f_{12} = \frac{f_9 - HXY1}{\max\{HX, HY\}}$$
Information measure of correlation 2	$$f_{13} = (1 - \exp[-2.0(HXY2 - f_9)])^{\frac{1}{2}}$$

Table 2. Second-order statistics [14].

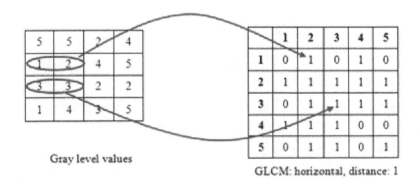

Gray level values   GLCM: horizontal, distance: 1

Figure 3. GLCM calculation.

The second-order statistics are derived from GLCM of images by using the methodology proposed by Haralick [26]. GLCM is the statistical method of examining texture that considers the spatial relationship of pixels [29]. GLCM measures how often a pixel p_1 occurs in specific spatial relationship to a pixel p_2 as shown in **Figure 3**. GLCM is a square matrix of size $N \times N$ where N is the number of gray level. Generally, the statistical measures are made from this matrix. When a single GLCM is not enough to describe the textural features of the input image, an additional parameter "*offset*" could be specified to allow detection of patterns in different direction [29]. The offsets define pixel relationships of varying direction and distance given in **Figure 4**. An offset array is defined to create a different GLCM for multiple directions.

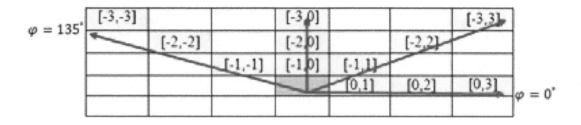

Figure 4. Offset directions.

The notations given in the following (Eqs. (3)–(6)) are used in the formulas for the second-order statistics of the image texture [26–28],

$p(i, j)$: (i,j)-th entry in a GLCM, and called as "*probability density*" with N being the number of gray levels.

$$p_x(i) = \sum_{j=1}^{N} p(i, j) \tag{3}$$

$$p_y(j) = \sum_{j=1}^{N} p(i, j) \tag{4}$$

$$p_{x+y}(k) = \sum i, j : i + j = k^{p(i,j)} \quad \text{for } k = 2,3,4\ldots\ldots\ldots 2N \tag{5}$$

$$p_{x-y}(k) = \sum i, j : |i - j| = k^{p(i,j)} \quad \text{for } k = 0,1,2\ldots\ldots\ldots N - 1 \tag{6}$$

where μ is the mean of $p(i, j)$, μ_x, μ_y are the means of p_x and p_y, respectively, and

$$\mu_{x-y} = \sum_{i=0}^{N-1} i p_{x-y} \cdot \sigma_x$$ and σ_y are the standard deviations, and HX and HY are the

entropies of p_x and p_y, respectively. They are calculated as follows:

$$HXY1 = -\sum_{i=1}^{N}\sum_{j=1}^{N} p(i, j) \log(p_x(i) p_y(j)) \tag{7}$$

$$HXY2 = -\sum_{i=1}^{N}\sum_{j=1}^{N} p_x(i) p_y(j) \log(p_x(i) p_y(j)) \tag{8}$$

4.3. Description of texture feature extraction method

The algorithm consisting of Discrete Wavelet Transform (DWT), Soft Wavelet Thresholding (SWT) and GLCM methods is formed to extract the required texture features of the defective fabric images. The procedure of the algorithm includes seven steps as follows:

i.   The image noises are removed by means of Wiener filter to get a smoother image.

ii.   The image is then decomposed into sub-images by applying DWT at level 2 with "db3" wavelet base. The approximation image is then applied to SWT (Eq. (9)) [30]:

$$Y = \begin{cases} sgn(X)(|X| - T_0), & |X| \geq T_0 \\ 0, & |X| < T_0 \end{cases} \tag{9}$$

where Y is the *wavelet coefficient* and T_0 is the threshold level. The *threshold value* "T_0" is determined according to Eq. (10):

$$T_{1.2} = mean\left[a(i, j)\right] \pm w * mean\left[std(a(i, j))\right] \tag{10}$$

T_1 is the upper limit, T_2 is the lower limit of the double thresholding processes, and "w" is the weighting factor which is determined experimentally between 2 and 4. The upper and lower thresholding limits are determined by using a defect-free fabric image as a template.

iii.   The regular texture patterns should be made smoother and the defective regions should be accentuated in order to distinguish the defect boundaries. The image frame applied to soft thresholding is convolved with *"Laplacian"* operator.

iv.   The first-order statistics (**Table 1**) are then extracted from the convolved image.

v.   The woven fabric pattern is produced by interlacing the warp and weft yarns with a perpendicular angle. They are arranged to the horizontal (weft yarns) and vertical (warp yarns) directions in the fabric. The co-occurrence matrices with offset [0, 1] are formed for horizontal and vertical detail coefficients of the defective fabric. Basically, they represent the latitude and the longitude properties of the fabric.

vi.   The second-order statistics are extracted from the co-occurrence matrices by using Haralick method.

vii.   The feature column vector having 32 elements is then formed by using the first- and second-order statistics.

The procedure given above is repeated for each defective fabric image.

5. Preparation of defect database

The material selected for defect classification is *"undyed denim fabric."* Denim is a strong and heavy warp-faced cotton cloth. The classical denim is made from 100% cotton and woven from coarse indigo dyed warp and gray undyed weft yarn. Weft yarn passes under two or more warp yarns and three and one twill construction is obtained. Generally, brown- or blue-colored yarns are used in warp and bleached yarns are used in weft [31, 32]. The name of denim comes from a strong fabric called serge, originally made in Nimes, France, which is then shortened to denim [31, 32]. Denim fabric is first produced as *"working cloths."* Since the denim fabric is strong and durable, it was used as a working cloth in the 18th century and as a mineworker cloth in the 19th century. The mass production of the denim fabrics was begun in 1853 by Levi Strauss. Overtime, the denim fabric was used in the production of different cloth types such as short, shirt, skirt, jacket, and different products such as hat and bag. It is being estimated that 85% of the produced denim fabric is used in the production of trousers.

The sample fabric used in this study has got the specifications given in **Table 3**. The material is supplied by Prestij Weaving Company in Gaziantep/Turkey, as an undyed denim fabric. It is woven on Picanol Gammax rapier weaving machines with a production speed of 450 rpm and a production efficiency of 85%. The fabric has got a size of 2000 cm length and 43 cm width. The fabric sample has four types of defects: warp lacking, weft lacking, hole, and soiled yarn (**Figure 5**). Since the required number of defect cannot be encountered on a fabric with such a length, some of the defects are made randomly with different widths and lengths on the sample [14].

Pattern	3/1 (s) twill
Warp yarn number	Ne 16/1 Open end
Weft yarn number	Ne 10/1 Open end
Warp sett	45 ends/cm
Weft sett	20 picks/cm
Warp crimp (%)	12
Weft crimp (%)	1.5
Weight per square meter (with sizing)	323 g/m^2
Cover factor	33.8
Reed number	110 dents/10cm

Table 3. Fabric sample specifications [14].

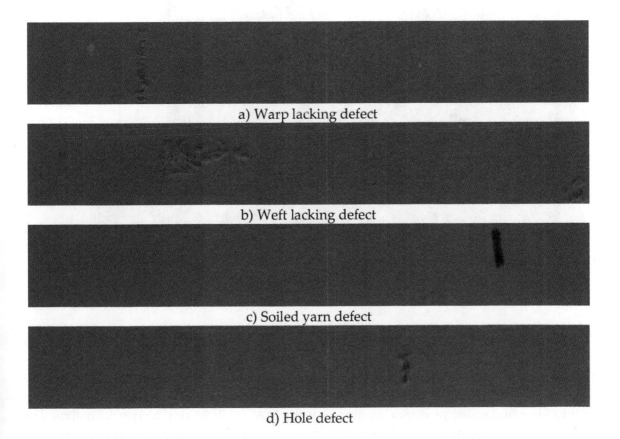

a) Warp lacking defect

b) Weft lacking defect

c) Soiled yarn defect

d) Hole defect

Figure 5. Fabric defect samples.

The image frames of the defective fabrics that will be used for network training and testing are acquired by using a prototype machine vision system [14] (**Figure 6**). The system consists of an industrial fabric inspection machine, a camera system, camera attachment equipment, an additional lightening unit, a rotary encoder, and host computer. The camera system includes charge-coupled device (CCD) line-scan camera, frame grabber card, lens, and camera link cable. The fabric sample was placed on a fabric inspection machine. As the fabric was wound, the image frames were captured and then memorized on the computer. The fabric motion and the camera exposure are synchronized with a rotary encoder via a frame grabber card.

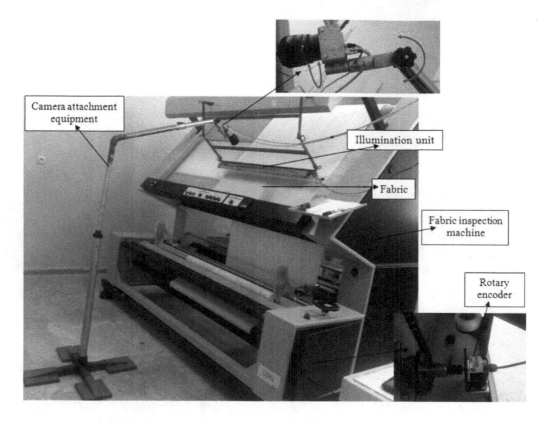

Figure 6. Machine vision system for fabric inspection.

6. Case study: neural network architecture for fabric defect classification

The most commonly preferred method in AI among the studies on fabric defect classification problem [9–13] is Artificial Neural Network. In this study, four defect types, hole, warp lacking, weft lacking, and soiled yarn are classified by using MATLAB® Neural Network Toolbox. The toolbox consists of some tools such as neural fitting, neural clustering, pattern recognition, and neural network. The pattern recognition tool is used to classify inputs into a set of target categories for the fabric defect classification problem. The pattern recognition tool consists of a two-layer feed-forward network (**Figure7**). The network is trained with scaled conjugate gradient back propagation. Tan-sigmoid transfer function is used in both the hidden and the output layers [21].

The input and target matrices are formed for each defect type. Twenty-five defective fabric images for each defect type are taken to be used for the feature extraction. This results in an input matrix with 32 × 100 size. Each feature vector of the input matrix is assigned to the target vector, which has a size of 4 × 1 (binary vector). It is defined in **Table 4**.

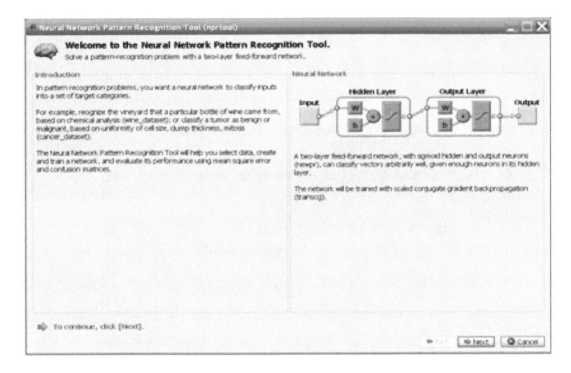

Figure 7. Pattern Recognition Tool GUI of MATLAB® NN toolbox.

Defect type	Column vector
Hole	[1; 0; 0; 0]
Warp lacking	[0; 1; 0; 0]
Weft lacking	[0; 0; 1; 0]
Soiled yarn	[0; 0; 0; 1]

Table 4. Defect type and corresponding vector definition.

Target vector is formed for each defective fabric image and the target matrix's size is 4 × 100. The input and target matrices are introduced into Neural Network Pattern Recognition Tool (nprtool) (**Figure 8**). The input data set is randomly divided as 80, 10, and 10% for training, validation, and testing samples, respectively (**Figure 9**). The number of neurons is then determined for the hidden layer of the network (**Figure 10**). The number of neurons in the output layer is determined automatically according to the number of elements in the target vector, and it is taken as four in this study. Since four defect types are to be classified having performed many trials, the best results are obtained for 37 neurons in the hidden layer after many trials. The network is finally trained using the scaled conjugate gradient back propagation (**Figure 11**). The Mean-Square-Error (MSE) algorithm adjusts the biases and weights so as to minimize the mean square error. MSE of training, testing, and validation operations is calculated by using Eq. (11). They are determined as 0.0021, 0.00014, and 0.00027, respectively (**Figure 12**):

$$E = \sum_j (t_i - o_i)^2$$

(11)

where t_i is the desired output and o_i is the actual output of neuron "i" in the output layer [10].

Figure 8. Input and target matrix introduction.

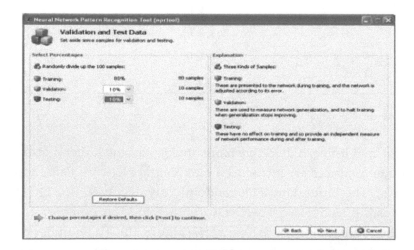

Figure 9. Random division of data set.

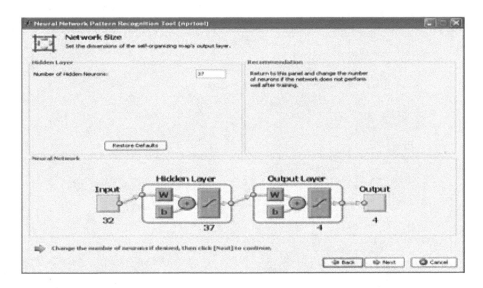

Figure 10. Number of neurons in the hidden layer.

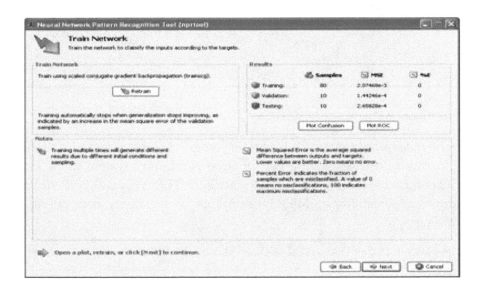

Figure 11. Network training.

6.1. Classification accuracy of the network

The classification accuracy of the network is specified by confusion matrices (**Figure 12**), and Receiver Operating Characteristic (ROC) curves (**Figure 13**) for training, testing, validation, and overall (three kinds of data combined). In the confusion matrices, the green squares indicate the correct response and the red squares indicate the incorrect responses. The lower-right blue squares illustrate the overall accuracies. As the number of green squares gets higher, the classification accuracy of the network increases. As in **Figure 12**, 100% correct responses are obtained for all confusion matrices with this network.

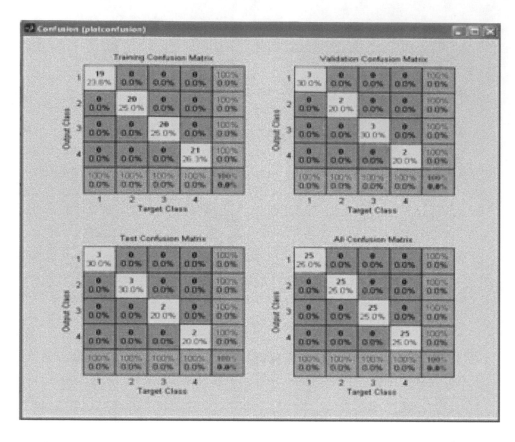

Figure 12. Confusion matrices [14].

Receiver Operating Characteristic curve is useful for recognizing the accuracy of predictions [33]. ROC curve illustrates the classification performance of a binary system as its distinguishing threshold level is varied. It is plotted as *True-Positive Rate* (TPR) versus *False-Positive Rate* (FPR). TPR is also known as sensitivity, and FPR is one minus the specificity. Four possible outcomes are seen as follows:

i.   If the sample is positive and it is classified as positive, it is counted as a *true positive* (TP).

ii.   If the sample value is positive and it is discriminated as negative, it is counted as a false negative (FN).

iii.   If the sample is negative and it is detected as negative, it is counted as a true negative (TN).

iv.   If the sample has a negative value and it is detected as positive, it is counted as a false positive (FP).

As the curve gets closer to the left upper corner, it means that the higher classification accuracy is obtained. A perfect test shows points in the upper-left corner, with 100% sensitivity and 100% specificity. When the true-positive rate of ROC value is 1, it means the true positives are perfectly separated from the false positives. For this classification problem, ROC value 1 is obtained for training, testing, validation, and overall (**Figure 13**). The network performs almost perfectly [34].

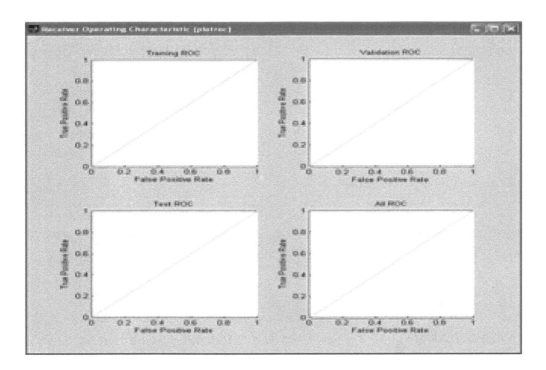

Figure 13. Receiver Operating Characteristic (ROC) curves.

6.2. Defect classification software

Finally, a user interface is prepared for the classification of the defective fabric images. It is automatically used to determine the defect type of a selected defective image. The user interface consists of three buttons as *"Exit,"* *"Reset Data,"* and *"Load-Defective Image"* as shown in **Figure 14**.

The exit button is used to exit the window. After the required image samples are classified, the counters of the defect classes can be made zero by using *"reset data"* button (**Figure 15**). The counts of the defect classes come to the initial zero number. The classification operation can be continued with a different defective image folder. The image to be classified is selected from the directory by using the *"load-defective image"* button. The folder browser window is opened and the required fabric image is selected when this button is activated (**Figure 16**). The selected image is applied to the feature extraction algorithm. The statistical texture features of the image are then extracted. The feature column vector is formed and it is simulated with the network previously built above. The selected image is displayed on the screen. The detect type is then titled for the image. The related defect-type counter is increased by one. These steps are shown in **Figures 17–20** [14].

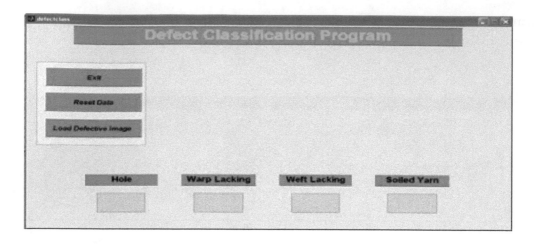

Figure 14. Defect classification program user interface.

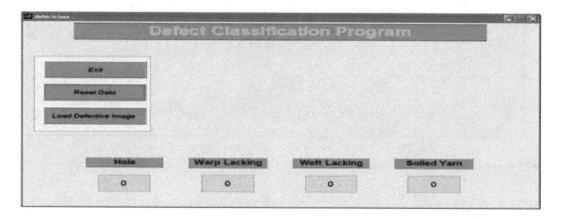

Figure 15. Reset the counters.

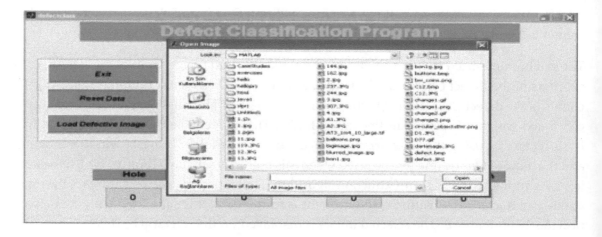

Figure 16. Selection of the defective image.

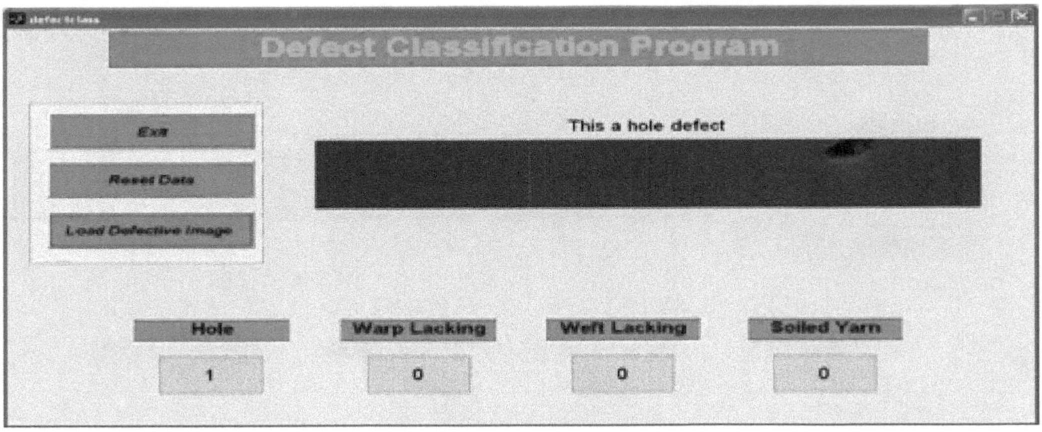

Figure 17. Classification of hole defect.

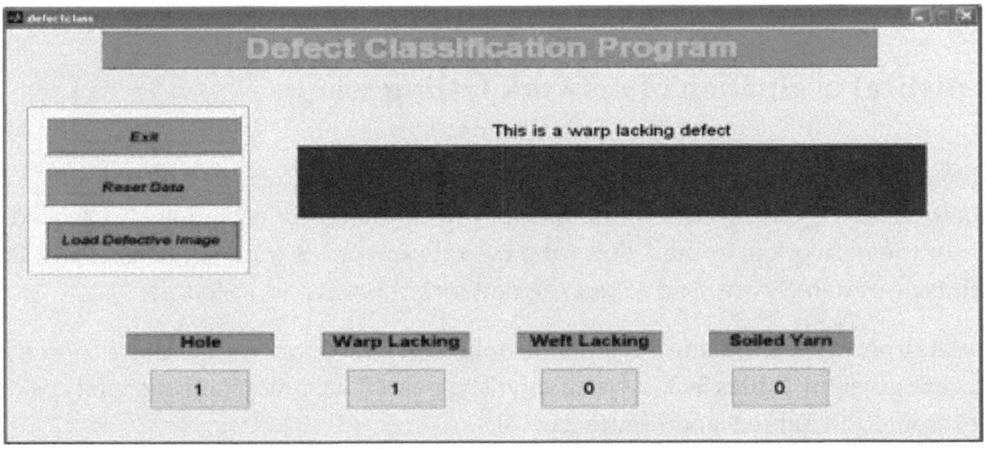

Figure 18. Classification of warp-lacking defect.

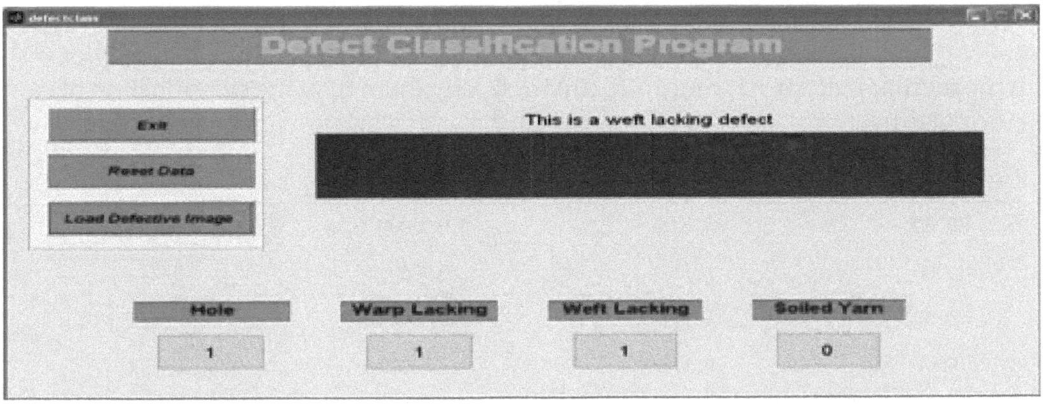

Figure 19. Classification of weft-lacking defect.

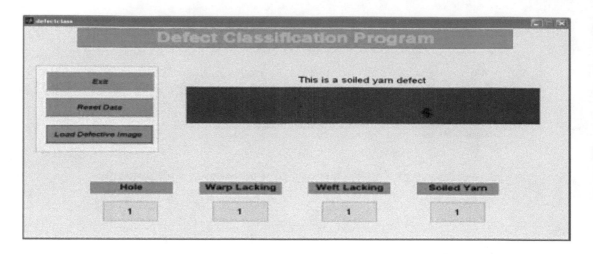

Figure 20. Classification of soiled yarn defect.

7. Statistical evaluation of network testing results

The defective fabric images are stored. They are then used for network training and testing. The features of the 25 defective fabric images are extracted for each defect type and the input matrix of the network is formed. After the neural network is trained successfully, 20 samples of each type of defects are used to test the network classification accuracy.

The neural network simulation results of hole, warp-lacking, weft-lacking, and soiled yarn defects are given in **Tables 5–8**, respectively. The overall accuracy rate of each type of defect is then presented in **Table 9** and **Figure 21** [14].

The defective images are classified with an average accuracy rate of 96.3%. As the hole defect is recognized with 100% accuracy rate, the others are recognized with a rate of 95%. Since many weft yarns are removed and the large spaces occur between the yarns, one of the weft-lacking images is recognized as the hole. One of the soiled yarn images is recognized as warp lacking because of having large vertical soil. Since only a small part of the fabric image is different from the regular pattern, it is more difficult to classify them than the classification of completely different textures.

1	1.0000	0.0090	0.0000	0.0000
2	1.0000	0.0004	0.0000	0.0000
3	1.0000	0.0000	0.0000	0.0000
4	1.0000	0.0000	0.0000	0.0000
5	0.9999	0.0001	0.0000	0.0000
6	1.0000	0.0000	0.0000	0.0000

1	1.0000	0.0090	0.0000	0.0000
7	0.9750	0.0000	0.0000	0.0495
8	0.9995	0.0000	0.0000	0.0009
9	0.9995	0.0000	0.0000	0.0005
10	0.9997	0.0000	0.0000	0.0022
11	0.6396	0.0033	0.0000	0.0036
12	0.8833	0.0003	0.0000	0.0311
13	1.0000	0.0009	0.0000	0.0000
14	0.9997	0.1108	0.0000	0.0000
15	0.8559	0.0087	0.0001	0.0000
16	0.9993	0.0004	0.0000	0.0000
17	1.0000	0.0001	0.0001	0.0000
18	0.9992	0.0025	0.0001	0.0000
19	0.8551	0.0020	0.3635	0.0000
20	1.0000	0.0000	0.0000	0.0001

Table 5. Classification results of *"hole"* defect.

1	0.0084	0.9601	0.0002	0.0000
2	0.0024	0.7283	0.0012	0.0000
3	0.0000	0.8354	0.1381	0.0000
4	0.0000	0.9938	0.0033	0.0000
5	0.0000	0.9997	0.0000	0.0001
6	0.0030	0.1955	0.0035	0.0001
7	0.0369	0.9362	0.0000	0.0000
8	0.0000	0.9824	0.0005	0.0024
9	0.0000	0.8589	0.5104	0.0000
10	0.0000	0.9983	0.0000	0.0003
11	0.0000	0.7221	0.0000	0.5606
12	0.0000	0.9999	0.0000	0.0000
13	0.0000	0.8850	0.0225	0.0000
14	0.0285	0.9988	0.0000	0.0000
15	0.0013	0.9998	0.0000	0.0000
16	0.0000	0.9910	0.0098	0.0000
17	0.0010	0.0099	0.0367	0.0042

1	0.0084	0.9601	0.0002	0.0000
18	0.0013	0.9238	0.0000	0.0001
19	0.0000	0.9993	0.0011	0.0000
20	0.0000	0.8986	0.1990	0.0000

Table 6. Classification results of *"warp-lacking"* defect.

1	0.0001	0.0015	0.9996	0.0000
2	0.0001	0.0017	0.9999	0.0000
3	0.9989	0.0003	0.0265	0.0000
4	0.0037	0.0127	0.9974	0.0000
5	0.0249	0.0467	0.9831	0.0000
6	0.0000	0.0014	1.0000	0.0000
7	0.0020	0.0094	0.2899	0.0000
8	0.0000	0.5929	0.8806	0.0000
9	0.0000	0.0001	1.0000	0.0000
10	0.0122	0.0476	0.8142	0.0000
11	0.0145	0.0004	0.9565	0.0000
12	0.0000	0.0000	1.0000	0.0000
13	0.0000	0.0001	1.0000	0.0000
14	0.0003	0.0010	1.0000	0.0000
15	0.0241	0.0846	0.5240	0.0000
16	0.0000	0.0001	1.0000	0.0000
17	0.0000	0.0036	1.0000	0.0000
18	0.0011	0.0007	0.9999	0.0000
19	0.0005	0.0006	0.9999	0.0000
20	0.0001	0.0007	0.9997	0.0000

Table 7. Classification results of *"weft–lacking"* defect.

1	0.0000	0.0000	0.0000	1.0000
2	0.0001	0.0024	0.0000	0.9991
3	0.0000	0.0003	0.0000	1.0000
4	0.0000	0.0002	0.0000	1.0000
5	0.0000	0.0233	0.0000	0.9897

1	0.0000	0.0000	0.0000	1.0000
6	0.0033	0.0916	0.0000	0.4757
7	0.0000	0.0010	0.0000	0.9999
8	0.0000	0.1733	0.0000	0.7789
9	0.0000	0.0392	0.0000	0.8368
10	0.0000	0.0008	0.0000	0.9995
11	0.0000	0.0000	0.0000	1.0000
12	0.0000	0.0000	0.0000	1.0000
13	0.0000	0.1266	0.0000	0.8657
14	0.0064	0.0073	0.0000	0.9998
15	0.0002	0.7885	0.0000	0.1102
16	0.0009	0.0000	0.0000	1.0000
17	0.0000	0.0075	0.0000	0.9987
18	0.0004	0.0000	0.0000	1.0000
19	0.0005	0.0149	0.0000	0.9924
20	0.0000	0.0001	0.0000	1.0000

Table 8. Classification results of *"soiled yarn"* defect.

Defect type	Hole	Warp lacking	Weft lacking	Soiled yarn	Number of sample	Classification accuracy (%)
Hole	20	0	0	0	20	100
Warp lacking	0	19	1	0	20	95
Weft lacking	1	0	19	0	20	95
Soiled yarn	0	1	0	19	20	95

Table 9. Defect classification accuracy rates.

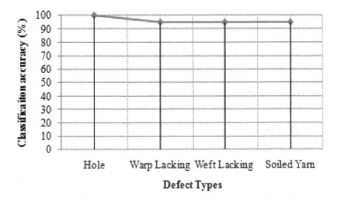

Figure 21. Classification accuracy rates of defects [14].

8. Conclusion

The experimental setup developed in this study has an operation speed of 7.5 m/min and it can detect the defects as small as 0.5 mm. This system was designed for the inspection of denim fabrics. The defective fabric images acquired via the developed machine vision system were classified by using ANN method. The classification was achieved according to their texture properties like a pattern recognition problem. The texture features of each defective image were extracted by using an algorithm based on DWT, SWT, and GLCM methods. Four defect types, hole, warp lacking, weft lacking, and soiled yarn, were classified. The first- and second-order statistical properties were extracted and the feature vector was formed for each defective fabric image. The feature extraction algorithm is applied for 25 images of each defect type. The input matrix with the size of 32 × 100 is obtained. The target vector indicated to which the input vector was assigned. It was made of a binary vector T (size = 4 × 1). The network was built by using MATLAB® Neural Network Toolbox and Pattern Recognition Tool.

Two layers were included in the network. The best results were obtained for 37 neurons in the hidden layer after many trials. The number of neurons in the output layer was determined automatically according to the number of elements in the target vector; it was taken as four in this study. The network was finally trained by using the scaled conjugate gradient BP method. Having trained the neural network successfully, 20 samples of each type of defects were used to test the network classification accuracy. The defective images were then classified with an average accuracy rate of 96.3%. As the hole defect was recognized with 100% accuracy rate, the others were recognized with a rate of 95%.

Acknowledgements

This study is a project supported by the Gaziantep University Scientific Research Projects Management Unit. The name of the project is "Development an Intelligent System for Fabric Defect Detection" and the project number is MF.10.12. The authors also thank Prestij Weaving Company in Gaziantep/Turkey for providing samples during tests.

Author details

H. İbrahim Çelik[1*], L. Canan Dülger[2] and Mehmet Topalbekiroğlu[1]

*Address all correspondence to: hcelik@gantep.edu.tr

1 Gaziantep University, Department of Textile Engineering, Gaziantep, Turkey

2 Gaziantep University, Department of Mechanical Engineering, Gaziantep, Turkey

References

[1] Stojanovic, R., Mitropulos, P., Koulamas, C., Karayiannis, Y., Koubias, S., and Papadopoulos, G. (2001). Real-time vision-based system for textile fabric inspection. Real-Time Imaging. 7, 507–518.

[2] Guruprasad, R. and Behera, B. K. (2010). Soft computing in textiles. Indian Journal of Fibre and Textile Research. 35, 75–84.

[3] Chattopadhyay, R. and Guha, A. (2004). Artificial neural networks: applications to textiles. Textile Progress. 35, 1, 1–42.

[4] Huang, C. C. and Chen, C. I. (2001). Neural-fuzzy classification for fabric defects. Textile Research Journal. 71(3), 220–224.

[5] Tilocca, A., Borzone, P., Carosio, S., and Durante, A. (2002). Detecting fabric defects with a neural network using two kinds of optical patterns. Textile Research Journal. 72(6), 745–750.

[6] Kumar, A. (2003). Neural network based detection of local textile defects. Pattern Recognition. 36, 1645–1659.

[7] Islam, A., Akhter, S., and Mursalin, T. E. (2006). Automated textile defect recognition system using computer vision and artificial neural networks. World Academy of Science, Engineering and Technology. 13, 1–6.

[8] Liu, S. Y., Zhang, L. D., Wang, Q., and Liu, J. J. (2008). BP neural network in classification of fabric defect based on particle swarm optimization. In: Proceedings of the 2008 International Conference on Wavelet Analysis and Pattern Recognition, Hong Kong. 216–220.

[9] Suyi, L., Liu Jingjing, L., and Leduo, Z. (2008). Classification of fabric defect based on PSO-BP neural network. In: Proceedings of the 2008 Second International Conference on Genetic and Evolutionary Computing. Hubei, China. 137–140.

[10] Suyi, L., Qian, W., and Heng, Z. (2009). Edge detection of fabric defect based on fuzzy cellular automata. In: Intelligent Systems and Applications. Wuhan, China. 1–3.

[11] Jianli, L. and Baoqi, Z. (2007). Identification of fabric defects based on discrete wavelet transform and back-propagation neural network. Journal of the Textile Institute. 98(4), 355–362.

[12] Kuo, C. J. and Su, T. (2003). Gray relational analysis for recognizing fabric defects. Textile Research Journal. 73(5), 461–465.

[13] Kuo, C. J. and Lee, C. J. (2003). A back-propagation neural network for recognizing fabric defects. Textile Research Journal. 73(2), 147–151.

[14] Çelik, H. I. Development of an intelligent fabric defect inspection system. Ph.D Thesis, Mechanical Engineering, University of Gaziantep Graduate School of Natural & Applied Sciences. 2013.

[15] Çelik, H. İ., Topalbekiroğlu, M., and ve Dülger, L. C. (2015). Real-time denim fabric inspection using image analysis. Fibers and Textiles in Eastern Europe. 3(111), 85–90.

[16] Çelik, H. İ., Dülger, L. C., and Topalbekiroğlu, M. (2014). Fabric defect detection by using linear filtering and morphological operations. Indian Journal of Fibre & Textile Research. 39, 254–259.

[17] Çelik, H. I., Dülger, L. C., and Topalbekiroğlu, M. (2013). Developing an algorithm for defect detection of denim fabric: Gabor filter method. Tekstil ve Konfeksiyon. 23(3), 255–260.

[18] Çelik, H. İ., Dülger, L. C., and Topalbekiroğlu, M. (2013). Development of a machine vision system: real-time fabric defect detection and classification with neural networks. The Journal of the Textile Institute. 105(6), 575–585.

[19] Graupe, D. (2007). Principles of artificial neural networks. 2nd edition. Advanced Series on Circuits and Systems. Vol. 6. Singapore: World Scientific Publishing Co. Pte. Ltd.

[20] Munakata, T. (2008). Fundamentals of the new artificial intelligence; neural, evolutionary, fuzzy and more. 2nd edition. London: Springer-Verlag London Limited.

[21] Beale, M. H. and Hagan, M. T. (2012). Neural network toolbox™ user's guide. Natick, MA: The MathWorks, Inc.

[22] Jain, A. K., Mao, J., and Mohiuddin, K. M. (1996). Artificial neural networks: a tutorial. Computer. 29(3), 31–44.

[23] Sonka, M., Hlavac, V., and Boyle, R. (2008). Image processing, analysis and machine vision. International student edition. Toronto, Ontario, USA: Thomson Corporation.

[24] Heijden, F. V., Duin, R. P. W., Ridder, D., and Tax, D.M.J. 2004. Classification, parameter estimation and state estimation an engineering approach using MATLAB. West Sussex, UK: John Wiley & Sons, Ltd.

[25] Gonzalez, R. C., Woods, R. E., and Eddins, S. L. (2004). Digital image processing using Matlab. Upper Saddle River, NJ: Prentice-Hall Inc.

[26] Haralick, R. M. (1979). Statistical and structural approaches to texture. Proceedings of the IEEE. 67(5), 786–804.

[27] Alam, F. I. and Uddin Faruqui, R. U. (2011). Optimized calculations of haralick texture features. European Journal of Scientific Research. 50(4), 543–553.

[28] Haralick, R. M., Shanmugam, K., and Dinstein, I. (1973). Textural features for image classification. IEEE Transactions on Systems, Man and Cybernetics, SMC 3(6), 610–621.

[29] The MathWorks. (2009). Image processing toolbox™ 6 user's guide. Natick, MA: The MathWorks, Inc.

[30] Misiti, M., Misiti, Y., Oppenheim, G., and Poggi, J. M. (1997). Wavelet toolbox for use with Matlab. Natick, MA: The MathWorks, Inc.

[31] Wikipedia the free encyclopedia. Available at: https://en.wikipedia.org/wiki/Denim. Accessed 17.02.2016.

[32] Gokarneshan, N. (2004). Fabric structure and design. New Delhi: New Age International (P) Ltd.

[33] Wikipedia. Available at: http://en.wikipedia.org/wiki/Receiver_operating_characteristic. Accessed 15.02.2016.

[34] Fawcett, T. (2006). An introduction to ROC analysis. Pattern Recognition Letters. 27, 861–874.

6

Neural Networks Applications for the Remote Sensing of Hydrological Parameters

Emanuele Santi

Additional information is available at the end of the chapter

Abstract

The main artificial neural networks (ANN)-based retrieval algorithms developed at the Institute of Applied Physics (IFAC) are reviewed here. These algorithms aim at retrieving the main hydrological parameters, namely the soil moisture content (SMC), the plant water content (PWC) of agricultural vegetation, the woody volume of forests (WV) and the snow depth (SD) or snow water equivalent (SWE), from data collected by active (SAR/scatterometers) and passive (radiometers) microwave sensors operating from space. Taking advantage of the fast computation, ANN are able to generate output maps of the target parameter at both local and global scales, with a resolution varying from hundreds of meters to tens of kilometres, depending on the considered sensor. A peculiar strategy adopted for the training, which has been obtained by combining satellite measurements with data simulated by electromagnetic models (based on the radiative transfer theory, RTT), made these algorithms robust and site independent. The obtained results demonstrated that ANN are a powerful tool for estimating the hydrological parameters at different spatial scales, provided that they have been trained with consistent datasets, made up by both experimental and theoretical data.

Keywords: microwave satellite sensors, soil moisture content, vegetation water content, snow water equivalent, woody volume

1. Introduction

Nowadays, global phenomena such as climate warning, stratospheric ozone depletion and troposphere pollution are threatening the long-term habitability of the planet. The Earth is a complex evolving system where regional as well as global processes at all spatial and temporal scales are strongly interrelated. These include surface exchanges of water, energy, carbon and other bio-geological processes, and exchange between land surface atmosphere, ocean and ground water. The human activity further complicated all these processes, because it transforms continuously the land surface to meet human needs associated with basic food production, population expansion and economic development.

Consequently, an ever-increasing interest in meteorological events and climate changes has led to a greater focus on the study of hydrological processes and their dynamics. The hydrological cycle involves the circulation of water from ocean to water vapour through the evaporation processes, the transformation of water vapour into precipitation and its return to the cycle through infiltration and evapotranspiration again. However, considering the spatial and temporal coverage needed to have reliable estimates, direct measurements of all the parameters involved in the hydrological cycle are difficult and extremely expensive. This led to an increasing interest for the observation from space, since it can meet the temporal and spatial requirements for an operational monitoring of the parameters related to the hydrological cycle. Earlier initiatives, such as the launch of a number of satellites having on-board sensors dedicated to the Earth's parameters observation, have already developed long-term applications and provided fundamental contributions in understanding global and regional ocean processes and enhancing land surface studies.

Among the instruments operating from space for the Earth surface observation, the sensors operating in the microwave portion of the electromagnetic (e.m.) spectrum have a great potential because these frequencies are capable of estimating some parameters of atmosphere, vegetation and soil that cannot be observed in the visible/near-infrared and thermal wavelength. Moreover, the scattering and emission at microwaves are related directly to the water content of the observed target. Microwave sensors, which can be classified in active (real aperture radar—RAR, and synthetic aperture radar—SAR), and passive (radiometers) are therefore particularly suitable for monitoring the key parameters of the hydrological cycle. In particular, these sensor represent a powerful tool for monitoring the soil water content or soil moisture content (SMC), the vegetation biomass, expressed as plant water content (PWC) for agricultural crops and woody volume (WV) for forests, and the snow depth (SD) or its water equivalent (SWE).

SMC is one of the driving factors in the hydrological cycle, being able to influence the runoff, the evapotranspiration, the surface heat fluxes and the biogeochemical cycles. The knowledge of SMC and its dynamics is mandatory in a wide range of activities concerning the forecasting of weather and climate, the prevention of natural disasters such as floods and landslides, the management of water resources and agriculture-related activities and many others. A huge amount of experimental and theoretical studies on the SMC retrieval from microwave acquisitions was therefore carried out since the late 1970s. The dielectric constant of soil (DC) at microwave frequencies is strongly dependent on the water content of the observed soil. At L-band, for example, the large variation in real part of the dielectric constant from dry to saturated soil results in a change of about 10 dB in radar backscatter and of 100 K in the radiometric brightness temperature. An important component required in the soil moisture inverse problem is the knowledge of the relationship between the soil dielectric constant to its moisture content: widely adopted empirical models for assessing such relationship are given in [1, 2].

Snow is another driving factor of the hydrological cycle, since it is able to influence the Earth's climate and its response to global changes. Snow is the main component of the cryosphere, and its accumulation and extension are related to the global climate variations. The monitoring of the snow parameters, and in particular SD and SWE, is essential for the forecasting of snow–water runoffs (flash floods) and for the management of the water resources. Currently, satellite microwave radiometers are employed for generating low-resolution SD or SWE products at global scale, while the operational mapping of snow at high resolution mainly rely with optical sensors, being the microwave application still at the research stage for this application. In both cases, the currently available snow products are based on the single sensors, and thus, the temporal and spatial coverage is given by the sensor characteristics, which may not fulfil the requirements for the operational use of remote sensing data in monitoring and management of snow.

Vegetation cover on the Earth's surface is an important variable in the study of global changes, since vegetation biomass is the most influential input for carbon cycle models. The frequent and timely monitoring of vegetation parameters (such as vegetation biomass and leaf area index) is therefore of vital importance to the study of climate changes and global warming.

The retrieval of the aforementioned parameters from active and/or passive microwave measurements is nonetheless not trivial, due to the nonlinearity of the relationships between radar and radiometric acquisitions and target parameters. Moreover, in general, more than one combination of surface parameters (SMC, surface roughness—HSTD, PWC and so on) give the same electromagnetic response. Thus, in order to minimize the uncertainties and enhance the retrieval accuracy from remote sensing data, statistical approaches based on the Bayes theorem and learning machines are widely adopted for implementing the retrieval algorithms [3–5].

In this framework, the artificial neural networks (ANN) represent an interesting tool for implementing accurate and flexible retrieval algorithms, which are able to operate with radar and radiometric satellite measurements and to easily combine information coming from different sources. ANN can be considered a statistical minimum variance approach for addressing the retrieval problem, and, if properly trained, they are able to reproduce any kind of input-output relationships [6, 7].

During the training, sets of input data and corresponding target outputs are provided sequentially to the ANN, which iteratively adjusts the interconnecting weights of each neuron, in order to minimize the difference between actual outputs and corresponding targets, basing on the selected learning algorithm.

Many examples of ANN application to inverse problems in the remote-sensing field can be found in literature, in particular concerning the retrieval of soil moisture at local scale from SAR [8–10] or radiometric [11] observations. The comparison of retrieval algorithms carried out in [9] demonstrated that ANN, with respect to other widely adopted statistical approaches based on Bayes theorem and Nelder–Mead minimization [12], offer the best compromise between retrieval accuracy and computational cost. Other comparison between ANN, Bayesian, SVM and other retrieval approaches can be found in [13–15]. All these works demonstrated that the ANN are able to provide accuracy results in line with (or better than) the other methods, with the advantages of a fast computation, that is mandatory for the online processing of high-resolution images, and the possibility of updating the training if new data are available. The cited publications refer to the retrieval of soil moisture; however, these considerations remain valid for the retrieval of the other parameters investigated here.

Basing the training on data simulated by forward electromagnetic models, namely models that are able to simulate the microwave signal emitted or scattered by the target surface, the ANN can be regarded as a method for estimating the hydrological parameters from satellite microwave acquisitions through the inversion of the given model. Following this approach, the ANN act for inverting the forward model, similarly to other physically based algorithms, but without the approximations needed for an analytical inversion. Moreover, the additional inclusion of experimental data in the training set allows retaining the advantages of the experimental-driven approaches in adapting the algorithm to the particular features of a given test site [16].

The main advantages of this technique consist of the possibility of quick updating the training with new datasets, thus adapting the algorithm to work on a given test area, but without losing the accuracy on a larger scale. Moreover, the method has the capability of easily merging data coming from different sources for improving the retrieval accuracy. The poor robustness to outliers represents instead the main disadvantage of ANN: outliers are input data out of the range of the training set. In such case indeed, the ANN may return large errors or fail completely the retrieval, requiring therefore a 'robust' training, which has to be representative of a variety of surface conditions as wide as possible.

Besides the other considerations, it should be remarked that the strategy adopted for setting up and training the ANN is fundamental for obtaining a valid retrieval algorithm. An inappropriate training can turn indeed the ANN from a powerful retrieval instrument into an inadequate approach to the given problem. Some examples can be found in literature, in which the training set is insufficient for defining all the interconnection weights of the complex architecture proposed, or in which the architecture definition and the related overfitting and underfitting have not been properly addressed. Another fundamental consideration is that ANN are able to represent any kind of input–output relationships, and therefore, a deep knowledge of the physic of the problem is mandatory for avoiding the risk of relating input and output quantities that are instead completely uncorrelated, thus generating relationships that have no physical basis.

In this work, a review of the main ANN-based algorithms developed at IFAC for estimating the soil moisture (SMC, in m^3/m^3), the water content of agricultural vegetation (PWC, in kg/m^2), the forest woody volume (WV, in t/ha) and the snow depth/water equivalent (SD, in cm, and SWE, in mm) is presented. These algorithms take advantage of an innovative training strategy, which is based on the combination of satellite measurements with data simulated by electromagnetic models, based on the radiative transfer theory (RTT).

2. Implementing and training the Artificial Neural Networks

The ANN considered in this work are feed-forward multilayer perceptron (MLP), having two or three hidden layers of nine to twelve neurons each between the input and the output. The training was based on the back-propagation learning rule, which is an iterative gradient-descent algorithm able to adjust the connection weights of each neuron, in order to minimize the mean square error between the outputs generated by the ANN at every iteration and the corresponding target values.

It should be noted that the gradient-descent method sometimes suffers from slow convergence, due to the presence of one or more local minima, which may also affect the final result of the training. This problem can be solved by repeating the training several times, with a resetting of the initial conditions and a verification that each training process led to the same convergence results in terms of R and RMSE, by increasing it until negligible improvements were obtained.

2.1. Defining architecture

In order to define the optimal ANN architecture in terms of number of neurons and hidden layers, the most suitable strategy is to start with a simple ANN architecture, generally with one hidden layer of few neurons. These ANN are trained by means of a subset of the available data, tested on the rest of the dataset, and the training and testing errors are compared. The ANN configuration is then increased by adding neurons and hidden layers; training and testing are repeated and errors compared again, until a further increase of the ANN architecture is found to have a negligible decrease of the training error and an increase in the test error. This procedure allows defining the minimal ANN architecture capable of providing an adequate fit of the training data, preventing overfitting or underfitting problems. NNs, like other flexible nonlinear estimation methods, can be affected indeed by either underfitting or overfitting. ANN configurations not sufficiently complex for the given problem can fail to reproduce complicated data set, leading to underfitting. ANN configurations too complex may fit also the noise, leading to overfitting. Overfitting is especially dangerous because it can easily lead to predictions that are far beyond the range of the training data. In other words, the ANN are able to reproduce the training set with high accuracy but fails the test and validation phases.

2.2. Selecting the transfer function

Another key issue for defining the ANN best architecture is in the selection of the most appropriate transfer function: in general, linear transfer functions give less accurate results in training and testing; however, they are less prone to overfitting and are more robust to outliers, that is input data out the range of the input parameters included in the training set. Logistic Sigmoid (logsig) and Hyperbolic Tangent Sigmoid (tansig) transfer functions are instead characterized by higher accuracies in the training and test; however, they may lead to large errors when the trained ANN are applied to new datasets. Logsig generates outputs between 0 and 1 as the neuron's net input goes from negative to positive infinity and describes the nonlinearity, g(a), as $1/(1+e^{-a})$. Alternatively, multilayer networks can use the tansig function, $\tanh(a) = (e^a - e^{-a})/(e^a + e^{-a})$.

2.3. Generating the training set

Nevertheless, besides these problems, the main constraint for obtaining good accuracies with the ANN approach consists of the statistical significance of the training set, which shall be representative of a variety of surface conditions as wide as possible, in order to make the algorithm able to address all the situations that can be encountered on a global scale. The datasets derived from experimental activities are in general site dependent and cannot be representative of the large variation of the surface features that can be observed on a larger scale. Therefore, a training set only based on experimental data is not sufficient for training the ANN for global monitoring applications.

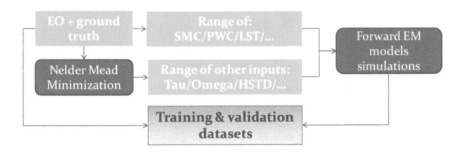

Figure 1. Strategy adopted for defining the raining and validation datasets, starting from the experimental data and using the forwards e.m. models (after [16]).

By combining the experimental in situ measurements with simulated data obtained from the e.m. models, it is possible to fill in the gaps of the experimental datasets and to better characterize the microwave signal dependence on the target parameter for a variety of surface conditions as wide as possible. The consistency between experimental data and model simulations can be obtained by deriving the range of model input parameters from the available measurements. After defining the minimum and maximum of each parameter required by the model, namely SMC, PWC, soil moisture, surface roughness (HSTD) and surface temperature (LST), the input vectors are generated by using a pseudorandom function, rescaled in order to cover the range of each parameter. Thousands of inputs vectors for running the model simulations can be generated by iterating this procedure, thus obtaining datasets of surface parameters and corresponding simulated microwave data for training and testing the ANN. The flowchart of **Figure 1** represents the main steps for generating the training from the experimental data. The same procedure allows generating the independent dataset for validating the ANN after training. In general, the available data are divided in two subsets with a random sampling; the first subset is divided again in 60–20–20% for training, test and validation phases, respectively, and the second subset is reserved for an independent test of the algorithm. The random sampling of the dataset is reiterated 5–6 times, and the training is repeated each time, in order to avoid any dependence of the obtained results on the sampling process.

This strategy has been successfully adopted for implementing and training the ANN-based algorithms that are presented in the following sections.

3. HydroAlgo ANN algorithm for AMSR-E and AMSR2

The 'HydroAlgo' algorithm [11] applies the ANN for estimating simultaneously SMC, PWC and SD from the acquisitions of the low-resolution spaceborne radiometers, like the Advanced Microwave Scanning Radiometer for the Earth observing system (AMSR-E) [17], which is no more operating, and its successor, AMSR2 [18]. We refer to [11] for a detailed algorithm description. The main characteristic of the algorithm is the exclusive use of AMSR-E/2 data, taking advantage of the multifrequency acquisitions of these sensors. It includes a disaggregation procedure, based on the smoothing filter-based intensity modulation (SFIM) technique [19], which is able to enhance the spatial resolution of the output SMC product up to the nominal sampling of AMSR-E/2 ($\sim 10 \times 10 \text{ km}^2$). The algorithm flowchart is represented in **Figure 2**: it should be noted that the algorithm applies the already trained ANN to the input data, without repeating the training for each new set of satellite acquisitions. The trained ANN are generated once, saved and recalled for processing the available data. In particular, specific ANN have been trained for each given output product, basing on training sets composed by a combination of experimental data and simulations from e.m. models, obtained following the scheme of Section 2.

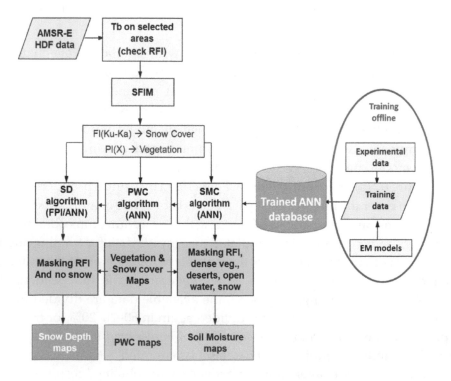

Figure 2. HydroAlgo flowchart.

3.1. SMC processor

The SMC processor was developed and tested using a set of several thousand of data, which was obtained by combining the experimental data collected in Mongolia and Australia with 10,000 values of Tb simulated by the 'tau-omega' model [20]. The experimental dataset was provided by JAXA, within the framework of the JAXA ADEOS-II/AMSR-E and GCOM/AMSR2 research programs.

The core of the algorithm is composed by two feed-forward multilayer perceptron (MLP) ANN, trained independently for the ascending and descending orbits, and using the back-propagation learning rule. Inputs of the algorithm are the brightness temperature at C-band in V-polarization, the polarization indices (PI) at 10.65 and 18.7 GHz (X- and Ku-bands), defined as $PI = 2 \times (TbV - TbH)/(TbV + TbH)$, and the brightness temperature at Ka-band (36.5 GHz) in V-polarization. C-band, that is the lowest AMSR-E frequency, was chosen for its sensitivity to the SMC, which is slightly influenced by sparse vegetation. The polarization indices at X- and Ku-bands are considered for compensating the effect of vegetation on soil emission [21], and for flagging out the densely vegetated targets, where SMC cannot be retrieved. The brightness temperature at Ka-band, V-polarization, was assumed as a proxy of the surface physical temperature, to account for the effect of diurnal and seasonal variations of the surface temperature on microwave brightness [22].

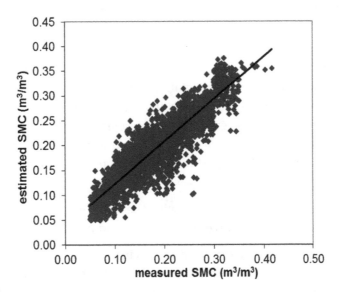

Figure 3. HydroAlgo SMC product validation (after [11]).

The SMC product validation on the Australian and Mongolian data, which were not used for the training, resulted in a determination coefficient $R^2 = 0.8$ (ANN output vs estimated SMC), root-mean-square error RMSE = 0.03 m³/m³, and BIAS = 0.02 m³/m³ (**Figure 3**).

The peculiar characteristics of ANN allowed adapting this algorithm for working on given test areas with a specific updating of the training process, which is devoted to maximize the performances of the algorithm on the area, losing something of the algorithm capabilities for the global retrieval. Following this approach, it was possible to obtain the algorithm for the SMC retrieval in central Italy, which was presented in [23]. In that work, HydroAlgo-derived SMC has been compared with simulated SMC data obtained from the application of a well-established soil water balance model (SWBM) [24] in central Italy (Umbria region), with the aim of exploiting the potential of AMSR-E/2 for SMC monitoring on a regional scale and in heterogeneous environments too. For this application, the 10% of about 450,000 AMSR-E acquisitions collected over the test area and corresponding SMC values simulated by SWBM, obtained with a random sampling, were added to the training set of the original HydroAlgo implementation. The algorithm trained with this updated dataset was validated on the remaining 90% of the available data, allowing an appreciable improvement of the accuracy with respect to the original implementation. In detail, this 'supervised' approach allowed obtaining an overall increase of the average R from 0.71 to 0.84 and a corresponding decrease of RMSE from 0.058 to 0.052 m^3/m^3, with respect to the original implementation of HydroAlgo applied to the same dataset.

3.2. PWC processor

The PWC processor was based on the well-demonstrated sensitivity of the polarization difference, expressed as the polarization index, at various AMSR-E frequencies to PWC. Past research has shown that the microwave polarization index (PI), defined as the difference of the first two Stokes parameters (H- and V-polarization) divided by their sum, especially at X- and Ku-bands, is directly related to τ and therefore to the seasonal changes in PWC and LAI.

It is generally known indeed that microwave emission, expressed as brightness temperature (Tb), depends on canopy growth but also on plant geometry and structure. Therefore, Tb temporal trends vary according to the vegetation type in terms of scatterer dimensions and observation frequency. Tb tends to increase as the biomass of plants characterized by small leaves and thin stems increases, whereas it has an opposite behaviour for crops characterized by large leaves and thick stalks. On the other hand, the PI at the same frequency usually decreases as the biomass of different vegetation types increases, resulting rather independent on crop type [25, 26].

This allowed using PI at higher frequencies with the twofold purpose of compensating the vegetation effect on soil emission at lower frequencies and of estimating directly the PWC.

The capabilities of ANN in merging different inputs into a single retrieval algorithm allowed making synergistic use of PI at C-, X- and Ku-bands from the AMSR-E acquisitions. In order to implement, train and validate the algorithm, we identified a suitable test area in a wide portion of Africa (0–20°N/16°–17°E), which extended from the Sahara desert to Equatorial forest, and therefore included a wide range of vegetation types, biomass amount and land-scapes. The area was also chosen for the presence of large and homogeneous regions, which allowed mitigating the effects related to the coarse resolution of AMSR-E. Several AMSR-E swaths on the area have been collected and resampled on a fixed grid, in order to be repre-sentative of the entire seasonal cycle of vegetation. This process resulted in a dataset of about 10,000 radiometric acquisitions at the considered frequencies, from C- to Ka-bands. Consid-ering the difficulties in obtaining 'ground truth' data of PWC for validating the algorithm on large or global scale, the validation was carried out referring to PWC values derived from NDVI thanks to the relationship established by [22]. Although this relationship was initially developed for corn and soybean crops, it can be considered valid for other types of vegetation too.

In detail, the 'reference' PWC was derived from NDVI data obtained from http://free.vgt.vito.be/home.php, resulting from 10 days of SPOT4 acquisitions on the African continent. These data were resampled on the fixed grid and compared with the corresponding satellite acquisitions, in both ascending and descending orbits. Two different ANN have been defined and trained independently, in order to better account for the large differences between Tb data collected in ascending and descending orbits.

A subset of 15% of the data available was considered for generating the datasets for training, testing and validating each ANN (60–20–20%, randomly sampled), and the remaining 85% of data (about 8500 samples) was considered for the independent validation of the algorithm, to which the result presented in **Figure 4** is referred.

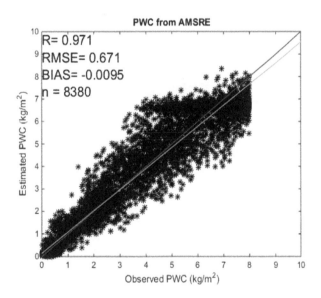

Figure 4. Validation results: PWC estimated by the algorithm as a function of the PWC derived from NDVI and considered as ground truth.

The ANN optimization process resulted in an architecture with two hidden layers of $11+11$ neurons, with a transfer function of type 'tansig'. The validation returned encouraging results, with a RMSE error on the PWC retrieval <1 kg/m^2, and a correlation coefficient $R = 0.97$.

3.3. SD processor

As per the SMC processor, the implementation of the SD processor was based on a dataset provided by JAXA and composed of AMSR-E acquisitions and direct SD and air temperature measurements collected in the eastern part of Siberia. The measurements covered a flat area of about 20' in latitude, 45' in longitude, at an average altitude of 300 m asl, covered by low vegetation. In this region, snow was generally present from the beginning of October to the end of May, with a depth that did not exceed 50 cm. The ground measurements were covering seven winter seasons, from October 2002 to May 2009. By combining the AMSR-E acquisitions and the related direct measurements of SD and air temperature, it was possible to obtain a dataset of 17,000 values for training and testing the ANN. As for the previously described processors, two ANN have been developed and trained separately for the ascending and descending orbits.

The validation was carried out on a different area of about 200×200 km located between Finland and Norway, obtaining the following statistics: R = 0.88, RMSE = 9.13 cm and BIAS = -0.95 cm.

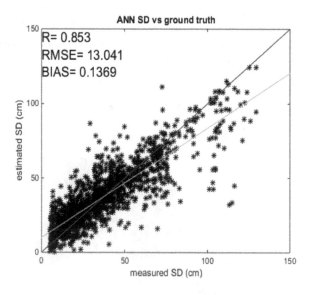

Figure 5. Validation results: SD estimated by the ANN algorithm as a function of the SD derived from ground measurements (after [26]).

The algorithm was then adapted for working on alpine areas, in which snow properties suffer dramatic spatial variations that cannot be easily reproduced by spaceborne microwave radiometers, due to their coarse spatial resolution. This limitation was overcome by setting up a method for evaluating and correcting the effects of the complex orography, of the different footprint in the different AMSR-E channels, and of the forest coverage. The detailed description of this method can be found in [27]. The test and validation were carried out on a test area of about 100×100 km^2 located in the eastern Italian Alps, using AMSR-E data collected during the winters between 2002 and 2011. The obtained results were encouraging: the correlation between SD estimated by the algorithm and the corresponding ground truth resulted in R = 0.85 and RMSE = 13 cm considering the descending orbits, while the retrieval accuracy worsened when considering the ascending ones (**Figure 5**).

In this case, the training of the ANN was updated by adding to the original training set a subset of the data collected on the area and the validation was carried out on the remaining part of the dataset, for a total of more than 1400 daily AMSR-E acquisitions and corresponding ground truth.

4. The SAR ANN algorithm for SMC, PWC and SWE

Similarly to HydroAlgo, a further ANN-based algorithm has been implemented for working with SAR data at C- and X-bands, aiming at generating SMC maps of bare or slightly vegetated soils, PWC maps of agricultural vegetation and SWE maps of snow covered surfaces. The algorithm takes advantage of the high resolution of the considered sensors, which can, however, provide data at local or regional scale, since SAR images cover usually areas not larger than 100×100 km^2. The other main difference in respect to HydroAlgo is that the existing SAR systems work at a single frequency and the obtainable product depends on the frequency, polarizations and ancillary information available. For instance, C-band cannot retrieve SD and it is more suitable for monitoring SMC, being less affected to the vegetation effects which drive instead the scattering mechanism at X-band. Depending on the input SAR data, the output resolution ranges between 10×10 and 100×100 m^2. **Figure 6** represents the algorithm flowchart: after a common pre-processing, the algorithm splits in three different branches, one for each output product. Details on the implementation of each processor can be found in [28, 29] for SMC processor [30], for PWC processor and [30] for SWE processor.

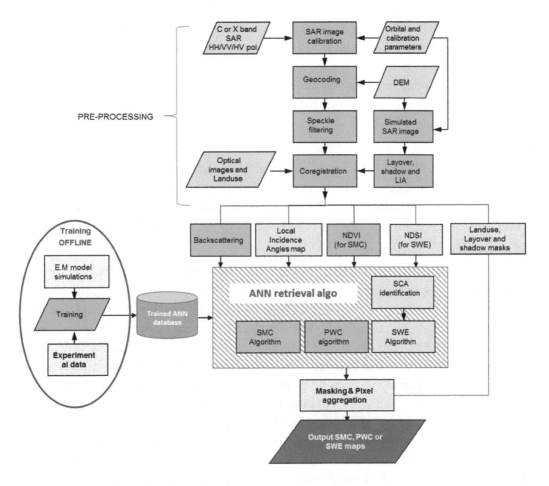

Figure 6. Flow chart of the SAR algorithm.

4.1. SMC processor

The recent generation of SAR sensors can operate in several acquisition modes and provide images at different polarizations and acquisition geometries. For enhance the retrieval accuracy, the algorithm has been implemented with a dedicated ANN for each configuration of inputs, namely the backscattering coefficients ($\sigma°$) in VV- or HH-polarization with and without the ancillary information on vegetation, represented by co-located NDVI from optical sensor, and VV + VH or HH + HV combinations. Consequently, the algorithm was composed by 6 + 6 ANN trained independently for C- and X-band, respectively. Following the strategy presented in Section 2, the dataset implemented for the ANN training was obtained by combining the available SAR images, the corresponding direct measurements of the surface parameters, and a large set of data simulated using e.m. forwards models.

Simulated backscattering values at all polarizations were obtained by coupling OH [31] and vegetation water cloud [33] models. This quite simple but widely validated combination offers several advantages with respect to more sophisticated formulations, namely the reduced set of input parameters needed for simulating the backscatter, the fast computation and the reliable accuracy. In detail, the OH model simulates the surface scattering from bare rough surfaces: with respect to IEM/AIEM, it is able to simulate both co- and cross-polarizations, accounting for the soil surface roughness by only using the height standard deviation (HSTD, in cm) parameter. The VWC model is a simplified implementation of RTT. It accounts for volume scattering of vegetation over the soil, for the attenuation effect on the soil scattering (simulated by OH model) and for the soil−vegetation interaction, requiring as inputs PWC and observation angle only. Inputs of the 'coupled' model are SMC, HSTD, PWC and the observation angle theta.

Minimum and maximum values of the soil parameters measured during the experimental campaigns (SMC, HSTD and PWC) were considered in order to define the range of variability of each soil parameter. Using a pseudorandom function drawn from the standard uniform distribution on the open interval (0, 1), rescaled in order to cover the range of each soil parameter, we generated input vectors for the e.m. model, in order to simulate the backscattering at VV, HH and HV/VH-polarizations.

This procedure was then iterated 10,000 times, thus obtaining a set of backscattering coefficients for each input vector of the soil parameters. The consistency between the experimental data and the model simulations was verified before proceeding to the training phase. The ANN training was carried out by considering the simulated $\sigma°$ at the various polarizations and the incidence angle as input of the ANN, and the soil parameters, in particular the SMC, as outputs. It should be remarked that the soil surface roughness parameter HSTD was added to the ANN outputs in order to enhance the training performances. However, an operational retrieval of surface roughness is not in the scopes of this algorithm and the roughness parameters are then disregarded in the algorithm. After training, the ANN were tested on a different dataset that was obtained by re-iterating the model simulations as described above. The use of a pseudorandom function prevented a correlation between these two datasets: this fact was particularly important in order to evaluate the capabilities of ANN to generalize the training phase and to prevent the overfitting problem. Incorrect sizing of the ANN or inadequate training could cause the overfitting: the ANN return outputs outside the training range (outliers) when tested with input data that are not included in the training set.

The algorithm was validated using a set of experimental data collected on several test areas, mainly agricultural fields and grasslands, located worldwide. The total dataset was composed by about 700 field-averaged values of $\sigma°$ at C-band from Envisat/ASAR and about 600 at X-band from Cosmo-SkyMed (CSK), collected at various polarizations.

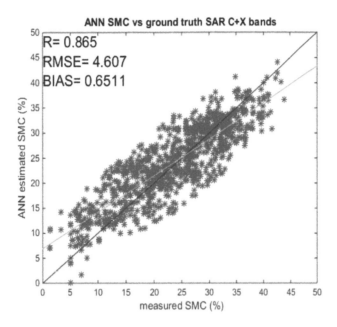

Figure 7. Validation of the SAR SMC algorithm.

Figure 7 shows the overall validation obtained by comparing the SMC values retrieved by the algorithm with the corresponding ground truth, and it corresponds to R = 0.86, RMSE = 4.6 and BIAS = 0.65. Analysing separately the two frequencies, the best results were achieved at C-band, which is more sensitive to SMC and less influenced by the vegetation than X-band. At the latter frequency, instead, the vegetation effect is dominant, although some sensitivity to SMC is detectable at least for bare and scarcely vegetated surfaces.

4.2. PWC processor

The algorithm for PWC estimate was very similar to the one for estimating SMC, and it is based on a feed-forward multilayer perceptron (MLP) ANN, trained by using the back-propagation (BP) learning rule and a RTT discrete element model, more sophisticated than the WCM [29].

The model was first validated with the experimental data collected in the 'Sesto' agricultural area located in central Italy, close to the city of Florence, mainly covered by wheat crops, and then used for generating the training set of ANN in combination with experimental data. Model simulations were iterated 10,000 times by randomly varying each input parameter in the range derived from experimental data, thus obtaining a training set able to complete the training phase and fully define all the neurons and weights of the ANN. The dataset was split randomly in two parts, the first part for training and the second one for testing the ANN. A configuration with two hidden layers of ten perceptrons each was finally chosen as the optimal one. The validation results gave R = 0.97 and RMSE = 0.345 kg/m² (**Figure 8**).

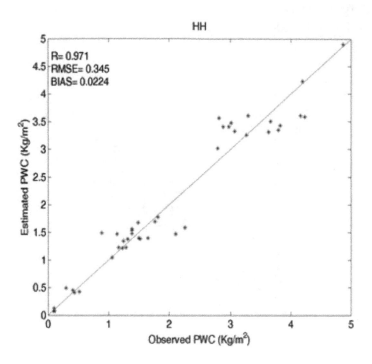

Figure 8. PWC algorithm validation: PWC estimated vs. PWC observed.

4.3. SWE processor

In the last years, the remote-sensing community has shown a growing interest in the new generation X-band SAR satellites, such as CSK and Terra-SARX (TSX), with the aim of better understanding if at this frequency, the information on snow parameters can be retrieved and under which conditions. Although X-band is not the most suitable frequency for the retrieval of SD or SWE, since the dry snow is almost transparent at this frequency, the freezing of dedicated missions such as the ESA cold regions hydrology high-resolution observatory (CoReH$_2$O), put more interest in evaluating the potential of such a frequency for snow parameter retrieval. Basing on encouraging experimental results pointing out the relationship between $\sigma°$ and SD for several winter seasons in the Italian Alps [30, 34], we have implemented an ANN-based retrieval algorithm able to estimate the SWE/SD of snow-covered surfaces from X-band SAR data.

This algorithm, which has been preliminary described in [30], is composed of two steps: first, the dry snow is identified and separated from the wet snow and from the snow-free surfaces using a well-known threshold criterion [35]. Then, the SWE retrieval by means of the ANN algorithm is attempted on the areas of the image identified as dry snow.

Inputs to the ANN are the X-band $\sigma°$ measured in the available polarizations, the corresponding reference value measured in snow-free conditions, and the local incidence angle information. SWE is the ANN output.

The main problem we had to face in developing this algorithm was related to the lack of extensive sets of measurements of snow parameters, which posed some constraints in defining the training set. The available measurements are indeed sparse, and, besides being site dependent, are numerically inadequate for training the ANN and define all its neurons and weights. The training of the ANN was therefore performed by using data simulated by the dense medium radiative transfer model implementation [36, 37]. As for the other algorithms, the training set was generated by running the model simulation for the input values of snow parameters in a range derived from the direct measurements, obtaining output backscattering coefficients at the given polarizations for each input vector of snow parameters. In order to match all the acquisition modes of CSK, several ANN have been set up and trained separately, according to the combination of polarizations available from the dataset.

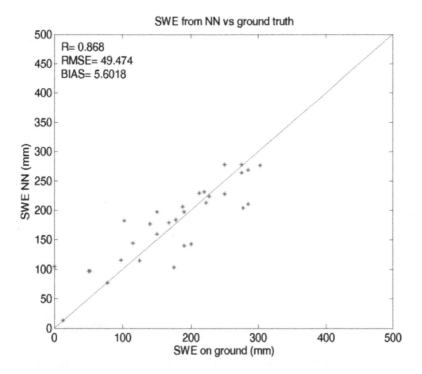

Figure 9. Validation of the SAR SWE algorithm.

Although the algorithm is not able to consider some model parameters, such the average crystal dimension, which are unavailable from in situ measurements, the training process converged successfully. In particular, for a configuration with 2 hidden layers of 13 neurons each and an activating function of 'tansig' type, assuming the availability of CSK data in two polarizations (co- and cross-polar), the validation resulted in $R > 0.9$, with an associated probability value (P-value) of 95% and RMSE = 50 mm of equivalent water [30]. After the test on simulated data, the algorithm was validated considering CSK images and corresponding ground truth available on the Cordevole and Bardonecchia test areas, located in the eastern and western part of Italian Alps, respectively. The direct comparison with ground truth data resulted in an R > 0.85, RMSE = 50 mm and Bias = 5.6 mm (**Figure 9**).

5. The P + L-band SAR ANN algorithm for WV

A final example of the ANN capabilities in adapting to the retrieval of hydrological parameters from microwave remote-sensing acquisitions is represented by this ANN application to the forest WV retrieval. The algorithm takes advantage of the well-known sensitivity of low microwave frequencies such as L- and P-bands to forest biomass. However, L- and P-band SAR data available from satellite and corresponding in situ measurements were not sufficient for implementing and validating such algorithm. Therefore, we selected a dataset of airborne SAR measurements derived from the ESA project BioSAR 2010, which has been obtained through the ESA eopi portal: https://earth.esa.int/web/guest/pi-community. The dataset was composed of airborne SAR fully polarimetric images at P- and L-bands acquired in fall 2010 in Sweden by the airborne system ONERA SETHI and corresponding LiDAR measurements of forest height, which were considered as target values for training and testing the algorithm.

The WV ANN algorithm considers as inputs the co- and cross-polarized backscattering at both P- and L-bands, along with the corresponding incidence angles, without any ancillary information from other sensors. The training set was implemented by considering as ground truth the WV estimated by LiDAR. In this case, the model simulations considered for increasing the training set were based on an implementation of the water cloud model with gaps, which was initially proposed in [38, 39] and it was based on the original VWC by [32]. The model has been modified by adding a term able to account for the backscattering dependence on the observation angle. The independent validation of this algorithm was carried out on some plots for which conventional measurements of WV were available. Although the validation set was limited, the results were encouraging, with R = 0.98, RMSE = 22 t/ha and Bias = 11 t/ha.

6. Generation of maps of the target parameter at regional and global scale

The fast computation is another important advantage of the ANN-based algorithms with respect to other statistical methods. The training represents indeed the only time-consuming process; however, it is only once carried out at the beginning and it deals with the algorithm implementation, not with its application. A trained ANN are indeed able to process the input satellite data in real or near-real time. This characteristic allows an operational application of the ANN for generating maps of the target parameter at high resolution and large or global coverage. In [27], the ANN retrieval algorithm was demonstrated to be able to process 200,000 pixels/s, which correspond to about 80 s for generating a SMC map at 25×25 m^2 resolution from an input SAR image of 100×100 km^2. Besides these considerations, the output maps represent also an effective tool for verifying qualitatively the validity of the training process, although these maps cannot be considered a real validation of the retrieval algorithms, since adequate ground truth for comparing extensively the algorithm outputs at large and global scale is barely available.

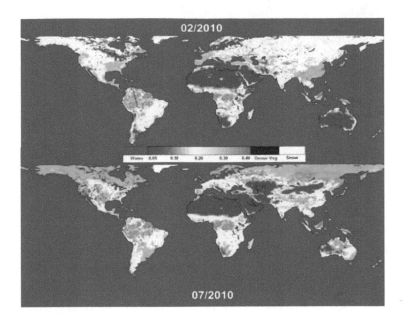

Figure 10. Global SMC and snow extent maps obtained as weekly average of AMSR-E acquisitions collected in February and June 2010 (after [11]).

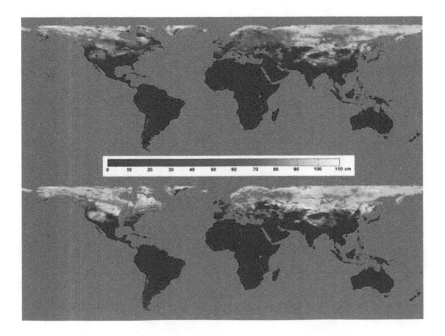

Figure 11. SD maps obtained as weekly average of AMSR-E acquisitions collected in different seasons between December 2009 and February 2010 (after [11]).

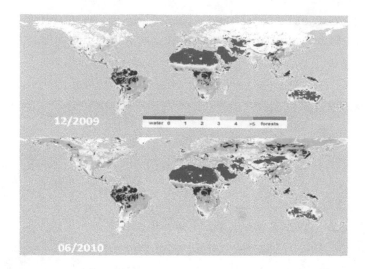

Figure 12. Global PWC maps (kg/m²) of agricultural and herbaceous vegetation from a weekly average of AMSRE ascending and descending orbits in February (top) and June (bottom) 2010.

Extreme variations of the target parameter between adjacent pixels, the presence of large percentages of outliers, and the absence of clearly detectable patterns indicate indeed that the training was not achieved successfully, although the validation in the control points resulted satisfactory. In these cases, the ANN should be retrained, by verifying that the training set is representative of the entire range of the input microwave data and output parameters considered for the specific application.

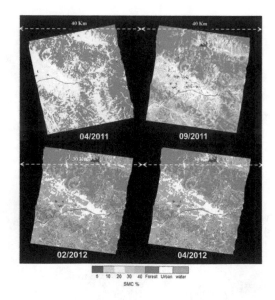

Figure 13. SMC maps from CSK images (© ASI)" for four different dates between 2011 and 2012 in the 'Sesto' test area.

As an example of the operational capabilities of the algorithms proposed here, **Figures 10** and **11** represent some examples of SMC and SD maps generated by using microwave radiometric data through HydroAlgo and reprojected on a fixed grid spaced 0.1° × 0.1°, while examples of outputs generated by the PWC processor are represented in **Figure 12**.

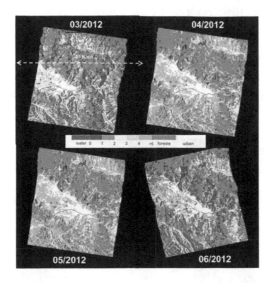

Figure 14. PWC maps from CSK images (© ASI) covering the entire seasonal cycle of wheat from march to June 2012 in the 'Sesto' test area.

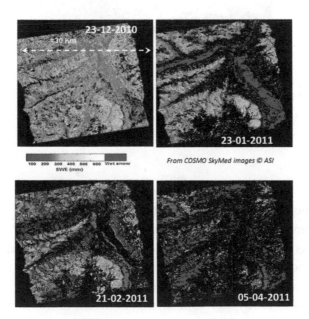

Figure 15. Maps of SWE derived from the proposed algorithm for a test area in the Italian Alps.

Maps have been obtained as weekly average of the AMSR-E acquisitions in both ascending and descending orbits for different seasons: winter and summer for SMC and PWC and two different winter periods for SD, in order to point out the sensitivity to the global spatial and temporal variations of the investigated parameter.

Examples of outputs maps generated by the SAR SMC and PWC algorithm from CSK images are represented in **Figures 13** and **14**, while maps of SWE derived from the proposed algorithm for a test area in the Italian Alps are shown in **Figure 15**. Map dimensions range between 30 × 30 and 40 × 40 km², depending on the input images. White and blue colours represent masking for urban areas and water bodies respectively.

Finally, a WV map (t/ha) has been produced for the area where SAR data at P-and L-bands have been acquired (**Figure 16**). Different colours represent different levels of forest biomass in accordance with the ground truth data collected simultaneously to the BioSAR acquisitions.

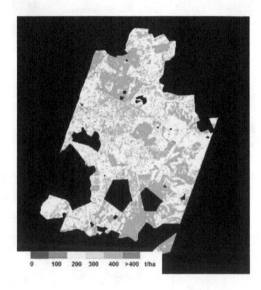

Figure 16. Forest biomass map (WV, in t/ha) from BioSAR data on the Sweden test site.

7. Conclusions

The overview of the retrieval algorithms presented here demonstrated that ANN are a powerful tool for implementing inversion algorithm, which are able to estimate the hydro-logical parameters from microwave satellite acquisitions, provided ANN have been trained with consistent datasets made up by both experimental and theoretical data. The flexibility of this method and the possibility of using it for both active and passive sensors with high accuracy and computational speed were confirmed. Moreover, the possibility of repeating the training with new datasets easily enables the improvement of the retrieval accuracy, making this technique flexible and adaptable to new datasets and sensors.

A further advantage of these algorithms is in their capability of merging data coming from different sources, as other sensors or ancillary information, into a unique retrieval approach. It was the case of the algorithm implemented for C- and X-band SAR, which takes advantage of the NDVI information from optical sensors (Landsat/Modis), when available, for improving the SMC retrieval accuracy.

The main constraint for accurate retrievals is due to the training process: the retrieval error may be large if the ANN are tested with data not correctly represented in the training. Large datasets are therefore needed for properly training the ANN, in order to cover the whole range of the microwave data and corresponding surface parameters. It should be noted that there is not a unique way for defining the training set. Some a priori knowledge and the support of model simulations help in setting the range of each surface parameter, in order to make the training set as representative as possible of the observed surface. Testing and validation on independent datasets (i.e. not related to the data considered for training) may indicate if the training has been achieved properly. In particular, the use of electromagnetic models for generating large training dataset is one of the best methods for avoiding the danger of 'black box' algorithms and to make sure that the results are based on physical assumptions. Since the training is performed off-line, before starting the data processing, the computational speed of ANN is not hampered by this procedure.

Acknowledgements

This research work was partially supported by the JAXA ADEOS-II/AMSR-E and GCOM/AMSR2 research programs, by the ESA/ESTEC Contract No. 4000103855/11/NL/MP/fk on GMES Sentinel-1 Soil Moisture algorithm development, by the EUMETSAT Contract No. EUM/C0/14/4600001368/JF on the use of SCA cross-pol for the Soil Moisture retrieval and by the ASI Hydrocosmo Proposal No. 1720 on the retrieval and monitoring of Land Hydrological parameters for Risk and Water Resources Management.

Author details

Emanuele Santi

Address all correspondence to: e.santi@ifac.cnr.it

Institute of Applied Physics, National Research Council (IFAC-CNR), Florence, Italy

References

[1] Dobson C., Ulaby F., Hallikainen M., El-Rayes M. 1985. Microwave dielectric behaviour of wet soil—Part II: Four component dielectric mixing models. IEEE Transactions on Geoscience and Remote Sensing. 23(4):35–46.

[2] Mironov V. L., Kosolapova L. G., Fomin S. V. 2009. Physically and mineralogically based spectroscopic dielectric model for moist soils. IEEE Transactions on Geoscience and Remote Sensing. 47(7):2059–2070.

[3]   Notarnicola C. 2014. A Bayesian change detection approach for retrieval of soil moisture variations under different roughness conditions. IEEE Geoscience and Remote Sensing Letters. 11(2):414–418.

[4]   Pasolli L., Notarnicola C., Bruzzone L., Bertoldi G., Della Chiesa S., Hell V., Niedrist G., Tappeiner U., Zebisch M., Del Frate F., Vaglio Laurin G. 2011. Estimation of soil moisture in an alpine catchment with RADARSAT2 images. Applied and Environmental Soil Science. Article ID 175473:12. doi:10.1155/2011/175473

[5]   Pierdicca N., Pulvirenti L., Pace G. 2014. A prototype software package to retrieve soil moisture from Sentinel-1 data by using a Bayesian multitemporal algorithm. IEEE Journal of Selected Topics in Applied Earth Observations and Remote Sensing. 7(1): 153–163.

[6]   Hornik K. 1989. Multilayer feed forward network are universal approximators. Neural Networks. 2(5):359–366.

[7]   Linden A., Kinderman J. 1989. Inversion of multi-layer nets. Proceedings of the International Joint Conference on Neural Networks. 2:425–443.

[8]   Del Frate F., Ferrazzoli P., Schiavon G. 2003. Retrieving soil moisture and agricultural variables by microwave radiometry using neural networks. Remote Sensing of Environment. 84(2):174–183. doi:10.1016/S0034-4257(02)00105-0

[9]   Elshorbagy A., Parasuraman K. 2008. On the relevance of using artificial neural networks for estimating soil moisture content. Journal of Hydrology. 362:1–18. Available at: http://www.sciencedirect.com/science/article/pii/S0022169408004204

[10] Paloscia S., Pampaloni P., Pettinato S., Santi E. 2008. A comparison of algorithms for retrieving soil moisture from ENVISAT/ASAR images. IEEE Transactions on Geoscience and Remote Sensing. 46(10):3274–3284.

[11] Santi E., Pettinato S., Paloscia S., Pampaloni P., Macelloni G., Brogioni M. 2012. An algorithm for generating soil moisture and snow depth maps from microwave spaceborne radiometers: HydroAlgo. Hydrology and Earth System Sciences. 16:3659–3676. doi:10.5194/hess-16-3659-2012

[12] Nelder J. A., Mead R. 1965. A simplex method for function minimization. Computer Journal. 7:308–313.

[13] Gruber A., Paloscia S., Santi E., Notarnicola C., Pasolli L., Smolander T., Pulliainen J., Mittelbach H., Dorigo W., Wagner W. 2014. Performance inter-comparison of soil moisture retrieval models for the MetOp-A ASCAT instrument. Proceedings of the 2014 IEEE International Geoscience and Remote Sensing Symposium (IGARSS), pp. 2455–2458. doi:10.1109/IGARSS.2014.6946969

[14] Mladenova I. E., Jackson T. J., Njoku E., Bindlish R., Chan S., Cosh M. H., Holmes T. R. H., de Jeu R. A. M., Jones L., Kimball J., Paloscia S., Santi E. 2014. Remote monitoring of soil moisture using passive microwave based techniques—theoretical basis and

overview of selected algorithms for AMSR-E. Remote Sensing of Environment. 144:197–213. doi:10.1016/j.rse.2014.01.013

[15] Paloscia S., Santi E., Pettinato S., Mladenova I. E., Jackson T. J., Bindlish R., Cosh M. H. 2015. A comparison between two algorithms for the retrieval of soil moisture using AMSR-E data. Frontiers in Earth Sciences. 3(16):1–10. doi:10.3389/feart.2015.00016

[16] Santi E., Paloscia S., Pettinato S., Fontanelli G. 2015. Application of artificial neural networks for the soil moisture retrieval from active and passive microwave spaceborne sensors. International Journal of Applied Earth Observations and Geoinformation. doi: 10.1016/j.jag.2015.08.002

[17] Lobl E. 2001. Joint advanced microwave scanning radiometer (AMSR) science team meeting. Earth Observer. 13(3):3–9.

[18] Imaoka K., Takashi M., Misako K., Marehito K., Norimasa I., Keizo N. 2012. Status of AMSR2 instrument on GCOM-W1, earth observing missions and sensors: development, implementation, and characterization II. Proceedings of SPIE 2012, 852815. doi: 10.1117/12.977774

[19] Santi E. 2010. An application of SFIM technique to enhance the spatial resolution of microwave radiometers. International Journal of Remote Sensing. 31(9–10):2419–2428.

[20] Mo, T., Choudhury, B. J., Schmugge, T. J.,Wang, J. R., and Jackson, T. J. A model for microwave emission from vegetation covered fields. J. Geophys. Res., 87, 11229–11237, 1982

[21] Paloscia S., Pampaloni P. 1988. Microwave polarization index for monitoring vegetation growth. IEEE Transactions on Geoscience and Remote Sensing. 26(5):617–621.

[22] Jackson T. J., Cosh M. H., Bindlish R., Starks P. J., Bosch D. D., Seyfried M. S., Goodrich D. C., Moran M. S. 2010. Validation of advanced microwave scanning radiometer soil moisture products. IEEE Transactions on Geoscience and Remote Sensing. 48(12):4256–4272.

[23] Santi E., Paloscia S., Pettinato S., Brocca L., Ciabatta L. 2015. Robust assessment of an operational algorithm for the retrieval of soil moisture from AMSR-E data in central Italy. Proceedings of IEEE International Geoscience and Remote Sensing Symposium (IGARSS). pp. 1288–1291. doi:10.1109/IGARSS.2015.7326010

[24] Brocca L., Camici S., Melone F., Moramarco T., Martinez-Fernandez J., Didon-Lescot J.-F., Morbidelli R. 2014. Improving the representation of soil moisture by using a semi-analytical infiltration model. Hydrological Processes. 28(4):2103–2115. doi:10.1002/hyp.9766

[25] Choudhury B. J., Tucker C. J. 1987. Monitoring global vegetation using Nimbus-7 37 GHz Data Some empirical relations. International Journal of Remote Sensing. 8:1085–1090.

[26] Paloscia S., Pampaloni P. 1992. Microwave vegetation indexes for detecting biomass and water conditions of agricultural crops. Remote Sensing of Environment. 40:15–26.

[27] Santi E., Pettinato S., Paloscia S., Pampaloni P., Fontanelli G., Crepaz A., Valt M. 2014. Monitoring of Alpine snow using satellite radiometers and artificial neural networks. Remote Sensing of Environment. 144:179–186. doi:10.1016/j.rse.2014.01.012

[28] Paloscia S., Pettinato S., Santi E., Notarnicola C., Pasolli L., Reppucci A. 2013. Soil moisture mapping using Sentinel-1 images: Algorithm and preliminary validation. Remote Sensing of Environment. 134:234–248. doi:10.1016/j.rse.2013.02.02721

[29] Santi E., Paloscia S., Pettinato S., Notarnicola C., Pasolli L., Pistocchi A. 2013. Comparison between SAR soil moisture estimates and hydrological model simulations over the Scrivia test site. Remote Sensing. 5:4961–4976. doi:10.3390/rs5104961

[30] Paloscia S., Santi E., Fontanelli G., Montomoli F., Brogioni M., Macelloni G., Pampaloni P., Pettinato S. 2014. The sensitivity of Cosmo-SkyMed backscatter to agricultural crop type and vegetation parameters. IEEE Journal of Selected Topics in Applied Earth Observations and Remote Sensing. 7(7):2856–2868.

[31] Pettinato S., Santi E., Brogioni M., Paloscia S., Palchetti E., Xiong C. 2013. The potential of COSMO-SkyMed SAR images in monitoring snow cover characteristics. IEEE Geoscience and Remote Sensing Letters. 10(1):9–13.

[32] Oh Y., Sarabandi K., Ulaby F. T. 1992. An empirical model and an inversion technique for radar scattering from bare surfaces. IEEE Transactions on Geoscience and Remote Sensing. 30:370–381.

[33] Attema E. P. W., Ulaby F. T. 1978. Vegetation modeled as a water cloud. Radio Science. 13:357–364.

[34] Brogioni M., Cagnati A., Crepaz A., Paloscia S., Pampaloni P., Pettinato S., Santi E., Xiong C., Shi J. C. 2014. Model investigations of backscatter for snow profiles related to avalanche risk. Proceedings of IEEE International Geoscience and Remote Sensing Symposium (IGARSS). pp. 2415–2418. doi:10.1109/IGARSS.2014.6946959

[35] Nagler T., Rott H. 2000. Retrieval of wet snow by means of multitemporal SAR data. IEEE Transactions on Geoscience and Remote Sensing. 38:754–765.

[36] Liang D., Xu X., Tsang L. 2008. The effects of layers in dry snow on its passive microwave emissions using dense media radiative transfer theory based on the quasicrystalline approximation (QCA/DMRT). IEEE Transactions on Geoscience and Remote Sensing. 46:3663–3671.

[37] Tsang L., Pan J., Liang D., Li Z. X., Cline D., Tan Y. H. 2007. Modeling active microwave remote sensing of snow using dense media radiative transfer (DMRT) theory with multiple scattering effects. IEEE Transactions on Geoscience and Remote Sensing. 45(4): 990–1004.

[38] Santoro M., Eriksson L., Askne J., Schmullius C. 2006. Assessment of stand-wise stem volume retrieval in boreal forest from JERS-1 L-band SAR backscatter. International Journal of Remote Sensing. 27:3425–3454.

[39] Fransson J. E. S., Israelsson H. 1999. Estimation of stem volume in boreal forests using ERS-1 C- and JERS-1 L-band SAR data. International Journal of Remote Sensing. 20:123–137.

Permissions

All chapters in this book were first published in ANN, by InTech Open; hereby published with permission under the Creative Commons Attribution License or equivalent. Every chapter published in this book has been scrutinized by our experts. Their significance has been extensively debated. The topics covered herein carry significant findings which will fuel the growth of the discipline. They may even be implemented as practical applications or may be referred to as a beginning point for another development.

The contributors of this book come from diverse backgrounds, making this book a truly international effort. This book will bring forth new frontiers with its revolutionizing research information and detailed analysis of the nascent developments around the world.

We would like to thank all the contributing authors for lending their expertise to make the book truly unique. They have played a crucial role in the development of this book. Without their invaluable contributions this book wouldn't have been possible. They have made vital efforts to compile up to date information on the varied aspects of this subject to make this book a valuable addition to the collection of many professionals and students.

This book was conceptualized with the vision of imparting up-to-date information and advanced data in this field. To ensure the same, a matchless editorial board was set up. Every individual on the board went through rigorous rounds of assessment to prove their worth. After which they invested a large part of their time researching and compiling the most relevant data for our readers.

The editorial board has been involved in producing this book since its inception. They have spent rigorous hours researching and exploring the diverse topics which have resulted in the successful publishing of this book. They have passed on their knowledge of decades through this book. To expedite this challenging task, the publisher supported the team at every step. A small team of assistant editors was also appointed to further simplify the editing procedure and attain best results for the readers.

Apart from the editorial board, the designing team has also invested a significant amount of their time in understanding the subject and creating the most relevant covers. They scrutinized every image to scout for the most suitable representation of the subject and create an appropriate cover for the book.

The publishing team has been an ardent support to the editorial, designing and production team. Their endless efforts to recruit the best for this project, has resulted in the accomplishment of this book. They are a veteran in the field of academics and their pool of knowledge is as vast as their experience in printing. Their expertise and guidance has proved useful at every step. Their uncompromising quality standards have made this book an exceptional effort. Their encouragement from time to time has been an inspiration for everyone.

The publisher and the editorial board hope that this book will prove to be a valuable piece of knowledge for researchers, students, practitioners and scholars across the globe.

List of Contributors

Ma. del Rosario Martinez-Blanco, Víctor Hugo Castañeda-Miranda, Gerardo Ornelas-Vargas, Héctor Alonso Guerrero-Osuna, Luis Octavio Solis-Sanchez, Rodrigo Castañeda-Miranda and José María Celaya-Padilla
Centro de Investigación e Innovación Tecnológica Industrial (CIITI), Universidad Autónoma de Zacatecas, Zacatecas, México
Unidad Académica de Ingeniería Eléctrica (UAIE), Universidad Autónoma de Zacatecas, Zacatecas, México

Carlos Eric Galvan-Tejada and Jorge Isaac Galvan-Tejada
Unidad Académica de Ingeniería Eléctrica (UAIE), Universidad Autónoma de Zacatecas,Zacatecas, México

Héctor René Vega-Carrillo
Unidad Académica de Estudios Nucleares (UAEN), Universidad Autónoma de Zacatecas, Zacatecas, México

Margarita Martínez-Fierro
Centro de Investigación e Innovación Tecnológica Industrial (CIITI), Universidad Autónoma de Zacatecas, Zacatecas, México
Laboratorio de Medicina Molecular, Unidad académica de Medicina Humana y Ciencias de la Salud (UAMHCS), Universidad Autónoma de Zacatecas, Zacatecas, México

Idalia Garza-Veloz
Centro de Investigación e Innovación Tecnológica Industrial (CIITI), Universidad Autónoma de Zacatecas, Zacatecas, México
Laboratorio de Medicina Molecular, Unidad académica de Medicina Humana y Ciencias de la Salud (UAMHCS), Universidad Autónoma de Zacatecas, Zacatecas, México

Jose Manuel Ortiz-Rodriguez
Centro de Investigación e Innovación Tecnológica Industrial (CIITI), Universidad Autónoma de Zacatecas, Zacatecas, México
Unidad Académica de Ingeniería Eléctrica (UAIE), Universidad Autónoma de Zacatecas, Zacatecas, México
Laboratorio de Innovación y Desarrollo Tecnológico en Inteligencia Artificial (LIDTIA), Universidad Autónoma de Zacatecas, Zacatecas, México

Jie Zhang, Junliang Wang and Wei Qin
School of Mechanical Engineering, Shanghai Jiao Tong University, Shanghai, China

Maosen Cao, Nizar F. Alkayem and Lixia Pan
Department of Engineering Mechanics, Hohai University, Nanjing, People's Republic of China

Drahomír Novák
Faculty of Civil Engineering, Institute of Structural Mechanics, Brno University of Technology, Brno, Czech Republic

Waylon G. Collins
National Weather Service, Weather Forecast Office Corpus Christi, TX, USA

Philippe Tissot
Texas A&M University—Corpus Christi, Conrad Blucher Institute, Corpus Christi, TX, USA

H. İbrahim Çelik and Mehmet Topalbekiroğlu
Gaziantep University, Department of Textile Engineering, Gaziantep, Turkey

L. Canan Dülger
Gaziantep University, Department of Mechanical Engineering, Gaziantep, Turkey

Emanuele Santi
Institute of Applied Physics, National Research Council (IFAC-CNR), Florence, Italy

Index

Printed in the USA
CPSIA information can be obtained
at www.ICGtesting.com
JSHW051321221024
72173JS00006B/1282